MANAGING PEOPLE IN THE PUBLIC SERVICES

David Farnham
and
Sylvia Horton

with contributions by Susan Corby, Lesley Giles,
Barry Hutchinson and Geoff White

First published 1996 by
MACMILLAN PRESS LTD
Houndmills, Basingstoke, Hampshire RG21 6XS
and London
Companies and representatives
throughout the world

ISBN 0–333–63044–0 hardcover
ISBN 0–333–63045–9 paper back

A catalogue record for this book is available from the British Library.

10   9   8   7   6   5   4   3   2   1
05   04   03   02   01   00   99   98   97   96

Printed in Malaysia

Contents

PART II   CASE STUDIES

List of figures and tables

Figures

Tables

List of contributors

Susan Corby is Senior Lecturer in Industrial Relations at the Manchester Metropolitan University. Previously she was a Senior Industrial Relations Officer with the Royal College of Midwives. She has published in the areas of trade union organization, collective bargaining and personnel management in the public sector.

David Farnham is a Professor at the University of Portsmouth, where he holds a personal Chair in Employment Relations. His books include *Personnel in Context* and *Employee Relations*. He has also co-authored, with John Pimlott, *Understanding Industrial Relations*. He is co-editor, with Sylvia Horton, of *Managing the New Public Services*.

Lesley Giles is Research Fellow at the Institute of Employment Studies, where she works in the Employment Policy Research Group. She was previously a research worker at the University of Central England in Birmingham and the University of Portsmouth.

Sylvia Horton is Principal Lecturer in Public Sector Studies at the University of Portsmouth. She is co-editor, with David Farnham, of *Managing the New Public Services* and has published in the areas of local authority budgeting, local government reform and human resources management in the public services.

Barry Hutchinson is Senior Lecturer in Personnel Management and Industrial Relations at the University of Greenwich. He became a university teacher in 1991, having previously worked in local government personnel management for 14 years.

Geoff White is Senior Lecturer in Personnel Management and Industrial Relations at the University of Greenwich. He became a university teacher in 1991, having previously worked in personnel management publishing, including over 11 years at Incomes Data Services (IDS). Whilst at IDS, he was responsible for establishing and running the IDS Public Sector Unit.

Preface

This book complements an earlier one, co-edited by the editors of this volume, *Managing the New Public Services* (1993 and 1996, forthcoming). Our starting point is identical with that of the earlier book: that the UK's public services have been subjected to considerable political, organizational and managerial changes since the late 1970s. The first book assessed the impact of these changes on the reformed public services, described how they are being managed and provided an analysis and critique of the new managerialism within them. This book takes the analysis further, by focusing on the principal people management issues associated with change in the public services. People management is concerned with the activities, processes and systems through which those in authority in organizations manage their workforces. It begins when staff are recruited and selected in organizations and ends when they are exited, due to resignation, retirement, dismissal or redundancy. The public services, in turn, are broadly defined as those organizations whose current and capital expenditure are funded primarily by taxation, rather than through the direct sale of their services to individual or corporate consumers. Within the UK public services, the Civil Service, National Health Service (NHS), local government, education and the police provide the focuses for this study.

We believe this book is a timely one. First, the public

services are large-scale employers of people and the ways in which people are being managed within them are changing rapidly. These changes are of interest to managers, staff and students of the public services and they need to be recorded, examined, compared with past practices and evaluated. Second, there is no current personnel management text which describes and analyses people management issues in the public services, either generically or by sector (Torrington and Hall, 1991; Armstrong, 1993; Sisson and Storey, 1993; Beardwell and Holden, 1994; Storey, 1994). Further, some personnel management texts tend to be prescriptive of what good personnel practice is and make only passing reference to the state as an employer. They make no distinction between how people are managed in the public sector compared with the private sector. They certainly do not explore the different contextual and philosophical assumptions underpinning the people management process in public-service organizations from those in the private sector. Third, the public services have claimed for many years to be 'model' employers, pursuing fair and reasonable employment policies and acting as exemplars of good practice for private employers to follow. That orthodoxy needs to be reassessed, in the light of recent changes and developments in people management in public-service organizations.

This book has three aims. The first is to describe and analyse past practices and current developments in the managing of people in the public services. The second is to compare and contrast current people management and employment practices amongst public-service organizations, in conditions of change. The third is to examine some of the factors making people management and employment relations in the public services both different from and similar to those in the private sector.

The book is in three parts. Part I examines the background to the UK's public services. Initially, the editors look at the elements of continuity and change in the public services. They discuss the distinguishing features of the public services, the impact of the new public management upon these organizations and the basic elements of people management within them (Chapter 1). The editors then explore the origins, genesis and maturation of traditional people management (TPM) and the legacy of history upon people management policies and practices, focusing particularly on central and local government. They go on to identify five essential features of TPM: an administrative personnel function; a paternalist style of management; standardized employment practices; collectivist patterns of industrial relations; and the state's role as a model employer (Chapter 2).

Part II consists of five case studies. These detail the most significant changes taking place in people management policies and practices in the public services, since the late 1970s. Horton examines the Civil Service, where she details the innovations taking place in recruitment and selection, equal opportunities, conditions of service, pay rewards, industrial relations and training and development. She concludes that, amidst continuity and change, a 'quiet revolution' has taken place over the last 15 years and that a system of 'new people management' (NPM) is emerging (Chapter 3). Corby analyses recent reforms and structural change in the NHS, focusing particularly on NHS trusts which are the major employers of health service staff. She highlights the impact of these reforms on the personnel function, personnel policy, staffing, employment resourcing, pay determination, staff organizations and training and staff development. In her view, strong elements of TPM remain in the NHS but TPM is not going unchallenged by managers. (Chapter 4).

The changing nature of people management in local government is examined by White and Hutchinson. They focus on the evolving structure of local government employment, the emerging personnel function, the changing cultures of local government – especially the impacts of compulsory competitive tendering and performance management – developments in collective bargaining and the ways in which training is being organized, now that the Local Government Training Board has been absorbed within the Local Government Management Board. Whilst observing a shift towards more proactive forms of managing people, they argue that local government has been the public service least affected by the new managerialism and NPM. They claim that this is largely due to the continued independence of local from central government and that control of public spending will continue to be a key influence in shaping personnel policies in local government (Chapter 5).

Farnham and Giles examine developments in people management in schools, further education and universities. They identify and discuss the major legislative changes which have resulted in Local Management of Schools and removed further education and the new universities, formerly polytechnics, from local authority control. The people management innovations analysed include the removal of collective bargaining for school teachers and the establishment of a pay review body, staff appraisal and staff development, new employment contracts, the personnel function in colleges and universities and collective bargaining reform in the new universities. They conclude that there has been a balkanization of people management in all sectors of education and a shift towards NPM, with important changes in the personnel function (Chapter 6).

Horton considers current people management issues in the police. Having identified the special nature of the police service, and its increased civilianization, she discusses the personnel function, recruitment, selection and promotion, and equal opportunities. She then considers pay and conditions of service, industrial relations and training and development. She concludes that although in some respects people management changes in the police have been distinctive, the general direction of change is following the pattern identified throughout the public services (Chapter 7).

In Part III, the editors assess the nature and extent of NPM. They contrast it with TPM and identify its essential features as: a strategic personnel function; a rationalist style of management; flexible employment practices; a mixture of collectivist and individualist patterns of industrial relations; and a new role for the state in people management (Chapter 8).

The completion of a book like this would not have been possible without the collaboration, commitment and goodwill of its contributing authors and the publishers. We would like to thank all our colleagues for meeting their deadlines and making our job as editors a relatively easy one. Our thanks are also due to colleagues at the University of Portsmouth, Andrew Massey, for reading Chapter 3, Steve Savage and Barry Loveday, for reading Chapter 7, and Jackie Cooper and Lesley Giles for providing editorial assistance at crucial times. We would also like to thank our editor at Macmillan, Stephen Rutt, for his support in commissioning this book, ensuring its smooth progress in-house and getting it published on time. As co-editors, we alone remain responsible for the final product.

University of Portsmouth   DAVID FARNHAM
September 1995   SYLVIA HORTON

Abbreviations

ACAS	Advisory Conciliation and Arbitration Service
ACC	Assistant Chief Constable
ACPO	Association of Chief Police Officers
AEEU	Amalgamated Engineering and Electrical Union
AHA	area health authority
AL	advanced level
APO	area personnel officer
APT&C	Administrative Professional Technical and Clerical
APSG	Accelerated Promotion Scheme for Graduates
ATL	Association of Teachers and Lecturers
AUCL	Association of University and College Lecturers
AUT	Association of University Teachers
BCU	Basic Command Unit
BMA	British Medical Association
BT	British Telecom
CAT	college of advanced technology
CC	Chief Constable
CCT	compulsory competitive tendering
CEF	Colleges Employers Forum
CFE	college of further education
CHE	college of higher education
CID	Criminal Investigation Department
CLA/EIS	College Lecturers Association of the

xvii

	Educational Institute of Scotland
CLEA/ST	Council of Local Education Authorities and School Teachers
COHSE	Confederation of Health Service Employees
CPIS	computerized personnel information system
CPSA	Civil and Public Services Association
CPU	Central Planning Unit
CRE	Commission for Racial Equality
CSC	Civil Service Commission
CSD	Civil Service Department
CSU	Civil Service Union
CSSU	Council of Civil Service Unions
CSMC	Civil Service Management Code
CSPCSC	Civil Service Pay and Conditions of Service Code
DCC	Deputy Chief Constable
DES	Department of Education and Science
DFE	Department for Education
DHA	district health authority
DHSS	Department of Health and Social Security
DLO	Direct Labour Organization
DoE	Department of the Environment
DoH	Department of Health
DDPO	Departmental Disabled Persons Officer
DSO	Direct Service Organization
DTC	District Training Centre
DVLA	Driver Vehicle Licensing Agency
EIS	Educational Institute of Scotland
EO	executive officer
EOC	Equal Opportunities Commission
EOG	Establishment Officers Guide
EOO	Equal Opportunities Officer
EOU	Equal Opportunity Unit
ERA 1988	Education Reform Act 1988
ESG	Education Support Grant
ESTACODE	Establishments Code
FBU	Fire Brigades Union
FDA	First Division Association
FE	further education

FEC	further education corporation
FHEA 1992	Further and Higher Education Act 1992
FHSA	Family Health Service Authority
FMI	Financial Management Initiative
FTE	full-time equivalent
GCHQ	General Communications Headquarters (Cheltenham)
GDP	gross domestic product
GEST	Grants for Educational Support and Training
GLC	Greater London Council
GMB	General Municipal and Boilermakers
GMS	Grant Maintained Status
GP	general practitioner
HE	higher education
HEC	higher education corporation
HEO	higher executive officer
HEOD	higher executive officer development
HM	Her Majesty's
HMIC	Her Majesty's Inspectorate of Constabulary
HMSO	Her Majesty's Stationery Office
HoD	head of department
HRD	human resources development
HRM	human resources management
IAC	Interim Advisory Committee
ICC	Intermediate Command Course
IDS	Incomes Data Services
IIP	Investors in People
INLOGOV	Institute of Local Government Studies
INSET	In-service Education and Training
IPD	Institute of Personnel and Development
IPM	Institute of Personnel Management
IPMS	Institution of Professionals Managers and Specialists
IRSF	Inland Revenue Staff Federation
IT	information technology
JCC	joint consultative committee
JNC	joint negotiating committee
LACSAB	Local Authorities Conditions of Service Advisory Board
LEA	local education authority

LEATGS	Local Education Authority Training Grants Scheme
LGA 1988	Local Government Act 1988
LGA 1992	Local Government Act 1992
LGEB	Local Government Examination Board
LGMB	Local Government Management Board
LGPLA 1990	Local Government Planning and Land Act 1990
LGTB	Local Government Training Board
LMS	Local Management of Schools
LNNC	Lecturers National Negotiating Committee
LPA	Local Police Authority
MBA	Master of Business Administration
MCG	management consultancy group
MCI	Management Charter Initiative
MoD	Ministry of Defence
MPS	Metropolitan Police Service
MSF	Manufacturing Science and Finance Union
NATFHE	National Association of Teachers in Further and Higher Education
NHSME	National Health Service Management Executive
NHSTA	National Health Service Training Authority
NHSTD	National Health Service Training Division
MINIS	Management Information System
NIPSA	Northern Ireland Public Service Alliance
NME	new mode employer
NUJ	National Union of Journalists
MPO	Management and Personnel Office
MP	Member of Parliament
NSG	National Steering Group
NAHT	National Association of Head Teachers
NALGO	National and Local Government Officers Association
NAS/UWT	National Association of Schoolmasters/Union of Women Teachers
NHS	National Health Service
NJC	national joint council/committee
NJCLFE	National Joint Council for Lecturers in Further Education

NJIC	national joint industrial council
NPM	new people management
NUCPS	National Union of Civil and Public Servants
NUPE	National Union of Public Employees
NUT	National Union of Teachers
NVQs	National Vocational Qualifications
O&M	organization and methods
OCSC	Office of Civil Service Commissioners
OECD	Organization for Economic Cooperation and Development
OFSTED	Office of Educational Standards
OMCS	Office of the Minister of the Civil Service
OPS	Office of Public Service
OPSS	Office of Public Service and Science
PA	police authority
PAMs	professions allied to medicine
PAT	Professional Association of Teachers
PCEF	Polytechnic and Colleges Employers Forum
PCFC	Polytechnics and Colleges Funding Council
PF	Police Federation
PI	performance indicator
PL	principal lecturer
PMCA 1994	Police and Magistrates Courts Act 1994
PMS	performance management system
PNB	Police Negotiating Board
PO	principal officer
POA	Prison Officers Association
PRB	'pay review body
PRP	performance related pay
PRU	Pay Research Unit
PTC	Police Training Council
RAS	Recruitment and Assessment Services Agency
RHA	regional health authority
RTA 1965	Remuneration of Teachers Act 1965
SC	Special Constable
SF	Superintendants' Federation
SL	senior lecturer
SLA	service level agreement
SOCPO	Society of Chief Personnel Officers

SOCS	Scottish Office Central Statistics
SCPS	Society of Civil and Public Servants
SHA	Secondary Heads Association
SOS	senior open structure
SPOA	Scottish Prison Officers Association
SSA	Standard Spending Assessment
SSC	Senior Command Course
SSRB	Senior Salaries Review Body
STSC	Scottish Teachers Salary Committee
STRB	School Teachers Review Body
TGWU	Transport and General Workers Union
TSRB	Top Salaries Review Body
TOPO	training of personnel officers
TOTO	training of training officers
TPCA 1987	Teachers Pay and Conditions Act 1987
TPM	traditional people management
TRIST	TVEI-related in-services training
TQM	total quality management
TUC	Trades Union Congress
TUPE 1981	Transfer of Undertakings Protection of Employment Regulations
TVEI	Technical and Vocational Education Initiative
UCATT	Union of Construction Allied Trades and Technicians
UMRG	Universities Manpower Review Group
UK	United Kingdom
WIRS	Workplace Industrial Relations Survey

Background

PART I

Background

CHAPTER 1

Continuity and change in the public services

David Farnham and Sylvia Horton

The modern public services in the United Kingdom (UK), defined broadly as the activities of central and local government, can be examined in two ways. They can be seen as 'providers', that is those state organizations which supply goods and services to its citizens, according to their personal needs and irrespective of their ability to pay for them. Alternatively, they can be viewed as the 'outputs' of state organizations, to which the state's citizens are entitled, normally free at the point of use, on the principle of either universality or, sometimes, selectivity. In this book, we use the term public services mainly in the former sense, namely as organizations providing a range of benefits to people, as citizens or members of the state, according to individual or collective need. This highlights the major distinction between the public services and private-sector organizations: the former have politically-driven goals and the latter market-driven ones.

The public services are now wide ranging but in their early days their activities were limited to policing and law enforcement, defence of the realm and basic areas of public administration. The latter included tax collection, the monitoring of state spending and the maintenance of

3

the public accounts. The history of the public services is characterized by four broad phases in their development: their relatively narrow base and slow emergence in mid-Victorian Britain; their steady growth in the early twentieth century; their subsequent expansion and widening scope in the 30 years after the end of the second world war; and their changing boundaries and systems of provision since the early 1980s (Farnham and Horton, 1993). This Chapter examines the changing nature of the public services, their main characteristics as organizations and the basic people management issues concerning those who manage and work in them.

Public Goods

Public services provide public or collective goods to citizens, which generate positive utilities or benefits to those using them. Collective goods, when provided by state organizations, are normally available to anyone wishing to use them, free at the point of consumption, and have two main features. First, they are characterized by 'non-rival consumption'. This means that normally where one individual uses a public good, such as education or public highways, this does not reduce its availability to others, although there may be a rationing system to allocate an equitable distribution of the good to those needing it. The consumption of a private or individual good, in contrast, such as the purchase of a motor car by a householder, precludes its consumption by another person. Second, public goods are 'non-exclusive'. In other words, once a public good is provided, such as street lighting, roads or clean air, the provider is unable to prevent others from using or consuming it. This feature of public goods prevents markets from functioning, because the 'seller' is unable to ensure that only those paying for the good obtain it. Since a public good can be obtained without payment, no one is willing to pay for it, unless forced to do so. Where consumption is not completely non-rival, or exclusion from it is possible, it is an 'impure' public good or a mixed good, which are quite common in practice. The provision of public goods is a matter of collective choice. Whilst public goods can be supplied by the state, and be paid for out of compulsory taxation, they can also be provided by the private sector, if society chooses to do so. The choice depends largely upon the political ideology of the government in power and the expectations and responses of the electorate. The provision of health care in the UK, for example, is largely in the public sector: in the United States of America (USA), in contrast, it is mainly in the private sector. Similarly, electricity, gas and water supply and telecommunications were formerly in the UK public sector but, since being privatized and sold to private investors during the 1980s, they are now in the private sector. The latter group of public goods are classified as 'public utilities'. These provide monopolistic services to the community at market prices but are subject to some degree of governmental regulation. Indeed, the boundaries between the public and private sectors are constantly changing and overlapping.

Scope of the Public Sector

The UK public sector, as currently structured, covers: central government; local government; and the public corporations. Central government comprises all those state bodies whose activities are accountable, through a Minister of the Crown or other responsible person, to Parliament. It consists largely of four sub-sectors: Her Majesty's Forces, the National Health Service (NHS), the Civil Service and non-departmental agencies. The armed services are made up of the Royal Navy, the Army and the Royal Air Force, with responsibility for 'defending the realm'. The NHS, with its various purchasers and providers of health care, includes: regional and district health authorities; hospital and community health trusts; directly managed hospitals; family health service authorities; and general practitioners. NHS trusts, however, are now technically classified as public corporations.

The Civil Service consists of the Home Civil Service and Diplomatic Civil Service but not the Northern Ireland Civil Service or Overseas Civil Service. The Civil Service incorporates the various departments of state and the recently created Next Steps agencies. Non-departmental agencies, such as the Advisory Conciliation and Arbitration Service, Equal Opportunities Commission and Commission for Racial Equality, have terms of reference determined by statute. Their responsibilities are to apply and monitor the law in their fields of competence. There are also a number of other public bodies which, whilst not government departments, are financially dependent upon and effectively controlled in policy matters by government. These include the national research councils, museums, art galleries and royal commissions.

Local government consists of all local authorities, with the power to raise revenue by local rates, levies or council taxes, which are required to make annual returns of income and expenditure, and are scrutinized by other public authorities, under successive local government acts. This sector also includes local authorities with special functions such as, with effect from 1 April 1995, the new statutory police authorities. Local authorities embrace all types of administrative functions, such as education, social services, planning, road construction and trading activities such as municipal theatres and leisure services. Areas previously under the control of local authorities, which are now in the private sector, include: municipal bus companies, since 1986; municipal airports, since 1987; and grant maintained status schools, since 1989. The former polytechnics (now the 'new' universities) and higher education (HE) colleges were transferred out of local authority control from April 1989, with all further education (FE) colleges and sixth-form colleges following them in April 1993. These HE and FE institutions are now technically part of the private sector, as non-profit making bodies, although most of their revenue and capital expenditure comes from taxation.

There were some 40 public corporations in 1995. These included the Audit Commission, British Broadcasting Corporation, Post Office, Welsh Fourth Television Channel Authority and Her Majesty's Stationery Office. Public corporations are public trading bodies which have substantial degrees of financial independence from central government. The Sovereign, Parliament or a Minister appoints the whole or part of their boards of management. They are free, however, to manage themselves without detailed control by Parliament. In particular, they have the power to borrow money, within limits laid down by Parliament, and maintain their own reserves. A handful of public corporations, such as the Post Office and the British Waterways Board, are nationalized industries but most nationalized industries have been privatized or are being privatized. Apart from NHS trusts, which are now classified as public corporations, the public corporations are not public services as defined here.

Characteristics of Public Services

The history of the UK's public sector illustrates that the boundaries between public organizations and private ones have changed continuously over time. In the immediate postwar period between 1945 and 1951, there was a large extension of the public sector, with the establishment of the Welfare State and the nationalization of the 'commanding heights' of the economy including the Bank of England and the coal, railway, gas, electricity and iron and steel industries. During the 1980s and 1990s, the public sector was reduced in scope by privatization, contracting out services and increases in private-sector provision of welfare and social services. The boundaries between the public and private sectors, however, do not fall neatly into a two-fold classification and should be viewed, rather, as a continuum (Tomkins, 1987).

The focus in this book is not the public sector generally but the major public services. Broadly, public services are those public-sector organizations providing public goods to citizens, excluding the public corporations. The main public services include central and local government, health care, education and the police. The strategic importance of central and local government in the national economy is illustrated by what was spent by them in 1993–94. This amounted to £209 billion by central government and £70.2 billion by local authorities, out of a total £286.4 billion general government expenditure. The latter represented approximately 45 per cent of gross domestic product (GDP) in 1993–94 (Cm 2519, 1994).

Put another way, central government, including the Civil Service, had a headcount of 1.2 million staff in 1994, local government 2.7 million – including 1.2 million in education and 207 000 in the police – and the NHS 1.2 million, including 966 000 in NHS trusts. The public services currently employ some 5.3 million people by headcount – about one in every four workers – or some 21 per cent of the total workforce (Hughes, 1995).

The public services have a number of characteristics distinguishing them from private organizations and these are critical in influencing how people are managed within them. These are: public accountability; scale and complexity; labour intensity; recognized unions and high membership density; monopoly provision; and public-service ethos.

Public accountability

Public-service organizations are, by definition, political institutions. Whether in central government or local government, public services are created by government, normally through legislation, are funded by individual and corporate taxpayers and exist primarily for the benefit of citizens. All public services have multiple goals, which tend to be complex, vague and often in conflict, but they are essentially politically-driven (Pollitt, 1993). Thus the goals of public services are ultimately political ones and the effectiveness of these services is normally measured in terms of their political achievements, not by market criteria. It also means, because of the dynamics of politics, that senior public servants, increasingly described as 'public managers', are faced, unlike their private-sector counterparts, 'with frequent changes of goals as either political pressures force a new negotiated order or changes in political leadership result in new priorities' (Farnham and Horton, 1993, p. 37).

As political organizations, public services are accountable to the public, both as taxpayers and users of services. As citizens, the public is interested in how the public services are run; the efficiency with which public money is used; the effectiveness and quality of provision; and how public power is utilized on their behalf. It is this exercising of public power which necessitates that the final accountability of public services in a liberal democratic state, like that of the UK, is to the electorate. Accountability takes various forms, 'legal, political, consumer and ... professional' (Farnham and Horton, 1993, p. 38), with the relative importance of each varying, according to circumstances.

First, the public services operate within a strict legal framework. Unlike private organizations, which can do anything which the law does not proscribe, public ones can only do what the law permits. The legal rule of *ultra vires* means that public officials must be able to demonstrate the legality of their actions and decisions to the community. Unlike in most western European countries, the UK has no constitutional court to decide what is lawful and legitimate in the public domain. It is the ordinary courts that hold public organizations to account, both for the actions of their officials and the procedures they use. Where there are disputes over the legality of their decisions, the public authorities have to demonstrate to the courts that they have complied with the substantive law, procedural law and rules of natural justice.

Second, political accountability takes different forms. As Elcock (1991, p. 2) indicates: 'central to the processes of government in the twentieth century has been the accountability of officials to elected representatives – in both central and local government.' All public officials are accountable to a political person or political body. Civil servants and public management boards are accountable to ministers and local government officers to elected councillors. This model of political accountability rests on the fact that powers are vested in ministers in central government, who are responsible for what public servants do, and ministers are accountable to Parliament for the actions of their civil servants. In local government, power is vested in elected local authorities which are responsible for the actions of their officials. Yet the reality of both ministerial and local accountability has long been disputed. In central government, civil servants are now more directly accountable to Parliament, through its specialist committees, than in the past (Drewry, 1989). In local government, local officials also deal directly with the public. In both cases, the ultimate accountability of the authorities is to the electorate, through the ballot box and periodic elections.

Third, the accountability of the public services to their users is through the institutions created to deal with public complaints. These include internal procedures, various tribunals, Ombudsmen and commissioners. Since the 1980s, the rights of 'public consumers' have come to the fore, with the publication of the *Citizen's Charter* (Prime Minister's Office, 1991) and other specific charters. All are aimed at making the public services more accountable and responsive to citizen and client needs.

Fourth, the issue of professional accountability is particularly pertinent in the public services. As discussed below, many public services are dominated by groups of professional workers, such as doctors, nurses, teachers, public accountants and social workers. These professional groups claim control over not only entry to professional training, the awarding of qualifications and methods of working but also the policing of their professional activities. Such groups argue that through their codes of professional conduct, codes of practice and internal disciplinary rules, they protect client interests by maintaining high standards of professionalism.

TABLE 1.1   Employment in the UK public services, 1994

	full-time equivalents	*per cent*
NHS Trusts	788 000	20.0
Central government[a]	1 087 000	28.0
NHS	163 000	[15.0]
Civil Service	529 000	[48.7]
Other	395 000	[36.3]
Local Authorities	2 055 000	52.0
Education	818 000	[40.0]
Social services	288 000	[14.0]
Construction	86 000	[4.2]
Police	201 000	[4.8]
Other	662 000	[32.0]
Total public services	3 930 000	100

a   excludes HM Forces
Source: derived from *Economic Trends*, 1995

Scale and complexity

The public services are large-scale organizations, whether measured in terms of their assets or numbers employed. Table 1.1 is based on data collected by the Central Statistical Office and indicates that there were almost four million full-time equivalent staff (FTEs) employed in the public services in 1994. This represented about 74 per cent of all public-sector employment at that time. In central government, the Civil Service was technically the largest employer, with something over half a million FTEs. But the NHS, with about 163 000 staff and over 788 000 in trusts, employed almost a million FTEs in total. This made the NHS second in size only to the local authorities as an employer. Within local government, with 2.1 million FTEs, education was by far the largest area of employment, with over 818 000, followed by social services with almost a third of a million, and the police with over 200 000, including civilian staff.

Table 1.2, which is based on public expenditure data, takes a slightly longer-term view by examining the FTE

TABLE 1.2   Public-sector workforce, 1978–93[a]

	000s (FTEs)							
	1979	*1981*	*1983*	*1985*	*1987*	*1989*	*1991*	*1993*
Central government	2194	2218	2211	2162	2113	2066	2039	1786
Local government	2325	2343	2274	2320	2352	2379	2280	2257
Nationalized industries	1843	1785	1538	1390	1043	775	659	465
Other public corporations	203	205	185	181	126	118	108	345
Total	6565	6551	6208	6053	5634	5338	5056	4853

a   these figures are based on public expenditure data, so the calculations differ slightly from those in Table 1.1
Source: derived from Cm. 2519, 1994

public-sector workforce for the period 1979–93. Table 1.2 identifies five main trends in the period 1979–93. First, the total public-sector work force fell by 1 712 000 or 26 per cent. Second, those employed in central government services, including the Armed Services, declined by 408 000 or 19 per cent. Within central government, civil service employment fell from 734 000 to 565 000 – or 23 per cent – whilst employment in the NHS, excluding health trusts, fell from 923 000 to 725 000 or 22 per cent (Cm 2519, 1994). Third, there was little variation in local authority employment, with numbers fluctuating around 2.3 million throughout the period. Fourth, due to privatization, employment in the nationalized industries fell by 1 378 000 or 75 per cent. Fifth, employment in other public corporations rose by 142 000 between 1979 and 1993, or 70 per cent, with most of this increase taking place between 1991 and 1993. In 1991, 108 000 people were employed in other public corporations, rising to 202 000 in 1992 and 345 000 in 1993 (Cm. 2519, 1994). These increases were largely accounted for by the creation of NHS trusts.

On any measure, the public services are large-scale employers. The 'top 10' UK companies, in comparison, employed in total just over a million employees in 1993. The largest of these was a former public corporation –

British Telecom (BT), with some 183 000 employees. BT was followed by BTR, with 135 000 employees, ICI with 117 000, British Aerospace – another former public corporation – with 108 000 and British Petroleum with 105 000. Only two of the next group of eight companies in the top 18, GEC with 105 000 employees and the Post Office – the only remaining nationalized industry in this group – with over 200 000, exceeded 100 000 employees each (Times, 1994). Compared with the main public services, top companies are relatively small-scale employers.

Public services are also complex organizations, with internal tensions and intricate structures. The division of responsibilities amongst the public services, for example, is a matter of political consideration, not of logic or consistency. It is not uncommon for one level of government to set goals and policies for another level to implement. Thus whilst the Department for Education develops educational policies, it is left to local education authorities, colleges and universities to implement them. This frequent separation of goal setting and policy implementation means that there is sometimes a lack of control by policy-makers over those carrying out policy. A power-dependency relationship emerges in which skill in exploiting political resources replaces any rational process of decision-making or hierarchical control.

Similarly, central and local government organizations have complex structures. They tend to be large bureaucracies, characterized by hierarchies of authority and status. This makes decision-making within them more consensual, mediatory and slower than in the private sector. The public services are rarely static but are constantly changing, largely in response to the demands and pressures of politics. They also tend to have complicated communication systems, distinguished by interrelated interdepartmental committees and multiple consultative and communication channels. One consequence is that those responsible for managing public services are often managing the interface between their own organization and external ones.

Labour intensity

Many of the UK's most successful businesses, such as those listed in the *Times 1000* companies (Times, 1994), are increasingly capital intensive. Their ratio of capital costs to labour costs, that is, is relatively high. Because of hard market competition, and pressures on company profits, they have to continuously review their unit labour costs, methods of working and personnel policies. This has resulted in shakeouts of labour, a shift towards flexible employment and smaller, 'downsized' organizations. The 'mean', 'lean' organization characterizes the private sector of the 1990s. The large corporate sector also requires large injections of investment spending, in order to respond to market competition and technological change, and this reinforces its capital intensity.

The public services, in contrast, tend to be labour intensive, with labour costs amounting to something approaching 80 per cent of costs. According to Pearson (1994), in 1983 there were 5.3 million staff employed by headcount in the public services, excluding the public corporations. By 1993, this had fallen to 4.3 million, a decrease of some 19 per cent over the decade. This fall in public-service employment is accounted for by the transfer of some services to the private sector, compulsory competitive tendering (CCT), external contractorization and increased efficiency by remaining workers.

The degree of labour intensity in the Civil Service is demonstrated by the size and structure of its labour force. Industrial civil servants, who now constitute only some 10 per cent of the workforce, consist of a number of groups. The main skilled groups include technicians, shipbuilding, building, engineering and printing trades. The unskilled include cleaners, caretakers, drivers and maintenance staff. The largest group of non-industrial civil servants is the Administration Group who range from top management grades to low rank officers doing routine clerical work. The remaining non-industrial grades consist of the Science Group, the Professional and Technology Group, Economists and Statisticians, Lawyers and Other Specialists.

These last five groups illustrate another feature of public-service employment, the relatively large number of professional workers employed within the sector. Civil servants, for example, have a wide range of professional qualifications and competences. They include: research scientists; architects and quantity surveyors; engineers; economists; solicitors and barristers; actuaries; linguists; medical and dental practitioners; veterinary officers; and psychologists.

The NHS is also a labour intensive organization, again with a wide range of professional and non-professional staff. The largest group is nurses, followed by doctors, administrative staff and paramedicals. The paramedical group is itself very heterogeneous, containing opticians, chiropodists, laboratory technicians, dieticians, ambulance personnel and so on. Another major group is ancillary or manual workers, doing portering, cleaning and domestic services.

The local government workforce is also marked by a multiplicity of occupations and professions. As Fowler (1988, p. 13) remarks: 'no comprehensive list of occupations has ever been compiled, but it certainly amounts to several hundred.' The workforce is crudely grouped into two categories: non-manuals and manuals. The non-manuals include administrators, clerical workers, technicians and professional workers. The largest professional group is school teachers but other professionals include social workers, accountants, solicitors, engineers, surveyors, valuers and planners. The manual groups consist of general manual workers, such as school meals staff, caretakers, cleaners, refuse collectors, labourers and transport workers, and skilled groups. Skilled workers include building and engineering craftworkers, fitters, electricians, heating engineers and maintenance staff.

A final feature of the public-service labour force is that it is predominantly a female one, of whom almost 50 per cent are part-time workers. In 1993, women made up some 51 per cent of civil service employment, 78 per cent in the NHS and almost 60 per cent in the local authorities, including 78 per cent of all employees in schools and 86 per cent in social services. The only public services where

TABLE 1.3   Trade union recognition in the public services, 1980, 1984 and 1990

	1980	*1984*	*Per cent 1990*
Establishments with recognized unions for any workers	94	99	87
Establishments with recognized unions for manual workers	76	91	78
Establishments with recognized unions for non-manual workers	91	98	84

Source: derived from WIRS, 1990

males predominate are HM Forces and the police, where men make up 93 per cent and 83 per cent of the workforces respectively (Pearson, 1994). In spite of the large numbers of women employed in the public services, they are concentrated in the lower ranks, with a marked underrepresentation in senior positions. In this respect, the public services mirror the private sector.

Recognized unions and high membership density

A characteristic of public-service employment has been the willingness of employers to recognize unions for the purposes of collective bargaining, over pay and conditions, especially in the period after the second world war. Table 1.3, derived from the Workplace Industrial Relations Survey of 1990 (Millward *et al.*, 1992), illustrates the broad pattern of trade union recognition in the public services, including the remaining public corporations which cannot be disaggregated from the figures, since 1980. It is clear that the overall level of union recognition for all establishments with recognized unions in the public services declined from 94 per cent in 1980 to 87 per cent in 1990, having risen to 99 per cent in 1984. The decline in recognition was especially noticeable for non-manual workers, which fell from 98 per cent of all establishments with recognized unions in 1984 to 84 per cent in 1990. This is 'almost entirely explained by the withdrawal by the Government of negotiating rights for teachers in state schools in England and Wales' (Millward et al 1992, p. 73).

There was still a relatively high level of union recognition in the public services in 1990, especially when compared with private manufacturing and private services. In private manufacturing, for example, union recognition in establishments with recognized unions for any workers fell from 65 per cent to 44 per cent between 1980 and 1990. In the private services, it fell from 41 per cent to 36 per cent (Millward et al., 1992).

Partly as a result of the state's policy of supporting union recognition, union membership has generally been high in public services. Another factor explaining high membership density is the large size of employing units and concentration of employment in public services.

There is a wide choice of unions which public-service workers can join. In 1992, nine out of the 20 largest unions in the UK, with over 100 000 members each, were predominantly public-service unions. In rank order of size, these were: the General Municipal and Boilermakers; National and Local Government Officers Association; Royal College of Nursing; National Union of Teachers; Confederation of Health Service Employees; National Association of School Masters and Union of Women Teachers; Assistant Masters and Mistresses Association; and Civil and Public Services Association. Collectively, these public-service unions had some 3.3 million members in 1992, which at that time was about one third of total union membership. Additionally, there were 14 other public-service unions in 1994, with less than 100 000 members each, which had a collective membership of almost 700 000 (Trades Union Congress, 1994).

These four million trade unionists exclude those public workers, especially in manual grades, who are members

TABLE 1.4   **Aggregate union membership density by sector of employment, 1984 and 1990**

	All workers		manuals		Per cent non-manuals	
	1984	1990	1984	1990	1984	1990
All industries	58	48	66	53	51	43
Manufacturing	56	48	70	60	32	22
Private services	30	27	40	32	23	24
Public services	80	72	82	72	79	72

Source: derived from WIRS, 1990

of large general unions, such as the Transport and General Workers Union, and of big occupational unions, such as the Amalgamated Engineering and Electrical Union and Union of Construction and Allied Trades. Although the majority of members in these unions are employed in the private sector, all have members in the public services (Certification Office, 1994).

A better measure of trade union voice in the public services is density of membership. Table 1.4 shows the aggregate percentages of union membership density, for all workers, manual workers and non-manual workers, by broad sector of employment at the time of the workplace surveys of 1984 and 1990. Density measures the proportion of a workforce who are members of a union, expressed as a percentage of total employment in that sector. From Table 1.4, it is clear that union density for all workers in all industries had dropped to under 50 per cent by 1990. Falls in union density in 1990, compared with 1984, were particularly observable amongst manual and non-manual workers in manufacturing, whilst the private services have never been very highly unionized. In the public services, however, the decline in union density was much less severe. Between 1984 and 1990, it fell by 10 per cent amongst manual workers and seven per cent amongst non-manuals. Union membership density in the public services, in short, remains relatively high.

Monopoly provision

The public services are monopolistic or near monopolistic providers of essential services to the community, where there is often only limited or even no alternative provision. This means that these organizations have strategic command of the 'market' or a strategic position within the economy as a whole. Individual citizens depend upon the state's willingness to supply such essential services at reasonable cost to taxpayers, to distribute them equitably and to prevent impediments to their provision.

This strategic command of supply, in turn, puts their workforces in a critical position in the labour market. This arises from the potential damage they can do, when the public services are disrupted, if public servants either withdraw their labour or fail to cooperate with management as a result of industrial action. Since the public services are monopoly or near monopoly providers, deprivation of them causes considerable hardship to the community and can even endanger life, health and safety. Although 'Britain stands apart from many other countries which have considered that public servants should be subject to greater [legal] restrictions than their private sector counterparts', when taking part in trade disputes, some groups are subject to specific restrictions. These are the armed services, police, postal workers and merchant seafarers (Fredman and Morris, 1989, p. 385). The Emergency Powers Act 1964 also enables government to ameliorate the consequences of any disruption, by using the armed services to substitute for striking workers.

Public-service ethos

The public-service ethos makes public organizations essentially different from private ones. Although it is difficult to define, it is generally identified with the normative principles guiding the behaviour of public servants and the decisions they take. The public-service ethos encapsulates a number of underpinning principles including:

political neutrality; loyalty; probity; honesty; trustworthiness; fairness; incorruptibility; and serving the public.

Senior public officials, and those working in politically sensitive areas, are expected to be politically neutral. This means serving their political leaders and implementing their policies, irrespective of their own political preferences or party position. 'This implies that in their official duties they should avoid personal identification with the political philosophy of any particular administration' (Williams, 1985, p. 18). Public servants are also expected to be loyal to their political leaders and do their best to protect and serve them.

Probity is the expectation that public officials will act as guardians of the public purse, ensuring that public money is spent without waste and on approved expenditure. Public officials are also expected to tell the truth in their professional roles and demonstrate their honesty by keeping full and accurate records of decisions.

The principle of trustworthiness in public servants is rooted in the expectation that they trust one another, there is trust between themselves and the politicians for whom they work and they act trustworthily in accordance with the law of the land and their public duties. Fairness is the expectation that public officials will not discriminate in the ways in which public services are provided and that their decisions will be equitable and in accordance with proper procedures, with rights of appeal to those who think that they have been treated badly.

The principle of incorruptibility is linked with the idea that public servants should act in the public interest and not use their public positions for personal gain. It is linked with the idea of serving the public and the view that public servants should be above reproach and be proficient at all times. As Wilding (1979, p. 185) puts it, the professional ethic of the public adminstrator includes 'two spoonfuls each of honesty, tenacity and obedience; and one . . . of humility.'

There is also the issue of secrecy. The Official Secrets Act 1989, and over 100 other statutes which apply especially to the Civil Service, make it an offence for civil servants and others to disclose information without authorization. This constrains the behaviour of civil servants, resulting in a relative lack of openness. Whilst secrecy may not be seen as a value *per se*, it has been described as a core feature of civil service culture, like 'calcium in the bones'. Other public services, although generally more open than the Civil Service, still tend to be cautious in divulging information to the public, unless required to do so by the law. Some secrecy in the public services is desirable, especially where it protects national security, the privacy of individuals and confidentiality of the state's relationships with its clients and individual citizens. But the blanket principle of secrecy is highly controversial and has been widely contested over the last decade, with moves being made towards greater openness (Ponting, 1986; Chapman, 1978; Chapman and Hunt, 1987; Pyper, 1991).

The New Public Policy

Since the 1970s the scope, organization and managing of the public services have changed radically. These changes have been driven largely by political forces, although economic, social and technological factors have provided the contexts within which the changes have occurred. During the 1970s, the UK economy faced problems stemming from increased competition from Europe, Japan and the USA, her major industrial rivals, as well as from third world economies. The UK's poor record of capital investment, combined with bad management and difficult industrial relations, especially in the private sector, had resulted in low productivity, high production costs, rising inflation, loss of exports, rising imports and recurrent balance of payments crises.

At the same time, public expenditure was rising rapidly, reaching almost half of GDP in 1975. Much spending was on the services forming the core of the Welfare or 'opportunity' State, introduced by the Labour government between 1945 and 1951. The expansion of most public services was fuelled by the growing expectations of the electorate and the demands for more public spending on welfare services. This led to increases in public employment and rises in taxation and public borrowing to finance it. With governments unable to manage the economy successfully or to curb public expenditure, there was a breakdown in the postwar consensus initiated in 1945. This was triggered largely by oil price rises in 1973, causing an economic crisis, and a rise in inflation to 25 per cent. The Labour government was forced to seek help from the International Monetary Fund which set down stringent conditions before agreeing to a loan. These conditions included reducing public expenditure and, in particular, government borrowing. From then onwards, new ideas about the role of government, as a manager of the economy and a provider of public services, came to the surface.

One set of ideas, those of the 'New Right'or neo-liberalism, took root in the Conservative party after the election of Margaret Thatcher as leader in 1975. Another set of ideas, those of the 'New Left', found a home in the Labour party and in a section of the Liberal party, particularly at local government level. Both constituted political challenges to the ways in which public services were organized and in particular to their domination by professionals and their perceived lack of responsiveness to public needs. The prescriptions of the New Right (Friedman, 1962; Brittan, 1973; Niskanen, 1973; Buchanan, 1975; Bacon and Eltis, 1976) and New Left (Holland, 1975; Benn, 1979; Hain, 1983) were quite different and it was the victory of the Conservatives in the 1979 general election which determined the policies that would be applied in practice. Only in local government did the ideas of the New Left have any impact (Blunkett and Jackson, 1987; Wainwright, 1987).

The Conservative government headed by Margaret Thatcher had no blueprint for the policies it implemented post-1979. But it had clear ideas and values in evolving its strategy for transforming the British economy and the

British state. First, the economic interventionism associated with Keynesian fiscal and monetary policies was rejected. Second, government was committed to rolling back the frontiers of the state, reducing its activities and transferring many of its functions to the private and voluntary sectors. Third, public expenditure and public employment had to be reduced, along with direct taxation. Fourth, government's view was that people should be free to choose whether or not to use public or private services and decide what they were prepared to pay for them. Fifth, public services had to become more efficient and accountable, guided by the principles of 'economy, efficiency and effectiveness', rather than by the inclinations of their professional staff. Sixth, the old administrative principles of procedural rectitude, mistake avoidance and lack of cost consciousness must be replaced by the concepts of 'business efficiency', 'quality service' and 'clientism'. The public services, in short, had to be more responsive to individual consumers and customers, whilst consumers, not suppliers, should be the ultimate quality controllers of what the public services provided.

The main strategies of successive Conservative governments from 1979 were based on four core beliefs. These were that: markets are superior to politics, in ensuring the most rational use of limited resources and maximizing consumer or customer choice; competition stimulates enterprise; enterprise ensures resources move to the most efficient organizations, responsive to customer needs; and responsibility for welfare should rest primarily with the individual and the family, with the role of the state a residual one. Private ownership and entrepreneurial capitalism were held to be the foundations upon which a successful market economy and a healthy liberal democracy should be built. The state's role should be to stimulate enterprise and competition. Government should prevent abuses of monopoly power, provide a legislative framework supporting free markets and protect the public interest. This includes providing a welfare safety net. Governments expected a deregulated economy to generate the wealth to provide rising living standards for all.

The public policies pursued by the Conservatives were founded upon these beliefs. The strategies adopted included: monetarism; the deregulation of capital, labour and money markets; the reduction of direct taxation, especially at higher levels; privatization; enforcing public-service competition through compulsory competitive tendering (CCT), market testing and the creation of 'internal' markets; introducing private-sector management techniques into the public services; reducing the power of unions and professional workers; and restructuring the state. This meant shifting the state from being a monopoly provider of traditional services to being a facilitator and creating a mixed economy of welfare comprising private, voluntary and public agencies. In its role as an employer, the government sought to set an example in overcoming union resistance to change, by pursuing initiatives supporting enterprise and the right to manage (Savage and Robins, 1990).

Not all governmental policies were successful and some were modified or abandoned (Savage, Atkinson and Robins, 1994). But the overall effect after four successive Conservative election victories in 1979, 1983, 1987 and 1992, and their New Right ideology, was a radical change in the scope, size and role of the state. This has had significant consequences for the ways in which the public services are financed, organized and managed.

The New Public Management

There are many definitions of the 'new public management' but in essence the term incorporates three basic elements. The first is rooted in the ideology of 'managerialism' or 'neo-Taylorism' (Pollitt, 1993). The second is that public management is identified with business-centred managerial practices and techniques, imported from the private sector (Hood, 1990). The third is that the new public management is the means for transforming a bureaucratic, paternalistic and democratically passive polity into an efficient, responsive and consumerist one (Ranson and Stewart, 1994). These are not mutually exclusive but are overlapping characteristics of the new public management.

The rise of the new public management is not confined to the UK and cannot therefore be seen as a Thatcherite or simply a UK phenomenon. It is a feature of international trends in public administration since the late 1970s (Hood, 1991; Organization for Economic Cooperation and Development (OECD), 1992; Eliassen and Kooiman, 1993; Massey, 1993). Changes in the postwar international order, variously described as post-Fordism (Murray, 1989; Jessop, 1989), post-industrialism (Bell, 1973; Toffler, 1980; Touraine, 1974) and post-modernism (Lyotard, 1984; Liepietz, 1992), have confronted all western societies.

Hood (1990; 1991) identifies a number of governmental responses to what he calls 'megatrends'. First, there have been attempts to cut back state expenditure and state expansion, though not always successfully (Dunsire and Hood, 1989; Massey, 1993). Second, there has been a redrawing of the boundaries of the public and private domains, as industries have been privatized, private organizations have been contracted to the public sector and new models of 'purchasers' and 'providers' have been developed (Dunleavy, 1989; Clarke and Langan, 1993; Johnson, 1990). Third, many changes in the operation of public services have resulted from the introduction of information technology. This has revolutionized the delivery of services and the methods of controlling public organizations and their constituent parts (Pitt and Smith, 1984; Bellamy and Taylor, 1994). However, the approaches adopted by individual countries vary as the OECD report (1992) demonstrates. The UK falls into the group adopting a market-oriented approach.

Managerialism

There is disagreement about whether managerialism is an ideology in its own right or whether it is a sub-set of the ideology of professionalism (Pollitt, 1993; Massey, 1993). Whichever view is taken, both are rooted in a belief in the centrality of knowledge in human affairs and its ability to transform society and to solve human problems. Managerialism is also closely related to scientific management and is 'neo-Taylorist' (Taylor, 1911). Managerialists assert that professional managers are better able to take decisions to solve business problems, including economic and administrative ones facing governments, than are those relying on experience and common sense alone. At the core of managerialism 'burns the seldom-tested assumption that better management will prove an effective solvent for a wide range of economic and social ills' (Pollitt, 1993, p. 1). Management and managing, therefore, are 'good' and should be left to managers alone to do.

Pollitt identifies five elements in managerialist analyses. These are: social progress requires continuing increases in economic productivity; productivity increases come from applying sophisticated technologies; the application of these technologies can only be achieved through a disciplined workforce; 'business success' depends on the professionalism of skilled managers; and to perform their crucial role managers must have the right to manage.

Managerialism is also predicated upon universal approaches to solving organizational and resource problems. The underlying assumption is that managers are involved in the same processes and activities, whatever organization they are in, and only the context varies. The private sector therefore provides a repertoire of management techniques and practices, which can be applied to the public sector. The rationalist, economistic and generic approaches of the private sector, it is argued, should be adopted and transmitted to the public sector (Farnham and Horton, 1993). Supporters of the managerialist position assume that the injection of private-sector management practices into the public services will improve their performance, make them more responsive to client needs and make them more effective organizations. The techniques of the classical public administrator, in contrast, are typically identified with slow decision-taking, risk avoidance and domination by professional workers.

As an ideology, managerialism has been promoted by management consultants and gurus, such as Peters and Waterman (1992), Deming (1986) and Juran (1989). It has been transmitted into organizations, both private and public, by university business schools and management trainers. In the public services, managerialism has also been introduced by ministers and public managers committed to its values and those who took advantage of the professional opportunities it provided for them.

The new management practices

In the early years of the new public management, there was a preoccupation with economy and efficiency, focusing on what the public services were doing and how they were doing it. The underlying purpose was to eliminate waste and shed activities which were no longer necessary or could be provided by the private sector. Private businessmen were recruited to advise on new management systems and initiate cultural change within public organizations. The areas of public management which were changed in that first period were those of strategic, financial and personnel management. By the late 1980s, the changes reflected a new emphasis on competition, performance, quality and customer care, drawing upon private-sector techniques in marketing, performance management, total quality management and organizational re-engineering. The ordering, timing and emphases placed on the new techniques vary amongst the public services but all have featured in the new public management since 1979. There has, in other words, been a cultural change in public-service organizations, bordering on what can be described as a 'quiet revolution' (Butler, 1993).

Mission statements, business plans and financial plans are now produced by all the public services and sub-units within them, reflecting the adoption of a rational approach to strategic management. With the use of IT, management information systems have been developed, often with the aid of outside consultants, to assist top managers in strategy determination and strategic implementation, as well as in coordinating and controlling their organizations (Elcock, 1993). The first management information system, MINIS, was introduced into the Civil Service, in the Department of the Environment, in 1980. Now all departments and agencies have Top Management Systems. Systematic planning is now a feature of all public services, as they have adopted strategic planning models from the private sector. Strategic planning has become important as the public services are faced with uncertainty, turbulence and increased competition. Many are using private-sector techniques such as SWOT analysis – the examination of the strengths, weaknesses, opportunities and constraints facing organizations (Lawton and Rose, 1994).

Effective strategic management requires good financial control and major changes have occurred in this area too. Business people were brought into government to assist in the development of financial procedures. In 1979, for example, Derek Rayner, from Marks and Spencer, was appointed as Margaret Thatcher's efficiency advisor in the Civil Service. After a series of efficiency scrutinies in individual departments, the need for a new financial initiative was evident. In 1982, the Financial Management Initiative (FMI) was introduced throughout the Civil Service (Cmnd. 9508, 1983). It looked remarkably like the systems of accountable management and cost-centred management found in the private sector. Once the FMI had been installed, it enabled other management techniques to be adopted. These included decentralized and devolved budgeting, performance indicators and performance management. Although FMI was a civil service policy, all public services followed a similar pattern. Financial information systems, devolved budgets, performance indicators and performance management were introduced into the NHS, local government, education, and, most recently, the police (Perrin, 1988; Rawlinson and Tanner, 1989). The main effect of developments under FMI was to instil greater cost control and introduce financial accounting techniques and new managerial tools into the public services, which were astonishingly absent until then (Flynn, 1993; Gray *et al.*, 1991).

Performance indicators (PIs) were used within the NHS and education before 1979 but tended to focus on quantifiable throughput results such as bed occupancies or the costs of educating students. PIs, which can be counted in their thousands in the public services, have been extended and refined and are now central in setting objectives, comparing efficiency and managing resources. They provide managers with hard data on what is being done, how much is being done and how much it costs. In the NHS, local government, education and the police, they are used to construct league tables of achievement, measured against performance criteria. These provide bases for comparisons over time, as well as for external comparisons. They are also a benchmark for setting targets and a means for comparing efficiency and effectiveness amongst subunits. PIs also enable central government to retain control and monitor public services, even where managerial functions are devolved.

Performance management has become an important feature of the public services since the mid-1980s. Performance management has various meanings but essentially it uses systems which help organizations to plan, delegate and assess the operation of their activities and services. Its aims are high standards of work, to achieve quality output and satisfy customer needs. It has three main elements. First, performance standards are set and actions planned to achieve these goals. Second, issues of day-to-day management, including monitoring, directing and coaching, are addressed to ensure that actions are translated into practice. Third, results are appraised and assessed in the light of the targets set (Local Government Training Board (LGTB), 1988; Bevan and Thompson, 1992). An important element of performance management is performance related pay.

Management of quality has dominated public-service

organizations in the 1990s. It was an idea which germi-
nated in the private sector, where intense market competition forced companies to look to the quality of their
products, rather than price or design, as the key to market success. Quality is defined as 'conformance to requirements' (Crosby, 1984), 'fitness for purpose' (Juran, 1989)
and 'meeting the requirements of the customer' (Oakland,
1989). The enthusiasm for quality was imported into the
public services through the *Citizen's Charter* (1991). The
management of quality reflects acceptance by public
managers that the users of public services are their 'customers' and 'clients'. The latter should be provided with
services meeting their expectations and eliciting high levels
of customer satisfaction. It is also considered that customers of the 'business' should be consulted about the
services they want and whether their needs are being met.
Techniques for managing quality, initially used in the
private sector, such as BS5750, quality circles and TQM,
have been widely introduced into the public services,
to meet the needs for 'continuous improvement' and
'customer care' (Koch, 1992; Sanderson, 1992; Skelcher,
1992).

Fundamental organizational restructuring has been a
further strategy adopted in the public services to bring
about continuous change. Restructuring has been done
by creating sub-units, such as Civil Service agencies, NHS
trusts, locally managed schools and basic command units
within the police. The reasons include: to break up monolithic bureaucracies into smaller, more flexible functional
units; to create internal markets; and to facilitate competition. In practice, the objectives for restructuring are
different in each service but restructuring has been
accompanied, in most instances, with the appointment of
general managers, some of them recruited from the private
sector. Structural change makes it easier to introduce new
private-sector management techniques, whether in agencies, NHS trusts, universities, further education colleges
or locally managed schools.

CCT, contracting out and internal markets have introduced competition and forced public services to adopt

strong marketing strategies and techniques, previously confined to the private sector. Public managers have had to set clear objectives and find new ways of designing and delivering services. Extensive use is made of customer questionnaires and opinion surveys, to enable public organizations to respond to the diverging and changing needs of different clients. Skills in developing service contracts have become imperative, as services are increasingly put out to the private sector or as contracts are used amongst internal business units, as in local government.

All the innovative management techniques outlined above, and the objectives underlying them, amount to a cultural reorientation in the public services (Metcalf and Richards, 1990). Senior public managers are both the subjects and agents of change. Many have been trained in the new management techniques and an increasing number are either recruited from the private sector or seconded for periods to private organizations. Increasing numbers of managers are engaged on personal contracts of employment and, like their private-sector counterparts, paid by performance, albeit to a limited extent. Increasingly, public managers are subject to regular performance reviews by their own senior managers. To bring about changes in employee behaviour, in turn, and to overcome resistance to change, public-service managers are using new human resources management (HRM) techniques, again imported from the private sector. A series of innovatory personnel management and HRM practices are being used as levers of change on supervisory staff and other employees. These include: non-standard contracts of employment; PRP; staff appraisal; and training and development.

People Management in the Public Services

Given the crucial importance of the public services, their costs to taxpayers and the large numbers they employ, the tasks associated with people management are enormous.

Those responsible for managing public services have to deal with diverging and conflicting pressures. Their role is essentially threefold: to ensure quality service to those using public services; to provide value for money or cost-effectiveness to those paying for them; and to promote fair employment standards for those working in them. In practice, a sensitive balance has to be struck between the disjunctures inherent in managing public organizations: management's accountability to its political masters; its responsibility for providing essential services to the public; and its responsibilities as an employer of people.

This marks out a further distinction between private-sector and public-service organizations. However good they are as employers, businesses employ people primarily as resources, for the purposes of producing goods and profits, since their ultimate goals are customer and shareholder satisfaction. There is always a potential conflict and trade-off in businesses between profits for shareholders and wages for workers. For businesses, the employment function is always a secondary activity.

The public services, in contrast, whilst employing people as resources, also have wider social duties to them. First, their employees can never be totally regarded simply as resources, since, as workers, they are agents for providing national welfare and delivery of essential services to the community, whilst, as citizens, they are part of the state. Second, state organizations, like other employers, require competent, qualified and committed workers, who, in turn, expect to be treated fairly, reasonably and consistently by those employing them. The standards by which public-service employers act in relation to their staff, however, may well be the minimal benchmarks by which the state authorities might expect private employers to treat their workforces. If the state is perceived to be a bad employer, it sets a poor example for those private employers having the lowest employment standards.

Third, in their own instrumental, self-interest, those ultimately directing public organizations, politicians, normally seek to avoid, as far as possible, overt conflicts between public employees and their employers. This is primarily because of the potentially damaging and far reaching economic consequences of disputes in essential public services. It is also because unregulated industrial conflict can turn into political conflict, undermine governmental authority and lead to social disorder. This means that people management in the public services is bounded by government's political agenda and a strategic framework within which people management takes place. This agenda and framework also affects the private sector, but to a lesser degree.

There are also similarities between managing people in public services and business organizations. The people management tasks within each sector are common, although how they are executed in practice varies amongst organizations, because of the different contexts within which public services and businesses operate. Public services, as indicated earlier, are driven by politics and ministerial imperatives, whilst businesses are driven by markets, prices and profits.

People management activities in both types of organizations are bounded externally by the labour markets from which they recruit, the law affecting employment relationships and trade union power. Although each organization has its own personnel policies, there is a common 'people management process' applying to all organizations. This has seven elements or basic managerial activities, as illustrated in Figure 1.1: procuring the workforce; structuring work; rewarding staff; controlling staff; training staff; staff participation; and exiting staff.

Personnel policy, labour markets and employment law

Public-service personnel policies tend, in comparison with some in the private sector, to be formal and detailed. Their strategic framework is determined by government, with operational policies determined by senior managers within each service. The public services generally operate in national labour markets in recruiting senior, professional and middle level posts, but in local ones for lower level and manual

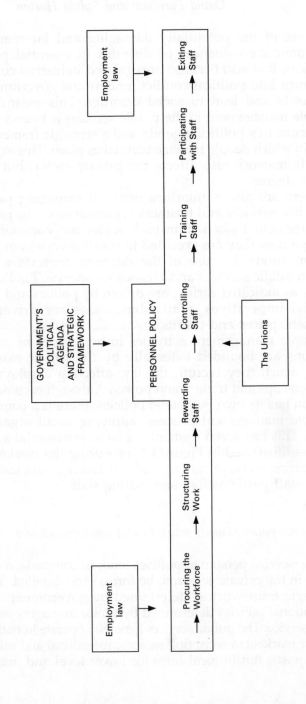

FIGURE 1.1 The people management cycle in the public services

staff. Traditionally, public services have had structured, internal labour markets, providing career pathways and career opportunities, especially for professional, technical and managerial workers. The impact of employment law on the public services varies. On the one side, many personnel policies in public organizations are in excess of the minimal standards required by legislation, such as maternity pay and leave, equal opportunities and health and safety. On the other hand, trade union law affects public employers and unions in the same ways as it does the private sector. Because of the special status of some public officials, there is also legislation relating only to them and their conditions of service, such as civil servants and police officers.

Procuring the workforce

Procuring the public workforce requires the managing of several tasks. Most recruitment takes place locally, beginning once a vacancy is established, either by creating a new post or replacing an existing one. In some cases, recruitment may be in response to human resources or 'manpower' planning but, more usually, it is in response to the immediate human resource needs of the organization, after the job requirements have been identified, analysed and defined. Managers involved in selection, like those in the private sector, short list applicants, evaluating them by a variety of methods – the 'classic trio' being the application form, the interview and references – and take employment decisions. The contracts to which staff are appointed vary, being either standard or non-standard ones. Many conditions of employment are negotiated through national collective bargaining machinery. With few exceptions, normally senior managers, it is the relevant collective agreements which become incorporated into the individual contracts of employment of most public servants. Graduate recruitment is more likely to be national and involves assessment centres and sophisticated selection techniques. An increasing feature is headhunting and using recruitment consultants for senior appointments.

Structuring work

The structuring of jobs and work takes place locally, through job analysis, job descriptions and job design. Organizational structures, on the other hand, are determined centrally. The structure of the Civil Service, for example, is determined politically and by means of orders-in-council, although individual agencies and units now have scope to determine their own structures within that framework. Structures in other public services are primarily a function of legislation, with detailed internal structures being determined by top management locally, in accordance with the needs of the service. Because of the scale and political accountability of public organizations, bureaucratic structures and standardized procedures have traditionally typified the public services, although during the 1990s there is evidence of more flexible, post-bureaucratic structures emerging. These have shorter hierarchies, *ad hoc* task groups and more managerial discretion locally.

Rewarding staff

Pay structures, pay rates and conditions of employment are normally determined by employer and staff side representatives through national collective bargaining. Some senior management staff are employed on personal contracts, linked to performance appraisal and performance pay, but the norm remains national pay and conditions agreements, interpreted locally by managers and unions. The major groups of public workers currently excluded from national bargaining are senior civil servants, doctors and dentists, school teachers, nurses and midwives and the professions allied to medicine. Other rewards for public workers include career paths, promotion opportunities and occupational pensions. Even today, employment security is relatively higher than in the private sector.

Controlling staff

Public employment tends to be bureaucratized. Employment rules, employment decisions and employment records are generally proceduralized and set down in manuals, handbooks and collective agreements. Disciplinary, grievance and other personnel procedures set out the stages and time scales for determining decisions, with union involvement being the norm. A recent trend has been the use of staff appraisal and performance reviews, in the NHS, education and the police, where previously there were none. Emphasis is now being placed on performance management, because of the pressures on employment costs, need for increased productivity, commitment to greater staff involvement and the opportunity provided for controlling people from a distance.

Training staff

The public services have generally had a good record for training staff, especially since the 1970s. Induction is the norm, with many opportunities for post-entry training, especially for professional, administrative and managerial groups. Management development is more common than in the past. Training is often facilitated by staff appraisal linked to staff development. A range of training methods is used: coaching and counselling; courses, seminars and workshops; studying for qualifications; distance and open learning; secondments; transfers, rotation and job enrichment; action learning; and projects and assignments. Increasingly, training is evaluated to assess its effectiveness and value for money. Most public services have national training centres, although most training takes place locally.

Staff participation

The main means for staff participation continues to be union organization. There are, however, exceptions. First, independent trade unions were banned at General Communications Headquarters, Cheltenham (GCHQ), in 1984, on the grounds of their potential threat to national security (Farnham and Pimlott, 1995). Second, under the Police Act 1964, police officers cannot join trade unions but are normally members of police federations. Third, in the armed services, union membership is not proscribed but unions are not recognized for collective or individual purposes. In most of the NHS and school teaching, there is no longer national pay bargaining but the unions present evidence to the pay review bodies and most have local recognition rights.

Collective bargaining and joint consultative machinery, frequently modelled on Whitley arrangements, remain the norm for providing indirect, power-based staff participation, with links between these channels at different levels (Farnham, 1978). Time-off-work provisions are agreed for local union officials and facilities for lay representatives are provided by the employers. There is also growing evidence of parallel channels of direct, task-based staff communication. These include vertical top-down communication between senior managers and subordinates, cascading of information through line managers, team briefings, staff questionnaires and opinion surveys.

Exiting staff

Staff leave public employment by resigning, retiring or on the grounds of dismissal or redundancy. Procedures exist for ensuring that staff exits are conducted and concluded in accordance with the basic legal requirements and good employment practice. Public employers have to be transparent in the ways in which they handle these sensitive people management issues. There was, for example, a massive public outcry in 1991 after the President of the Board of Trade, Michael Heseltine, failed to comply with the law regulating collective redundancies, when he announced the government's intended closure of 31 coal mines without consulting the staff and their unions.

Conclusion and Evaluation

Public services are important providers of essential services and national welfare. They carry out their statutory duties in government departments, Next Steps agencies, health service units, the local authorities, education establishments and police forces. They are also large-scale employers which utilize a wide range of professional, managerial and other skills to carry out their wide responsibilities to the UK's citizens and those organizations paying for and using them.

The public services are undergoing radical changes in terms of their scope, functions, structures, the ways in which they are financed, how they are managed and who manages them. After reorganization, there were 'at least 20,000 managers in the NHS in England' in 1994, an increase of some 13 per cent over the previous year, whilst the number of nursing staff had fallen by 4.6 per cent over the same period. Published figures also indicated that between 1989–90 and 1993–94, NHS managerial salary costs in England increased by 284 per cent and administrative and clerical costs by 49 per cent, whilst those of nursing staff increased by only 25 per cent (Brindle, 1995, p. 3). Growth of managerial cadres has also been experienced in the Civil Service, especially in Next Steps agencies, locally managed schools, further and higher education corporations and, to a lesser extent, in police forces. This has followed restructuring, budgetary devolution and the introduction of performance management systems into them.

The injection of private-sector management techniques into the new public services (Farnham and Horton, 1993) is undeniable and has been both wide ranging and intrusive. These include strategic, financial and quality initiatives, as well as the introduction of internal markets, CCT and market testing. No part of the public services has been exempt from the economic and ideological fundamentalism of successive Conservative governments regarding the purposes, financing and managing of these services.

This managerial revolution has created tensions between those who manage them – and are increasingly highly paid – and those who are managed within them, especially professional groups such as doctors, nurses and teachers, who are paid less. This tension was highlighted during a series of often intense and bitter industrial disputes between the public authorities and public-service unions during the 1980s. Although some of these disputes were explicitly over pay, others reflected more implicit anxieties about the possible impacts of managerial changes on job security, conditions of employment, promotion prospects and work loads. Between 1979 and 1991, a cumulative total of some nine million working-days were lost in the public services, including the NHS (1979 and 1982), Civil Service (1981), public administration (1986), school teachers (1986) and local authorities (1989 and 1991) (Farnham and Pimlott, 1995).

The language of 'public administration' has been transformed into the language of 'business management'. Within the new managerialist hegemony, 'public administrators' become 'public managers'; 'forecasting' becomes 'strategy'; 'statistics' become 'performance indicators'; 'inspection' becomes 'quality assurance'; 'staff' become 'resources'; and 'personnel management' becomes 'human resources management'. Above all, the public services are increasingly being described as 'businesses', by those determining policy and managing them. Thus NHS trusts are increasingly described as being in the 'business of health care' and the new universities in the 'business of higher education', whilst police authorities formulate strategies and business plans, incorporating 'mission statement[s] . . . which comprehensively describe the business of the [Police] Force' (Home Office,

1994, p. 3). To what extent this linguistic rhetoric represents organizational reality is examined later in this book.

The forces for change in the public services are managerial innovations. These are driven by government policy, top civil servants and senior managers responsible for setting corporate targets in their own organizations. These innovations, whether in central or local government, are challenging the traditional ways in which people are managed. The implications are that in procuring, structuring, rewarding, controlling, training and participating with their workforces, those responsible for managing public servants are looking for new approaches to their tasks.

In the 1990s, the overarching issue appears to be government's goal of reducing spending on public services, whilst forcing employers to utilize the people they employ more intensively in customer-oriented, cost-effective 'public businesses'. These initiatives have resulted in public employers developing new people management strategies and entrepreneurial and assertive styles of management, based on what is perceived to be 'good practice' in leading-edge businesses. Senior public managers, concerned with performance, quality and value for money, are injecting private-sector people management techniques into their organizations. Senior managers are also introducing flexible employment patterns, performance management systems, work intensification and new styles of management into the public services. Unlike in the private sector, however, where there are examples of union derecognition, public employers appear to be neither encouraging nor actively discouraging union membership.

Yet the forces for continuity in the public services are deep-rooted. They include: resistance to change by those long identified with the public-service tradition; the bureaucratic procedures of public services; the strategic importance of key professional groups within them; their depth of trade union organization; and the scarcity of resources to facilitate absolute organizational and cultural change. It is to the forces of tradition in people management to which we turn in the next Chapter, before examining some detailed case studies of people management change in Part Two of this book.

CHAPTER 2

Traditional people management

David Farnham and Sylvia Horton

Traditional people management (TPM) and the collectivist institutions of industrial relations evolved in the public services out of the legacies of political patronage in the nineteenth century and political reforms in the twentieth century. TPM developed, over many years, as the demands placed on the state grew and expanded. It is characterized by: an administrative personnel function; standardized employment practices; paternalist styles of management; collectivist patterns of industrial relations; and the view that state employers should be 'model' and 'good practice' employers. These classical features of managing people finally came to maturity after the second world war. They grew out of the nineteenth century 'nightwatchman state', developed in the twentieth century 'social service state' and reached their peak in the post-war 'Welfare State' during the 1960s and 1970s.

The embryonic public services, which were largely creations of mid-Victorian Britain, evolved coherent but pragmatic people management policies. It was because of the political accountability, growing scale and complexity, labour intensity and monopolistic provision of the early public services that people management issues were continuously brought to the fore, for both politicians and senior public officials. As politically accountable bodies, the early Civil Service and the new local government had to be more open, transparent and sensitive in the ways they managed people than did many of their private-sector counterparts. The relatively large-scale and labour intensive nature of the prototypical public services meant that politicians and those responsible for administering these services were continuously concerned with the costs of employing staff and the implications of this for the public purse. The senior administrators of the early period also had to find effective ways of providing these services, as well as procuring, rewarding and retaining appropriate staff.

The steady growth of white-collar staff associations, professional associations and trade unions in the late nineteenth and early twentieth centuries eventually gave rise to demands for union recognition. But it was not until after the first world war that unions were recognized for the purposes of national collective bargaining for the first time, in the Civil Service, local government and education. It was these developments which led to another distinguishing feature of public employment: union recognition and high density of membership.

During the interwar period, the elements of TPM and the early institutions of industrial relations were successfully established and took root, pragmatically and piecemeal. After the second world war, with the creation of the modern Welfare State, which now included the health services and extended social services, the characteristic features of TPM in the public services were finally settled, continuing virtually unchallenged for the next 25 years. This Chapter traces the origins, development and maturation of TPM and outlines the legacy of history upon it.

People Management in the Early Civil Service

The Civil Service was the first public service. Yet even by 1800, there was no recognizable Civil Service or permanent body of 'full time salaried officials, systematically recruited, with clear lines of authority and uniform rules on such questions as superannuation' (Parris, 1969, p. 22). There was a collection as civil offices, grouped together into departments of varying sizes. The sale of offices was still common and recruitment was largely by patronage and nomination, at the disposal of ministers and Members of Parliament (MPs). At the highest levels, there was also a fusion of political and administrative roles, with officials changing positions as governments changed. The separation of permanent administrative officials from temporary political ones, and the clear distinction between ministers and civil servants, evolved between 1780 and 1830 (Parris, 1969). Only then were the elements of a constitutional bureaucracy achieved, consisting of a permanent body of officials, loyal to government and politically neutral. But the other characteristics of the modern Civil Service took much longer to achieve.

Pay and conditions

It was the pay of public officials which dominated the debates about the Civil Service during the first half of the nineteenth century. The main issues were the principles upon which payment should be based, levels of pay and whether pensions should be contributory or noncontributory. As early as 1808, a select committee of the House of Commons stated that 'the public ought unquestionably to be served as cheaply as is consistent with being served with integrity and ability'. In 1828, the same committee enunciated the principle of 'what the market will bear' or the competitive market rate for public officials (Cohen, 1941).

By 1850, some departments had introduced salary scales and adopted the market principle for determining the pay of lower level staff but there was no consistency amongst the graduated scales of remuneration for similar offices. Neither was there standardization of hours worked, paid leave or sick leave. Some departments had a six-hour day;

others seven. The length of annual holidays also varied. This absence of unified salary scales, apart from making it difficult to control expenditure on pay, restricted the transfer of staff amongst departments.

A more rational rewards system slowly developed in the last decades of the nineteenth century. In 1873, the government imposed a new policy on the terms upon which 'established' and 'unestablished' clerks could be employed. Unestablished clerks would not be superannuated, although standard terms were introduced for them. The unestablished 'writers' were aggrieved, because this meant a deterioration in their conditions of service. They formed the first staff association and were successful in getting policy changes. These resulted in a salary scale for all established writers and a weekly wage for unestablished staff. It was not until after 1920, however, with the establishment of the civil service national Whitley Council, that pay scales were first negotiated nationally.

Superannuation

By 1816, the principle that all civil servants should be entitled to a pension had been established and a uniform scale of payments set down. Pensions were not to exceed two-thirds of average salary over the previous three years and the maximum could be reached only after 45 years' service. There was wide disagreement, however, over whether pensions should be financed by funded contributions or out of revenue. Practices varied amongst departments and Parliament was inconsistent in the policies it sought to impose. In the 1820s, deductions from salaries were introduced but then rescinded. They were reintroduced in 1834, although only for staff joining after 1829.

The issue of contributions was only finally resolved when the Superannuation Act 1859 stated that all permanent civil servants should receive a pension on retirement. This was defined as a person holding an appointment directly from the Crown or admitted into the service with a certificate of the Civil Service Commission (CSC). No pension would be payable under the age of 60, other than for medical reasons, and pensions would be non-contributory. The 1859 Act remained the basis of superannuation until the twentieth century and the principle, that the pay of civil servants consists of a salary plus a retirement allowance, has survived to this day.

Superannuation has an important place in the history of the Civil Service and has served a number of purposes (Cohen, 1941). First, it provided a means of removing patronage and reducing the numbers of 'placemen' or people in post *via* patronage or personal nomination. Second, it was an inducement to continuous service and underpinned a permanent career structure. Third, it served to enforce discipline, since dismissal for misconduct meant loss of pension. The Civil Service was undoubtedly in advance of other institutions in the provision of pensions and set an example for other public bodies to follow.

Structure and grading

The Northcote-Trevelyan report (1853) is generally recognized to mark the origins of the meritocratic Civil Service. Its four main recommendations were:

- work should be divided into intellectual and mechanical tasks
- recruitment into each division should be by open competitive examinations, conducted by an independent board
- promotion should be based on merit and reports of superiors
- mobility between departments should be encouraged, with common entry points to each division

Northcote and Trevelyan envisaged the emergence of a profession of civil servants, comparable to those of the law and the Church. This, it was felt, would attract the best brains of the universities into the highest levels and the ablest, literate young men into the lower levels. Their report met with strong resistance by the politicians but their ideas gradually took root.

With standard recruitment systems emerging after 1870, it became possible to reform the fragmented grading structure. Each department still had its own internal structure and determined the work officials did. Although each department had a hierarchy, reflected in its recruitment and pay, there was no consistency across departments or even within them. There was clearly a need to match the type of work done and pay awarded across the Service. After 1859, the distinction between 'established' and 'unestablished' civil servants rested upon certification by the CSC and entitlement to superannuation. Unestablished staff escaped any control by the CSC and their numbers increased rapidly, as the work of departments expanded. Yet there was often no difference between the work which they did, or in their other rewards, from those of established staff.

By the 1890s, it was possible to discern a four class structure: a first division; a second division (formerly the lower division); an intermediate class, equivalent to a lower clerical division; and boy clerks. The last three classes were common to the Service and were found in all departments, but the first division remained departmentalized until 1920. The first division consisted of three grades and the second division of two. It was possible to move between grades and from one level to another by promotion and this led to a career Civil Service. Entry to the classes was standardized, based upon merit and closely linked to the educational system. Notably, the growing number of professional civil servants were outside this structure and confined to specific departments. After the first world war, a largely unified Civil Service was established but a fully integrated structure has never been achieved.

Staff associations

During the first half of the nineteenth century, the main way for officials to present their individual or collective grievances was in the form of a 'memorial' to their immediate superior or the minister of the department. After 1850, officials began to organize petitions to the Treasury. This practice was challenged on the grounds that it infringed the principle of ministerial responsibility, although petitions continued to be used. If petitions were not successful, then staff sometimes sought the help of MPs. This system politicized civil service pay and conditions.

The changes taking place in the Civil Service during the second half of the century, and the growing awareness of their common interests, led civil servants to combine into staff associations. 'By the 1890s permanent associations were demanding official recognition and the right to bargain on matters relating to their members' (Humphreys, 1958, p. 2). The years between 1870 and 1914 were significant in the history of staff relations. The grading reforms made strong staff associations possible, whilst standardized classes made the associations necessary if staff were to influence conditions of work. By 1914, there were 73 active staff associations. They had high levels of membership, ranging from 75 per cent to 100 per cent density. Although there was no official policy on recognition, staff associations were at no time forbidden by the authorities.

It was becoming evident that petitioning departments, the Treasury and Parliament was no longer appropriate. Neither was the device of the parliamentary committee, which, throughout the nineteenth century, had been the method of arbitration used in settling disputes between government and civil servants. A select committee of the House of Commons, investigating the wages and conditions of postal workers in 1912, recommended that an expert body should be appointed to advise on future relations between the state and its employees. This was delayed because of the outbreak of war in 1914. But anxious to avoid confrontation over wages, and to placate the unions, government set up an arbitration tribunal, in 1916, to decide on questions of wages for civilian employees.

The Genesis of People Management in Local Government

The remits of British local government, like those of central government, steadily expanded throughout the nineteenth and early twentieth centuries. Like the Civil Service, local government was largely the product of political pragmatism and incremental reforms. Industrial change and urbanization gave rise to problems of poverty, public health and law and order. In responding to these, Parliament approved the setting up of locally elected boards, with taxing powers, to provide services. These included: Boards of Guardians to enforce the poor law; School Boards to provide elementary education; Highway Boards to build and maintain roads; and Sanitary Authorities to provide clean water and sewage disposal. But there was no coordination or overall control, in spite of the existence of the central government Board of Health and Poor Law Commissioners.

In the last quarter of the century, there was an attempt to rationalize the chaotic structure of *ad hoc* boards, town councils and quarter sessions making up local government (Smellie, 1968). In 1871, central government established a Local Government Board which set about creating 'a logical pattern of local authorities each responsible for providing a wide and varied group of services in its locality' (Griffiths, 1976, p. 4). Under the Local Government Acts 1888 and 1894, six types of local authority were created: counties, county boroughs, boroughs, urban districts, rural districts and parishes. The larger cities were given county borough status and the authority to provide all local government services. In the rest of the country, services were divided between counties and districts or boroughs, with rural parishes having very limited powers and London having a separate two-tier arrangement.

By 1902, most of the *ad hoc* boards had been abolished and the new structure had absorbed their functions. This system lasted, in modified form, until 1974 and still underpins today's local government structure. The services provided by local authorities expanded continuously after 1870. Many embarked upon municipal trading and provided gas, electricity and public transport in addition to the poor law, public health, highways and police services. Later education, housing, libraries, town planning, health and personal social services were added, plus economic development and leisure activities after 1945.

Recruitment, pay and conditions

The growth in local government led to a major expansion in employment. There was a need for clerks, lawyers, engineers, surveyors, doctors, teachers, police officers, accountants, architects, librarians and manual workers. Each of the 1400 major local authorities and the 10 000 and more parishes in 1900 was responsible for recruiting its own staff. Because of the technical nature of most services, departments were staffed by specialists. This distinguished local government from the Civil Service which was, and is, dominated by generalists.

Recruitment was left to committees and chief officers and was characterized by patronage. Political considerations weighed heavily in appointments to senior posts but also influenced junior positions. Each council committee controlled its staff numbers, constrained only by financial limits set by the full council. There was 'an almost complete lack of uniformity and consistency of either entry standards, methods of selection or conditions of service' (Fowler, 1975, p. 41).

There were no standardized payments to officials in the nineteenth century and individual local authorities determined their own policies. The only exception was the police. From 1839, the Home Secretary had powers to make rules regarding the pay, clothing and equipment of the Metropolitan police and this was extended to cover all police authorities after 1919.

Central government involvement in the payment of school teachers also dates from the 1830s, when education was provided mainly by religious societies in the voluntary sector. Government grants were given to aid the training and remuneration of 'certificated' teachers (Tropp, 1957), although most teachers were 'non-certificated' and were paid according to the decisions of each individual school. After 1861, a new 'Revised Code' was introduced, abolishing all direct payments to teachers and pupil-teachers and introducing 'Payments by Results'.

Government grants were based upon numbers of children attending school, their attendance and the results they achieved in public examinations, supervised by the schools inspectorate. The creation of local government Board Schools in 1870 did not alter the system of payment by results, which continued until 1896. When education boards were absorbed by local authorities in 1902, many larger local education authorities sought to place their teachers under a comprehensive scale of salaries but there was no uniformity of scales until the formation of the Burnham Committee, after the first world war.

In other local authority occupations, committees decided on payment, subject to keeping within their budgets. The result was great variations amongst authorities, although the salaries of senior officials were related to authority size and the functions it carried out. Chief officer salaries were always high and rose steadily with length of service (Redlich and Hurst, 1903). This, plus the fact that there was no standard superannuation scheme, restricted staff mobility. Eventually, towns began to compare salaries, at least for higher posts, but 'it was not until the influence of [staff] organizations entered into local government that any attempt was made to get scales of salaries drawn up that were in any way comparable' (Hill, 1935, p. 132).

Superannuation

Superannuation came gradually to local government. The first pensions were for the Metropolitan police in 1829 and this was extended to all the police in 1890. Poor Law Authorities were empowered to grant pensions in 1864 but it was not until 1896 that compulsory superannuation was established. School teachers became entitled to superannuation in 1898 and asylum workers in 1909. Some local authorities had obtained statutory authority to superannuate their own officers but it was the Local Government and Other Officers Superannuation Act 1922 which enabled authorities to introduce schemes, if they wished. Not all did and this, along with the disparities of pay and other conditions, impeded the development of a uniform service.

Trade unions and staff associations

Collective organizations of manual and non-manual workers grew during the nineteenth century. From the beginning, manual workers joined unions which represented both private and municipal employees. These started as local associations of gas workers, dockers and engineers but grew into national unions after 1889 and the birth of the 'new unionism'. Gas workers and dockers were successful in gaining better pay, largely through industrial action and attempts to impose closed shops on employers (Clegg, 1964). It was where unions organized themselves politically and had representation on local councils that their influence was greatest. 'The attitudes of local authorities to trade unionism varied greatly from one area to another; but, where the unions managed to build up some political strength, they could exert an influence which was not available in private employment' (Clegg *et al.*, 1964, p. 88).

During the 1890s, a number of unions were established for local authority employees and one, founded in 1894 for London County Council workers, became the Municipal Employees Association in 1899. By 1905, its membership had grown to over 8000, with branches all over the country. It organized manual workers in electricity, gas, tramways, cleaning, and highways. Unlike rival unions, it was rarely involved in strikes, although this may have been because of the legal restrictions placed upon workers in essential gas and water services by the Conspiracy and Protection of Property Act 1875.

Local associations and professional associations of municipal and local government officers grew during the nineteenth century, as means of furthering the interests of newly emerging occupations. One theory is that the encouragement of professionalization was a deliberate strategy of reformers who wished to overcome the corruption and nepotism dominating local councils (Laffin and Young, 1990). Certainly, the emergence of professional corps, relatively immune from the manipulation of local influences, was an outcome of local government reform. New statutory posts of town clerk, civil and sanitary engineer, medical officer of health and education officer, were created and this became a pattern in later legislation.

The professionalization of local government staff was furthered by the formation of professional associations, seeking to control entry and maintain educational standards through qualifying examinations. Some of the earliest were the Institution of Municipal and County Engineers, formed in 1870, and the Chartered Institute of Public Finance and Accountancy in 1885. Associations of County Council Surveyors and Women Housing Managers followed in 1916. The earliest local government profession was lawyers. Solicitors were appointed to act as town clerks to municipal authorities after 1835 and to all local authorities, except parishes, after 1888. This tradition of the most senior officer being a lawyer has only recently been abandoned.

The strategy adopted by the professional associations, like those of the school teachers, was to gain control over entry to the profession, rather than by seeking to influence pay directly. They also petitioned MPs and submitted evidence to Parliament when matters of local government were being investigated. The Municipal Officers Association, encompassing administrative staff as well as some professionals, operated on issues of pay and conditions. An attempt was made in 1904 to form a single national organization of officials. The National Association of Local Government Officers (NALGO) emerged in 1905 and became a general trade union for all white-collar workers in local government (Spoor, 1964). It was only after Whitley that national collective bargaining began to emerge.

Lack of uniformity

The main characteristic of people management in local government before 1919 was absence of any standardization of pay, conditions and employment policies. Each local authority recruited its own staff and determined its own pay and conditions of service. Like the Civil Service, pay was generally based on the principle of 'what the market would bear', although there were attempts to match the salaries of senior officers in similar types of authority. The overall responsibility for leading and coordinating staff in a local authority rested with the Town Clerk. He was generally expected to advise committees on appointments, grading of work and remuneration, even though he was a trained lawyer. He was *primus inter pares* amongst senior officers, with no control over them. Until the interwar years, there was no single body or department responsible for staffing establishments within local authorities.

People Management in the Interwar Years

The interwar years were a watershed in the evolution of people management policies and the foundations of TPM were laid in the period after 1919. There were three key developments in the Civil Service and local government during these years. Each built on the prewar period and each provided a bridge with further developments at the end of the second world war. First, attempts were made to develop collective bargaining wage-fixing machinery, based on the principles of 'Whitleyism'. Second, there was the emergence of establishment work, aimed at controlling 'manpower' levels and employment costs. Third, there was growing pressure for equal pay and conditions for women, although these issues were not finally resolved until after the second world war.

Whitleyism and the public services

The Committee on Relations between Employers and Employees was a subcommittee of the Ministry of Reconstruction, set up by the War Cabinet in October 1916. It met under the chairmanship of J. H. Whitley, at that time Deputy Speaker of the House of Commons, with terms of reference (Ministry of Reconstruction, 1918, p. 3):

1. To make and consider suggestions for securing a permanent improvement in the relations between employers and workmen
2. To recommend means for securing that industrial conditions affecting the relations between employers and workmen shall be systematically reviewed by those concerned, with a view to improving conditions in the future.

The origins of the Committee lay in the growth of labour militancy and demands for workers' control of industry, made by some powerful rank-and-file trade unionists, before and during the first world war. It was during the war that the so-called 'Shop Stewards' Movement' emerged in those 'industries mainly concerned in the production of munitions of war' (Cole, 1923, pp. 26 and 28). And 'the actual spark which set the movement alight was the rise in prices, uncompensated . . . by any effective official movement for a corresponding rise in wage rates'.

The basic task of Whitley was to advise the Ministry of Reconstruction on the ways in which industrial relations between employers and workers might be stabilized and improved after the war. The Committee issued five reports between spring 1917 and summer 1918: an interim report; a report on 'joint standing industrial councils'; a 'supplementary' report on works committees; a report on conciliation and arbitration; and a final, summary report.

Initially, the 'Whitley Scheme' did not include government or local government within its remit. Whitleyism was to be limited to the private sector alone. Indeed, there is no evidence that the Treasury, as the department responsible for the Civil Service, had been concerned with the inquiry. Nor is it apparent that the Civil Service, or any other public service, had been examined regarding the scheme. Due to the protests of the civil service unions, the War Cabinet set up an interdepartmental committee in July 1918, under the chairmanship of the Minister of Labour, J. H. Roberts, to examine the situation. In the end, it recommended a watered down system of consultative councils which, it argued, was more appropriate to the needs of the Civil Service.

Unable to withstand the pressures of the 200 staff associations, and persuaded that its hard line could undermine the whole policy, the Cabinet approved a revised constitution for a Whitley system in the Civil Service, in June 1919. On 23 July, the first meeting of the National Joint Council (NJC) for the Administrative and Legal Departments of the Civil Service was held. As *The Times* wrote some years later (quoted in Armstrong, 1969, p. 153):

> So the principle of 'Whitleyism', which in theory was unsuited to the public service, where 'employers' and the 'employed' sides of a Whitley Council of their nature are absent, was accepted by the Treasury, and, as with many English institutions, in spite of apparently illogical foundations, it has worked well.

The objects of the national council were embodied in its constitution. These included (White, 1933, p. 10):

> ... to secure the greatest measure of co-operation between the state in its capacity as employer, and the general body of Civil Servants in matters affecting the Civil Service, with a view to increased efficiency in the public service combined with the well-being of those employed; to provide machinery for dealing with grievances, and generally to bring together the experience and different points of view of representatives

of the administrative and clerical and manipulative Civil Service.

The proposed activities of the council were wide-ranging: using the ideas and experience of staff; securing for staff a greater share in, and responsibility for, determining wages and conditions; determining the general principles governing conditions of service, such as 'recruitment, hours, promotion, discipline, tenure, remuneration, and superannuation'; encouraging the 'further education' and training of civil servants; improving 'office machinery and organization'; and discussing proposed legislation, 'so far as it has a bearing upon the position of Civil Servants in relation to their employment.' It was, for its time, a radical and innovative set of proposals for people management in the Service.

By the early 1930s, in addition to the NJC, some 70 departmental Whitley councils had been formed, as well as a number of district and office committees. The functions of these joint committees paralleled the national council and, according to White (1933, p. 25), the bulk of the work in these bodies 'in effective influence ... [equalled] or [surpassed] the national body.'

At the time of the Whitley reports, there was, as in the Civil Service, no collective bargaining machinery in local government for manual or non-manual workers or amongst those municipal and local authorities providing electricity, gas, water and tramway services. The employers were badly organized and not convinced of the desirability of national organization, even where the unions were strong. What influenced the setting up of Whitley national joint industrial councils (NJICs) was the Ministry of Labour. In industries where there were no disagreements amongst employers concerning union representation, the situation was straightforward but the municipal and local authorities were not generally in this position. Charles (1973, p. 138) summarizes the position amongst manual workers:

> The vast range of employments constituted under 'local authority manual workers', and the great variety of conditions

and places in which they were employed, combined with the weakness of unions and the previously localised outlook of the employers to make the problems of the JIC in this field unusually great and complex, and it was later emphasised that only the insistence and the intervention of the Ministry of Labour made it at all possible.

The outcome, unlike that of the Civil Service, was that the authority of the NJIC for local authority manual workers, once established, was weak. Although holidays with pay were granted by the NJIC in 1925, and most authorities provided superannuation by 1937, it was the district or 'Provincial' councils which determined wages structures, basic rates and differentials. Generally, 'it was in the urban areas or those in which the tradition of collective bargaining had been established that they were most effective' (p. 185). The attempt to set up a Whitley council to cover the administrative staff in local government, in 1919, however, was not successful.

The establishment of collective bargaining for school teachers and for teachers in technical education was more successful. After two months' negotiations in the summer of 1919, the Standing Joint Committee on a Provisional Minimum Scale of Salaries for Teachers in Public Elementary Schools, chaired by Lord Burnham, was established. It consisted of equal numbers of representatives from the local education authorities and the National Union of Teachers (NUT). Committees were also set up to deal with teachers' pay in secondary and technical schools. On a number of occasions, however, especially 1921–23 and 1931, the NUT was forced 'to devote all its energies to a defence of the schools and the teachers against those who wished to cut education ruthlessly' (Tropp, 1957, p. 217).

There was no collective bargaining for the police. An outbreak of discontent and strikes amongst police officers in 1918 led to the abolition of their union and the dismissal of its leaders. The Police Act 1919 made it unlawful for police to join trade unions or any association having as one of its objects the control or influencing of pay and

conditions of service. To compensate for this loss of freedom, police officers were permitted to establish police
federations, representative of senior, intermediate and
lower ranks, for the purposes of consultation and advice
on welfare and efficiency, but pay and conditions were
determined by the Home Office.

Establishment work

During the interwar years, one of the antecedents of public-
service personnel management was conceived of as
'establishment work'. It was out of the activities of establishment committees and establishment officers in both
the Civil Service and local government that, first, management services and, then, the professional personnel
management function eventually emerged.

Traditionally, Treasury control over civil service departments was rooted in the power of the purse and 'the
various Royal Commissions . . . had approved of the grad-
ual increase in Treasury control' (MacDonnell, 1914, p.
181). The MacDonnell Commission (1914) attributed de-
fects in coordinating recruitment with the educational
system to the absence of a controlling authority, with
information and powers of oversight and initiative. To
remedy this, it proposed the creation of an Establishments
Branch of the Treasury, entrusted with watching over the
general conditions of the service and providing recommendations to departmental heads and facilitating transfers.

War deferred action on these proposals and it was the
Haldane Committee (1918) which advocated the appointment of a special officer in each large department to study
'all questions of staff, recruitment, classification . . . and
routine business generally' (Haldane, 1919, p. 21). This
branch was to keep in touch with officers employed on
establishment work in other departments. In 1919, the
Establishments Department of the Treasury was created,
under the Controller of Establishments, and was entrusted
with sanctioning pay rates, controlling salaries and issuing regulations governing conduct in the Service. As the

department of finance, the Treasury had power to approve expenditure on staff, creation of new posts and regulations relating to recruitment. This latter power meant that it could set down qualifications for entry and the nature of examinations for general Treasury classes, although recruitment and selection were carried out by the CSC. Finally, the Treasury was responsible for pensions and superannuation: 'the only branch of Civil Service staff management which is comprehensively governed by statute' (Bridges, 1966, p. 115).

The day-to-day management and control of the Civil Service was undertaken by departments. Each had an establishment division and establishments officer for dealing with work, promotions and discipline. The main function, however, was enforcing the rules set down by the Treasury and liaising with it on the staffing needs of the department. On pay and conditions there were standard rules, determined mainly by collective bargaining in the Whitley Council. Most departmental and specialist classes were also linked to the general classes, by agreement or custom. There was a limited industrial relations role for departmental establishments divisions, though a more important one for the Treasury's Establishment Division.

In local government, it was the Hadow report (1935), set up to inquire into the qualifications, recruitment, training and promotion of staff, which recommended that every authority should have a single committee responsible for questions affecting the recruitment and training of staff. In smaller authorities, the finance or general purposes committee undertook this work, whilst in larger ones discrete establishment committees were created. Over time, most authorities set up establishment committees. Although the scope of early establishment work was narrow, being limited to administering conditions of service and examining staffing proposals of departments, this proposal was the first formal recognition of the personnel function in local government. For Fowler (1980, p. 43), it was 'the first acceptance that at least one officer in an authority might be needed for staff management on a full time basis.'

Establishment control work was subordinate to the finance function, since availability of funds was a prime condition for procuring staff, but its importance grew within local authorities over the next 30 years, in parallel with what happened in national bodies, such as the NJCs and the Local Authorities Conditions of Service Advisory Board, especially after the second world war. Establishment committees became responsible for a range of activities, including: recruitment, job advertising, training, probation, grading and salaries, conditions of employment, staff transfers, reviews of staff performance and disciplinary procedures.

Equality issues

Soon after the first world war, the issue of women's rights, especially in the Civil Service, was first formerly recognized. A subcommittee of the Ministry of Reconstruction in 1919 concluded that women temporarily employed during the war should be eligible for selection to permanent posts, on the same footing as candidates from HM forces. It also recommended, without success, that women should enjoy equal rates of pay and equal opportunity for promotion with men. In 1929, the Tomlin Commission examined pay differentials between men and women, as well as the conditions requiring the retirement of women civil servants on marriage. Although the report (Tomlin, 1931) concluded that all posts should be open to men and women, it wanted the marriage bar retained and was almost equally divided on the question of equal pay for men and women.

In local government, demands for equal rights for women were more muted. First, there was less segregation between 'men's' and 'women's' work and, second, the staff associations, such as NALGO, were relatively weak. In school teaching, however, the question of equal pay had become important during the first world war, although it was defeated at the NUT's conferences of 1917 and 1918. A referendum held by the union in 1919, however, approved the principle. The Burnham standard scales did not include the principle of equal pay and 'the more militant women members accused the N.U.T. of betraying its principles' (Tropp, 1957, p. 216). As a result, the National Union of Women Teachers increased its membership and, between 1919 and 1922, the National Association of Schoolmasters moved away from the NUT, seceding completely in 1922. The pressures on teachers' pay, and other problems facing the profession during the 1920s and 1930s, resulted in the equal pay issue receding from the teachers' agenda until after the second world war.

Public Services and the Postwar Settlement

The postwar settlement, which was politically mediated at the end of the second world war, provided another crucial influence on the development of TPM. In essence, the postwar settlement resulted in an expansion of the public services, an increase in public employment and a growing interest in management techniques and public administration. New issues of people management surfaced too. It was these factors, examined below, which eventually led to the professionalization of people management and creation of specialist personnel departments, staffed by personnel professionals, during the 1970s.

The postwar settlement

The postwar settlement, which lasted effectively until the mid-1970s, consisted of three elements: demand management economic policies, based on Keynesian principles; a Welfare State with universal services; and a political consensus between the two major political parties. Keynesian economic policies were targeted at creating high levels of aggregate demand, so as to maintain full employment and steady growth, without inflation or an adverse balance of payments. A wide range of public services, based upon the Beveridge report (1942), was provided by central and local government including: a universal system of social security and pensions; a comprehensive NHS, free at the point of use; free, compulsory education up to the age of 15; and subsidized public housing.

One outcome of the postwar settlement was the steady growth in public-sector employment. The public sector now included the newly nationalized industries, such as coal, electricity, gas and railways, and, in addition to the 'old' public services such as the Civil Service, local government, education and the police, 'new' ones such as the NHS and personal social services were created. A second outcome, arising from the government's policy of full employment, was an increase in trade union bargaining power in both the private and public sectors. There were, as a result, continuous attempts by governments to impose a series of incomes policies on employer and union negotiators. These policies were aimed at keeping wage increases in line with national productivity, constraining public spending and avoiding damaging industrial conflict (Farnham, 1993). This created tensions between government and the unions, especially during the 1970s, since they felt that their members were being treated less favourably than those in the private sector.

The expanding public services also had to balance the need for containing public spending with those of recruiting, rewarding and retaining a skilled and effective workforce, necessary for providing essential services to the public. These factors provide the background to the main developments affecting people management during the postwar settlement. These led eventually to a professionalized, standardized approach to people management, seeking to meet the requirements for cost-effective public services with their social responsibilities as large-scale and fair employers. Indeed, as early as 1917, in response to demands for Whitley councils in the Civil Service, the Chancellor of the Exchequer had declared: 'the Government fully realise the importance of setting an example in this matter' (Armstrong, 1969, p. 137). This statement pressaged the adoption of a model employer role for the public services, discussed subsequently by the Tomlin Commission (1931), which became deeply entrenched in TPM values and practices.

The growing importance of the professions

A main change in the structure of the public labour force after 1945 was the growing numbers of professional workers. These included, in the Civil Service, scientists, technologists, architects, planners, surveyors, lawyers, statisticians and economists. The Scientific Civil Service was created in 1946, followed by the Work Group of Professional Classes covering non-scientific professional staff. In the NHS, the largest professional group was nurses and midwives. They comprised about 40 per cent of all NHS staff and were some 400 000 strong by the late 1960s. In addition to doctors and dentists, other professional groups in the NHS included opticians, pharmacists, biochemists, occupational therapists, physiotherapists, chiropodists and radiographers.

The largest professional group was school teachers. There were some 500 000 teachers employed in schools, further education colleges and universities by the late 1960s. Local authorities also employed other professional workers including: engineers, accountants, solicitors, town and country planners, social workers, architects, surveyors and legal executives. Like their counterparts in the Civil Service and NHS, these groups were professionally qualified, with their own professional bodies. The major exception were the teachers who, though qualified, were state certificated professionals, not independently registered ones.

All professional groups were well unionized, with most using their professional associations to represent them in wage determination and other professional issues. By the 1970s, the main professional associations included: the Institution of Professional Civil Servants in the Civil Service and the Royal College of Nursing, British Medical Association, British Dental Association and the various bodies representing the professions allied to medicine, in the

NHS. In local government, professional bodies were less important in wage bargaining, apart from teachers. The main teachers' bodies were the National Union of Teachers, National Association of Schoolmasters/Union of Women Teachers, Assistant Masters and Mistresses, Secondary Heads' Association, National Association of Head Teachers and, in Scotland, the Educational Institute of Scotland.

The feminization of the workforce

During the second world war, large numbers of women had been recruited into the private and public sectors to replace men mobilized into the armed services, thus beginning the slow feminization of the workforce which has continued up to the present day. With demobilization and the return of men to the labour market at the end of the war, some women stopped working, whilst others ceased looking for employment. Nevertheless, the view that 'a woman's place is in the home' had finally been rejected and, in the fully employed economy of the postwar settlement, women entered the labour market in increasing numbers. As shown in Table 2.1, the labour force increased in size and the numbers of women, and their relative proportion within it, increased too. There were some seven million women out of a civilian labour force of some 23 million in 1949 – about 31 per cent of the total – rising to over eight million (34 per cent) in 1960 and almost nine million (36 per cent) in 1968.

Table 2.2 shows the numbers employed in public administration for selected years between 1949 and 1968, excluding the armed services, education, medical and dental services. Although female employment fell, in line with total employment in public administration, between 1949 and 1953 and 1957 and 1960, it rose slowly after 1960. Females made up 28 per cent of employees in public administration in 1960, 29 per cent in 1964 and 31 per cent in 1968.

Workforce data of those employed by local authorities

TABLE 2.1   Distribution of the civilian workforce in the
UK by gender, 1949–68, selected years

					000s	
	1949	*1953*	*1957*	*1960*	*1964*	*1968*
Males	15 641	15 920	16 237	16 264	16 546	16 285
Females	7 130	7 524	8 009	8 261	8 722	8 948
Total	22 771	23 444	24 246	24 525	25 268	25 233

Source: derived from Department of Employment and
Productivity, 1971

TABLE 2.2   Numbers of male and female employees in
UK public administration, 1949–68, for selected
years

					000s	
	1949	*1953*	*1957*	*1960*	*1964*	*1968*
Males	1 012	996	973	932	942	995
Females	416	366	370	353	377	445
Total	1 428	1 362	1 343	1 285	1 319	1 440

Source: derived from Department of Employment and Productivity, 1971

and the police, for the period 1952–68, show, on a headcount basis, more significant increases of female workers.
Table 2.3 indicates, first, an increase of 58 per cent in
total employment between 1952 and 1968. Second, it also
shows that women made up 49 per cent of all employees
in these sectors in 1968, a rise of over half a million jobs,
compared with 42 per cent in 1952. But it was in teaching and the NHS that most women were employed, con-
stituting about two-thirds of staff. Many of the new female
jobs were part-time but the growth in full-time jobs was
also significant.

These labour force trends meant that women's issues,
such as equal pay for work of equal value, occupational
pensions and equal opportunities in recruitment, promotion and training could not be neglected by public-ser-

TABLE 2.3   Numbers employed by the local authorities and police forces, 1952–68, for selected years

	Total males full time	part time	Total females full time	part time	000s Total males and females
1952	798	45	395	211	1449
1956	821	54	425	256	1556
1960	875	68	452	313	1708
1964	964	89	492	419	1964
1968	1051	107	574	555	2287

Source: derived from Department of Employment and Productivity, 197

vice employers. Although the record for these had not necessarily been worse in the public services than in the private sector, and sometimes they had been better, the agenda for equal opportunities could no longer be ignored by public-service employers. This was especially the case given the size, importance and visibility of public employers.

Staff training in the civil service

Staff training became an increasing concern in the public services during the postwar settlement. In 1968, for example, the Fulton Committee reported that 'great efforts have been made to increase the amount of training that civil servants receive' (Fulton, 1968, p. 35). Earlier, the Assheton report (1944) had recommended that there should be better training for all staff, to improve job performance. Assheton recommended the setting up of a staff college for senior civil servants but government rejected this on the grounds that the generalist tradition only required on-the-job training, not specialist training. Senior staff were developed principally by job rotation and occasionally by secondments to the Administrative Staff College, at Henley, and private industry. Post-Assheton, a training division was set up in the Treasury and, in the larger departments, training divisions were established and training officers appointed. Training in the Civil Service, however, was very uneven and unsystematic until the 1960s.

A number of things led to greater interest being shown in training. One was skill shortages and recruitment difficulties. A second was the introduction of new, mechanized technologies, such as automated accounting and record systems. A third factor was the increased and diverse workloads of departments, arising from new policies and legislation. Further, there was growing criticism of the lack of effective management in the Civil Service, especially at higher levels. The Plowden Committee (1961), for example, 'became increasingly conscious of the importance of management', adding that it was necessary 'to ensure proper training for junior ranks', to provide a 'wide variety of experience' for middle ranks and to maintain 'a careful system of selection and interchange between Departments in order that the best individuals may ultimately emerge in the most senior posts' (Plowden, 1961, pp. 16–17).

Following Plowden, the Centre for Administrative Studies was set up in London during 1964. It was designed to train new entrants to the administrative class, especially in economics and statistics, and to provide short courses for middle and higher civil servants. A few years later, the Fulton Committee (1968) proposed the creation of a Civil Service College with three main functions: courses in management and administration; short courses for other staff; and research.

The creation of the Civil Service College in 1970 gave a new impetus to training. Although it never developed in the way that Fulton had envisaged, the College expanded the range, diversity and availability of training and was a source of fresh ideas on developing managers and managerial skills. It only accounted for between six to ten per cent of training but included most of that offered to fast entry recruits, top civil servants and other key personnel, such as finance and establishment officers. The Civil Service College undoubtedly stimulated the expansion of training within departments, where, post-Fulton, most changes in training took place.

Staff training in the NHS

In the NHS, the training of professional groups, such as doctors and nurses, had long been supervised by the professionals themselves, within boundaries defined by the state and the law, whilst post-entry training for managers and white-collar staff was provided internally and externally. The high quality of professional training was generally recognized, whilst 'newcomers to the [service] at all levels . . . [were] attracted by the offer of proper training facilities'. This factor was borne in mind when people were being recruited (Cuming, 1978, p. 140–1).

In the new NHS in 1948, a wide variety of other training needs also had to be met, because of diversity of occupations, skills and jobs. Prior to reorganization in 1974, training provision was largely disparate and diffuse. An official analysis of training needs, incorporated within the Department of Health and Social Security's (DHSS, 1975) policies on education and training, classified what needed to be done. The areas were: induction training; post-entry training; updating knowledge; developing skills; management and supervisory training; and training for implementing new policies.

The need for coordinating the multiplicity of training in the reformed NHS was obvious and to this end a National Training Council was set up in 1975. Its aim was to advise the Secretary of State on the strategy, development and coordination of training for the NHS and on the training needs common to different staff groups. The Council worked closely with four National Staff Committees – for nurses, administrators, ambulance personnel and support services – and took full account of the responsibilities of the statutory and professional bodies involved in educating and training staff.

Up to and immediately following reorganization in 1974, training expertise was heavily concentrated at departmental and regional levels. Subsequently, it was recognized that operational managers should be able to call on training help, as part of local personnel services, to meet their immediate needs. According to Cuming (1978), the development of appropriate training infrastructures at area and district levels was no easy task. Further, the appointment of local training officers was inhibited, owing to scarcity of expertise and financial resources. At regional level, training branches of personnel departments formulated training strategies, in accordance with national policies and local needs, and implemented them.

After reorganization, new training needs became apparent, especially for managers. These derived from the introduction of 'consensus management', systematic planning and growing emphasis on the people management responsibilities of line managers in districts and areas. According to the white paper on reorganization (DHSS, 1972, para 149), management education and training would have to be designed 'to equip all the decision-makers with an understanding of the needs of the Service as a whole' and 'with the skills enabling them to make the best use of available resources.' Seven principles underpinned the new strategy for management education and training which was to be: comprehensive; integrated with work; linking theory and practice; progressive; collaborative between 'students', immediate superiors and trainers; directly related to organizational and individual needs; and monitored and evaluated (Health Service Circular 189, 1975).

Training in local government

Traditionally, training in local government was concerned with acquiring professional and other qualifications by examination, mainly for white-collar staff. The responsibility for training rested largely with professional associations and individual officers, rather than the employers (Fowler, 1980). Yet even before the creation of the Local

Government Training Board (LGTB) in 1967, formal training existed. In 1946, for example, the scheme of conditions of service, negotiated within the newly formed NJC
for administrative, professional and technical staff, virtually compelled authorities to make grants to officers studying for qualifications, although day release was almost
non-existent. The NJC also established the Local Government Examination Board which, until its functions were
transferred to the LGTB in 1968, developed and administered qualifications for clerical and administrative staff.
Additionally, provincial councils undertook training by
providing short courses for officers. They also facilitated
group training schemes, enabling smaller authorities to
form joint training groups.

The LGTB was set up in 1967, following the Industrial
Training Act 1964. It was a non-statutory, voluntary body
whose role was to assess training needs, take action to
meet them and spread the costs of training through a
levy-grant system involving employers. Its overall policy
was to increase the efficiency of local government, by
encouraging the extension of training, improving its quality
and spreading its cost fairly amongst local authorities.
The LGTB followed four principles in training: it should
be based on thorough analyses of occupations or work,
stated standards of performance and specified methods
of evaluation; it should be provided during working hours;
it should be part of personnel policy and related to future 'manpower needs'; and training and further education provision should be linked.

The LGTB excluded from its remit those for whom,
'adequate arrangements already existed and teachers,
police, firemen and civil defence workers were thus omitted
from the LGTB's terms of reference' (Fowler, 1980, p. 187).
Until its abolition, in 1991, the work of the LGTB centred
on seven activities: the levy-grant system; manpower planning; training training officers; training in personnel
management; management development; examinations; and
training recommendations.

Management services

The Civil Service was a pioneer of management services in the UK. Soon after its creation in 1919, the Treasury's Establishment Division set up an 'Investigation Section'. Its function was to carry out improvements in office management, clerical methods and use of office machines. This section became the Organization and Methods (O&M) Division in 1941 and was transferred to the Civil Service Department (CSD) in 1969, becoming its Management Services Division. After 1945, most large departments set up their own O&M divisions, within establishments divisions.

Prior to Fulton (1968), O&M units were largely concerned with clerical efficiency. The Committee made several recommendations on departmental management services units, concluding that although the Civil Service had played a major part in developing O&M in the UK, 'the work of departmental O and M divisions in promoting efficiency is at present inadequate' (Fulton, 1968, p. 55). It recommended that efficiency units should involve all aspects of departmental work and that management services should be responsible for promoting the best management techniques. It also wanted O&M to be combined with staff inspection.

Some years later, the Expenditure Committee's eleventh report on the Civil Service (1977) re-emphasised the central relevance of management services to efficiency but concluded, despite Fulton, that: 'there is still a tendency to give management services insufficient weight' (House of Commons Expenditure Committee, 1977, vol. 1, para. 112). Whilst progress in management services was encouraging, its impact had been slow and, in 1979, it fell victim to cuts in public expenditure.

In the NHS and local government, management services were closely linked with establishment control work and a range of specialist management techniques and activities. These included: work study, method study, O&M, job evaluation, computer applications, operations research, network analysis and cost-benefit analysis. The

Maud report (1967) commented favourably on the record of local government in introducing and making use of such techniques. In the same year, the Local Authorities Management Services and Computer Committee was set up by the local authority associations, with government support, to promote computer applications and management services throughout local government.

A review of the Greater London Council's (GLC) management services in 1967 demonstrated that management services were aimed principally at: getting the right staff for the employing authorities; employing them economically and efficiently; and providing them with 'fair and equitable treatment' in the workplace (Knowles, 1971, p. 171). Yet the Bains Committee (1972) recommended that management services and personnel work should be kept separate, with coordination being exercised at higher levels. In Bain's view, whilst management services comprised a number of heterogeneous analytical activities, personnel management was a body of knowledge in its own right.

The Professionalization of People Management

The final stage in the evolution of TPM was the setting up of specialist departments or personnel management divisions, largely during the 1970s, in the Civil Service, NHS and local government. The driving forces behind the changes in the Civil Service were the recommendations of the Fulton report (1968), the creation of the new CSD and the staffing problems associated with recruitment, retention and training. In the NHS and local government, the growth in professional personnel management arose out of similar factors: structural reorganizations in 1974; growing trade union power, especially amongst manual workers; the introduction of local incentive bonus schemes for manual workers; and concern to establish a comprehensive approach to managing people, by employing authorities.

The civil service

The Fulton Committee, set up to examine the structure, recruitment and management of the Home Civil Service, reported in 1968. It was very critical of all aspects of civil service management and placed responsibility for this on the Treasury and establishments divisions. The Fulton Management Consultancy Group (MCG) contrasted the impoverished form of establishment control within the Civil Service with the more human relations approach of personnel management in the private sector. Most personnel reforms suggested by the MCG were accepted by the Committee. In particular, Fulton recommended the creation of a Civil Service Department, 'as a centre of expertise in personnel management and efficiency services ... and it proposed that the Service should devote far more effort to that part of personnel management concerned with understanding and developing the abilities of the individual' (Garrett, 1980 p. 152).

The government accepted all but one of Fulton's 158 recommendations and immediately created the CSD with responsibility for central management of the Service and for implementing Fulton's recommendations. The pay and management divisions of the Treasury were transferred to the CSD, which also absorbed the CSC. From the outset, the functions of the CSD were identified as personnel management, administrative efficiency and terms of service. For the first time in the Civil Service, one department was given responsibility for the management of people, and a strategic role in developing personnel policies and personnel systems. It set down its perception of its role and its relationship with other departments in its first report. These were that (Civil Service Department, 1970, p. 10):

The CSD's role in fulfilling these responsibilities has several facets: planning and policy making, regulating, coordinating, advising and providing central services ... [but] the size of the Civil Service limits the extent to which direct management from the centre is possible or desirable. While, therefore, the

CSD must take a central and leading role in the processes of management and reconstruction, its work must be carried out in partnership with the other departments.

The CSD sought to make an impact on the Civil Service and to steer it in new directions. It grew from 1627 staff in 1969 to over 5000 by 1975 (Horton, 1976). This was partly due to an expansion of the CSD and the creation of the Civil Service College, Central Computer Agency and Catering Agency in 1970–71. There was a general expansion of staff, as the CSD developed its role. Further, throughout the Service, there had been a 30 per cent increase in staff providing personnel services over the same period (CSD, 1975).

From the outset, the CSD worked closely with the unions through the National Whitley Council. This enabled it to get agreement to structural changes and a reduction in the number of separate classes between 1968 and 1973. But there was widespread discontent mainly, but not wholly, about pay. There was industrial action in 1973 and the CSD set up a Wider Issues Review Team to investigate the causes of low morale. Its final report (CSD, 1975) acknowledged that many improvements in organization and management had taken place since Fulton and it showed evidence of developments in personnel management.

In particular, many of the barriers to career advancement had been removed by the creation of a unified pay and grading structure at the top of the Service and within the new Administrative, Science and Professional and Technology Groups. A new system of job appraisal reviews had been devised, for career interviews and identifying training needs. The effort devoted to training by departments had been substantially increased and the Civil Service College had expanded central training. These, and other developments, provided departments and the Service with systems for developing individual opportunities and for injecting departments with steady supplies of talent.

The Wider Issues Report spurred on attempts by the CSD to introduce modern personnel management systems and organizational development into the Service. Central personnel records were introduced, providing for personnel planning and matching staff to particular jobs. Job satisfaction studies were carried out by the Behavioural Sciences Research Division and its accomplishments were reviewed by its director in 1977 (Anstey *et al.*, 1977). From 1973, the Civil Service began to experiment with flexible hours and, in the same year, an experiment was carried out into the 'New Model Office', providing open planning and more relaxed working arrangements (Burden, 1976).

The progress made in introducing professionalized personnel management slowed down after 1975, mainly because of cash limits and the government's voluntary pay policy. Industrial relations deteriorated and 'the new ideas of progressive personnel management were overtaken by the old establishments function of cost control and cutbacks' (Garrett, 1980). However, departmental personnel divisions developed new skills and the CSD resisted any return to the establishments role. By 1979, professional personnel management was clearly in evidence in the Civil Service: it was a legacy which the Conservatives inherited.

The NHS

Cuming (1978, p. 10) records that professional 'personnel management emerged in the National Health Service as a phenomenon of the 1970s.' It was strongly linked with reorganization and, in 1972, a departmental circular (DHSS, 1972) proposed that:

> The Personnel Department of the future will differ both in approach and scope from the former Establishment Department. Instead of being mainly regulatory, it will be wider, more comprehensive, and more skilled. Whereas establishment work has been largely concerned with determination and control of complements, pay and grading, and management of appointments procedures, personnel work – while

including the whole range of establishment work – will also include . . . advice on recruitment sources and methods, on selection techniques and induction processes; staff appraisal and counselling; training, including the identification of training needs and arrangements to meet them; industrial relations; and wider staff welfare arrangements.

The circular also made it clear that line managers were to retain executive authority over their staff, whilst personnel would work in an advisory capacity.

A further circular (DHSS, 1973) identified five aims of the new personnel organization in the reformed NHS. These were: (1) to determine future staffing requirements to meet the objectives of the service in the most economic ways, and ensuring the recruitment and retention of suitable staff; (2) to develop and deploy staff so that individual and organizational needs would be satisfied, through career development, training, counselling and health safety and welfare; (3) to develop effective communications, consultation and relations with staff, including joint consultation; (4) to provide organizational structures suitable for successful task performance; and (5) to develop policies and procedures to achieve these objectives, with maximum efficiency.

A fundamental principle of reorganization was maximum delegation of authority downwards. This was to be achieved through a complex hierarchy involving the DHSS, regional health authorities (RHAs), area health authorities (AHAs) and district health authorities (DHAs), all of which had specific personnel management functions. The DHSS was to provide personnel policy guidelines, drive the national negotiating machinery and develop national training policy. In RHAs, personnel was to take the lead in developing, in conjunction with AHAs, regional-wide personnel policies, as well as maintaining regular contact with the DHSS. At AHA level, area personnel officers (APOs) had similar roles, whilst their links with the regions and districts were also defined. Finally, personnel officers in the DHAs had four main functions: helping to formulate district plans; providing specialist advice to district management teams; liaising with APOs; and advising line managers on personnel issues.

The net outcome of the 1974 reorganization was a proliferation of personnel posts in the NHS, at district, area and regional levels. The DHSS set up 'Training of Personnel Officer' programmes (TOPO) and 'Training of Training Officer' (TOTO) programmes to meet the demands arising from reorganization. Many new posts were filled from TOPO and TOTO personnel within the service but some attracted external candidates. By,the late 1970s, the dominant activities of personnel departments were recruitment and selection, industrial and employee relations and training, especially management development.

Local government

The Bains' report (1972), like Fulton, identified the need to raise standards of personnel management in local government. It viewed the establishment role as involving the day-to-day administration of rules about pay and conditions and acting as a watchdog on departmental demands for staff. But it inhibited development of a professional personnel management function. In the professional world of local government, the Committee argued, the non-professional establishment function offered little to those seeking the most senior posts in the service.

Bains identified six areas where developments in the personnel management function were necessary: (1) manpower planning, recruitment, selection, placement and termination; (2) education, training and career development, including staff appraisal; (3) working conditions and employee services; (4) formal and informal communications between employer and employee representatives; (5) negotiation and application of collective agreements on wages and conditions and procedures for avoiding disputes; and (6) the human and social implications of change. Whilst arguing that management services and the personnel function should be kept separate, the report concluded that personnel management should not be the exclusive preserve of personnel departments. The personnel role was to advise, coordinate, provide services and assist in applying personnel policies.

As in the NHS, many personnel appointments were made in the reformed local government service, post-Bains, with 'the top personnel job at top management level', not at the third or fourth tiers. Contrary to Bains, however, the personnel management and management services functions 'remained closely linked' (Fowler, 1980, p. 55). Growth in the activities of the personnel function was also stimulated by trends not limited to local authorities alone. These included increased union power locally, the extension of employment legislation during the 1970s, covering job protection, health and safety and trade union law, and demands for better training amongst all levels of staff.

Conclusion and Evaluation

As early as the 1950s and 1960s, the underpinning philosophy and principles of TPM were well established, having gestated and emerged over many years. But during the 1970s, TPM reached its apogee. From the political point of view, the overarching goals of government – as tax collector, provider of services and employer of people – appeared to be two-fold: first, to recruit and retain the necessary staff, including key professional workers, to enable it to provide a range of essential public services at a reasonable cost; and, second, to avoid damaging industrial conflict between the state and its employees.

The five essential features of TPM were: an essentially administrative personnel management function; a paternalist style of management; standardized employment practices; collectivist patterns of industrial relations; and a view that the state and its agencies should be model and good practice employers.

The administrative personnel function was derived from the manpower planning role of Whitehall and the fact that strategic personnel policies were determined by ministers and top civil servants. These policies operated within the constraints of public expenditure estimates and in response to the needs of the Treasury and central departments to control public spending. They were formal and wide ranging, covering union recognition, pensions, equal opportunities and, crucially, the principles upon which pay should be determined. These policies were then implemented and monitored departmentally in the Civil Service and through the various health, local and police authorities, with little policy discretion delegated to senior and operational managers involved in people management.

Policies on issues such as recruitment, promotion, union recognition and pensions, for example, were, by the 1970s, relatively uncontroversial and long established. The principles governing pay policy, on the other hand, were always more problematic, across the public services. This was largely because pay was a cost to the Exchequer. But it was also because of tension between two principles underpinning pay determination: one was the worth of groups of public servants in the labour market, the 'market pay' principle; the second was what they ought to be paid, in comparison with others, the 'fair pay' or 'comparability' principle.

These tensions are most clearly recorded in the history of the Civil Service where, until the 1950s, pay determination was based on the 1931 'Tomlin formula', which comprised three linked elements, incorporating both the market and fair pay principles (Tomlin, 1931, pp. 81–85). The first was embodied in the Fair Wages Resolution 1909, which held that the state should pay its workers not 'less than the current rates of pay recognised outside for certain types of labour.' Second, there was the Anderson Committee's view (1923) that the state 'should pay what is necessary to recruit and retain an efficient staff.' Third, the Industrial Court, in determining the wages of postal workers in 1927, upheld the principle of maintaining 'a fair relativity' between this group's wages 'and those in outside industries as a whole ... with due regard ... to the responsibilities undertaken.'

Senior officials at that time appeared to be more supportive of the market pay principle. The Joint Consultative Committee of higher grade civil servants, for instance, told Tomlin that remuneration 'should be such as is sufficient to recruit men [*sic*] appropriate to the particular duties and retain them in the Service without losing their keenness or efficiency.' For the Controller of the Establishments Department of the Treasury, the fixing of pay should have due regard 'to those other factors in the conditions of civil servants, notably security of tenure, prospects of promotion, leave and sick leave privileges, and pensionability.' Otherwise, pay and other conditions of employment 'shall be adequate to ensure the recruitment ... of a fully qualified staff, and the maintenance of an efficient and healthy public Service.'

In examining the principles governing civil service pay in 1955, the Priestley Commission (1955, pp. 23–32) identified the fair pay principle as the key one, when it concluded that 'there should be one set of principles of pay for the whole Service' and that 'the State is under a categorical obligation to remunerate its employees fairly.' For Priestley, 'concepts of fairness and ... a wage and salary framework not governed solely by the "law of the market"' should play an increasing part. The Commission defined fair pay comparison as 'the current remuneration of outside staffs employed in broadly comparable work, taking account of differences in other conditions of service.' A secondary principle was that internal relativities should be used in settling civil service rates in detail. Lastly, in any comparisons based upon rates paid by 'good employers', the civil service 'provisional rate' should lie near the median of the range of outside 'money rates' (p. 45–46).

The arguments of 'fair pay comparisons' and fair relativities were used by trade union negotiators when bargaining with other public employers during the 1960s and 1970s. But union leaders were also influenced by the 'going rate' in the private sector during annual pay rounds and by 'cost of living' increases, based on rises in the retail price index. With the introduction of incomes policies, especially between 1965 and 1979, some groups considered that they were being treated unfairly, because pay guidelines were easier to evade in the private sector. In attempting to resolve pay disputes involving manual workers in the local authorities and NHS in 1978–79, the Labour government set up a Standing Commission on Pay Comparability 'to examine the possibility of establishing appropriate comparisons with the pay of workers in the private sector' (Advisory Conciliation and Arbitration Service, 1980, p. 38). This policy was abandoned, however, with the return of the Conservatives to power in May 1979.

Given centralized personnel policies, people management activities at operational level were largely resourced by personnel departments which provided routine advice and services to line managers. Only limited personnel tasks were devolved to line managers. Personnel departments also often acted as buffers or mediators between employers and unions, on the one hand, and managers and staff, on the other. The essential role of personnel departments was to help manage stability and steady growth, with much personnel work routinized. The personnel function was rarely integrated into corporate management and personnel specialists often exercised an independent, professional role, acting as corporate consciences of their organization, though this varied in practice.

Paternalist styles of management were reflected in the bureaucratic, procedural and constitutional methods by which employment and other decisions were taken. Decisions were made and implemented in accordance with established rules, regulations and collective agreements. The preference was for decision-making by consensus, whether in dealings amongst managers, between managers and unions or between managers and staff. Managers were often concerned with staff welfare, the need to act fairly in dealing with staff and the obligation to consult their union representatives. Above all, those in authority accepted the softer norms and conventions of public employment, which differed from the more thrusting, market and sometimes anti-union values of the private sector.

The authority of senior public officials was based on their status or rank in public bureaucracies. Those in top positions were themselves servants of the state and ultimately accountable to their political masters. They spent their professional lives working in public bureaucracies, or sometimes even a single organization, as specialists and administrators rather than as risk-taking entrepreneurs. High employment security and promotion rooted in the seniority principle bred an institutional conservatism in such individuals, who often viewed people management as an activity based on experience, 'knowing the rules' and 'common sense' – not on prescriptive management ideologies and techniques found in the private sector.

As public office-holders within hierarchical structures, senior officials were normally expected to be protective of subordinates and their employment interests. The best would counsel, advise and coach subordinates and manage by example and leadership. The worst would demand conformity. There was no attempt to use staff to expand organizational activities or to drive them through patronage or fear of losing their jobs. Rather they were expected to suppress demand and personal reliability was the key to job security and promotion. Senior staff also sat on national Whitley councils, as representatives of the official or employers' side, and, certainly during the postwar settlement, they encouraged subordinate staff to participate in the Whitley system. As the Chief Inspector of Taxes wrote in the foreword to a booklet on Whitleyism at that time (Callaghan, 1953, p. 29):

> I am led to believe that there are genuine fears . . . that to take a prominent part on a Whitley Committee is to risk incurring official displeasure. I am sure that this fear should be groundless and that those in authority may be relied on to remove it where it exists. It is the essence of Whitleyism that opinions should be freely expressed and discussed in a friendly and helpful spirit.

The public services had their own standardized employment practices, covering procedures, terms and conditions, and details relating to job regulation and the wage-work bargain. These included open recruitment and selection methods, applied as fairly as possible. Recruitment to higher grades incorporated the use of written and objective tests, extended interviews and panel interviews. Standard contracts of employment provided full-time employment, job security and life-long employment for large numbers of workers, although there were also many part-time jobs in the NHS, local government and education, mainly employing women. White-collar staff had national pay structures and conditions of service, where individuals were in standard salary bands with incremental pay scales, whilst manual workers had national grading systems and national job structures. Opportunities existed in many areas for promotion to higher grades, based on merit, seniority and qualifications.

Staff appraisal was confined to white-collar workers and was concerned more with the personal qualities and promotion prospects of staff than with job performance. There were opportunities for on-the-job training, staff development and career development, although mainly for white-collar workers. There was sick pay, holiday pay and occupational pensions for all full-time staff, although part-time staff were less advantaged. Whilst there was concern with staff efficiency and the effective use of 'manpower', increasing attention was also paid to the health, safety and welfare of staff.

Collectivist patterns of industrial relations, based on the primacy of collective bargaining, took root after the Whitley reports were implemented in the interwar years. Whitleyism was extended to other public services, such as the NHS and local government, after the second world war, through national, sector-wide joint industrial councils. These covered virtually all staff grades in each public service. The major exception was senior, first division civil servants. The latter's pay was recommended by the Standing Advisory Committee on the Pay of the Higher Civil Service, established in 1957, after the Priestley report. In 1971, its duties were transferred to the Top Salaries Review Board which included other groups of senior public servants, such as the higher judiciary and chairmen of nationalized industries.

After 1945, national collective bargaining was the norm in public employment. Union membership was encouraged by the public authorities and the joint regulation of the wage-work bargain was based on the principles of industrial relations pluralism and 'management by agreement' (McCarthy and Ellis, 1973). These upheld trade unions as legitimate representatives of employee interests, with the right to be involved in the detailed regulation of the wage-work bargain (Clegg, 1975). During the ascendancy of TPM, recognition of unions and staff associations was never a matter of controversy. All staff, including most senior staff, such as assistant secretaries in the Civil Service, top administrators in the NHS, chief officers in the local authorities, principals of colleges and head teachers, were encouraged to join appropriate unions. As the handbook issued to new civil servants by the Treasury in the 1950s stated (Callaghan, 1953, p. 32):

> You are not only allowed but encouraged to belong to a staff association . . . it is . . . a good thing for Departments and for the Civil Service as a whole. . . . When [staff] get together in representative associations, their collective wish can be democratically determined and passed on to 'management' with real force and agreement behind it.

Joint consultative committees (JCCs) also existed locally, with varying success, in civil service departments, the health authorities and local authorities. Although distinctions between negotiation and consultation are sometimes difficult to distinguish in practice, these forums had specific terms of reference and detailed agenda. JCCs of managerial and staff representatives discussed matters of common interest such as welfare, health and safety and training. They also provided opportunities to communicate on local issues and for information exchange between management and staff. Wages and conditions of employment were normally excluded from joint consultation, since these were subject to national bargaining.

Even in the police, with its militaristic structure, a soft form of collective bargaining existed after 1948. Police officers were members of the police federations and a Whitley type structure performed the same functions as negotiating and consultative bodies in other public services.

The tradition that state employers should be models of good practice can be traced back at least as far as the Whitley Committee in 1917–18. One interpretation of the model employer role is provided by Fredman and Morris (1989, p. 25). They argue that, from about 1918 onwards, British governments became conscious of this role. For the next 60 years, the basic assumptions were that: 'the government sought to set a "good" example to the private sector by encouraging trade union organisation, supporting collective bargaining and offering a high degree of job security.'

In its evidence to the Tomlin Commission in 1929, the Civil Service Clerical Association indicated the variety of meanings given to the model employer notion (Beaumont, 1981, p. 11). These ranged from providing conditions of employment as 'an example' for private employers to follow, to those 'as good as those provided by good outside employers', to the view that 'the State should afford conditions not "out of scale" with those of outside industry.'

The Priestley Commission (1956, p. 39) redefined the 'good employer' role, as it applied to the Civil Service, not necessarily as the one offering 'the highest rates of pay'.

> He seeks rather to provide stability and continuity of employment, and consults with representatives of his employees upon changes that affect both their remuneration and their conditions of work. He provides adequate facilities for training and advancement and carries on a range of practices which today constitute good management, whether they be formalised in joint consultation along civil service lines or not.

Priestley added that such employers were likely to be amongst the more progressive ones 'in all aspects of management policy', with their pay comparable with that of the 'generality of employers'.

The good employer concept was not conceived of as being necessary for its own sake. It had the very practical objective of attracting, retaining and motivating the best staff. In the mid-1970s, the Wider Issues Review Team (CSD, 1975, p. 8) argued that, as an employer, the Civil Service should ensure that it:

— offers satisfactory **economic rewards** – pay, pensions, security and so on
— provides a **worthwhile job** and the means to do it; so that in the short-term the individual can give of his best from day-to-day **and** in the longer term can have **opportunities** for advancement
— provides a good **working environment**
— in other ways shows **fairness and consideration** towards staff, and respects their aspirations and needs
— and provides a sense of **common purpose**

Unless the employer meets these basic requirements, it concluded, staff commitment would be adversely affected and 'the quality of their work and the service they give the public will decline by degrees.' The Civil Service, therefore, should provide fair rewards but 'never excessive' ones, whilst 'in fairness and consideration towards its staff *it should be in the forefront of good employers*' [editors' italics].

Whilst the good employer concept was applied across the public services, it was not always practised consistently. For example, there were pockets of low pay within all public services, especially amongst manual workers, part-time workers and female staff, and not all public employers had effective training, staff development and career opportunities. Further, the quality of management varied.

In summary, it was in the postwar period, after 1945, that TPM finally became normalized in the public services. It had evolved piecemeal and pragmatically out of earlier people management policies and procedures. TPM arose, too, out of the increasing need for governments, and public employers, to harmonize people management practices, if they were to provide uniform public services across the country, as the state expanded. It was also necessary for governments to impose some uniformity of personnel policy upon the growing public services. This was largely because they were becoming more costly to support and public expenditure had to be controlled.

Case Studies

Case Studies

CHAPTER 3

The civil service

Sylvia Horton

The Civil Service is at the core of the public services, as it constitutes the administrative arm of central government. The radical changes in the public services since 1979, affecting the NHS, local government, education and the police, have been imposed, steered and monitored by civil servants, as agents of government and the state. But the Civil Service has itself been the target of governmental reforms which it has implemented and executed. A series of initiatives has reduced the size of the Civil Service, changed the way in which it is managed and transformed its culture.

The first initiative was designed to eliminate waste, increase efficiency, make civil servants cost conscious and ensure value for money. By imposing manpower targets and forcing departments to shed staff, government reduced the number of civil servants by 20 per cent between 1979 and 1988. In 1982, government introduced the Financial Management Initiative (FMI), designed to delegate budgetary responsibility to cost centres, operational units and individual managers. FMI, in turn, laid the foundations for a system of performance management (Fry, 1988; Metcalfe and Richards, 1990). Top management information systems (MINIS) were also developed, providing the means for central control to be made easier. These changes, with their emphasis on value for money, required new skills and attitudes by civil servants and were accompanied by major training programmes.

The second initiative stemmed from a review of the progress in improving management by the Efficiency Unit. The resulting Ibb's report led to a new strategic approach and a major programme of structural change. It recommended that 'agencies should be established to carry out the executive functions of Government within a policy and resources framework set by a department' (Efficiency Unit, 1988, p. 9). Since 1988, over 100 agencies have been created and most civil servants now work within them. The Next Steps initiative paved the way for further cuts in public expenditure and jobs, fragmentation of the Service, recruitment of managers from the private sector and major changes in personnel policies and industrial relations. It also led to a much stronger focus on performance management, quality of service and the efficiency and productivity of staff.

The third government initiative, introduced in 1991, was the *Citizen's Charter* (Prime Minister's Office, 1991). This marked a move away from efficiency in controlling the use of resource inputs towards a focus on outputs. The aim of the Charter is to raise standards of service, whilst improving value for money. It sets down principles of service which citizens as 'consumers' and 'clients' should expect, including standards, information and openness, choice and consultation, courtesy and helpfulness, and value for money. Next Steps agencies are the vehicles for implementing the Charter, improving performance and increasing the responsiveness of civil servants at every level.

Closely linked to the Charter was the fourth initiative, *Competing for Quality* (Cmd 1730, 1991). In the belief that competition is the best guarantee of quality and value for money, this white paper set out proposals for promoting fair and open competition. All departments and agencies must identify activities for contracting out or market testing to ensure that they are provided in the most cost-effective way. The options include privatization, contracting out or agency provision.

Taken together these governmental initiatives have brought about what Sir Robin Butler, Head of the Civil Service, describes as a 'quiet revolution'. The revolution is not yet over, since government proposes more privatization, market testing and restructuring (Cm. 2627, 1994; Cm. 2748, 1995). All these changes have had profound effects on people management, although there are elements of continuity amongst the changes.

Scope and Features

In the absence of a 'Civil Service Act', clearly defining what the Civil Service is and who civil servants are, the most widely used definition is that of the Tomlin Commission (Cmd. 3909, 1931) which stated: 'Civil servants are servants of the Crown, other than holders of political or judicial offices, who are employed in a civil capacity, and whose remuneration is paid wholly and directly out of monies voted by Parliament.' This distinguishes civil servants from the armed forces, MPs, judges, local government officers and employees of nationalized industries but it still leaves the boundaries unclear as the status of 'civil servants' can be changed by political decisions affecting the organizations in which they work. 'Civil Service' is the collective term for those civilian employees employed in government departments and establishments, subject to Treasury control, which appear in *Civil Service Statistics*.

Functions

The main functions of the Civil Service are to: assist government in formulating public policy and support ministers in their activities; manage the machinery of government and ensure that policy is carried out economically, efficiently and effectively; and provide services to the public. The policy role involves analysing and evaluating the options available to government and advising on the cost implications of alternatives. Civil servants support ministers in explaining government policy by providing information and briefings. In addition, they may be involved in representing ministers to outside groups, drafting legislation and assisting it through Parliament. Finally, they implement policy, monitor it and evaluate its effects. Around 10 per cent of civil servants are involved in this policy role.

Managing the machinery of government involves designing organizational structures, controlling public expenditure and manpower and monitoring the work of departments. There is clearly an overlap with the policy role and top civil servants are involved with both.

The vast majority of civil servants, however, are engaged in providing services to the public, supervising activities of other public bodies or doing research. They issue passports and driving licenses, pay pensions and social security benefits, staff prisons, assist people in finding jobs and inspect schools and police forces.

Structure

The work of government is allocated to departments, which are the major administrative units, headed by a minister accountable to Parliament. There is no logic to the number of departments or their range of responsibilities. In 1994, there were about 50 departments of varying size; the seven smallest had fewer than 40 staff each, whilst the largest six accounted for over 75 per cent of all civil servants (Treasury, 1994a). Most large departments are highly dispersed with some, such as Employment, Social Security and Inland Revenue, having more than 1000 local offices each.

Since 1988 and Next Steps, each major department has hived off activities to executive agencies, headed by chief executives. The numbers vary amongst departments but, at the beginning of 1995, there were over 100 agencies, employing over 65 per cent of all civil servants. By 1996 there will be about 150 agencies accounting for more than 80 per cent of civil servants.

The internal structures of departments reflect their size, responsibilities and numbers of executive agencies. They all have policy divisions and central units which support operational divisions. These units include finance, personnel, legal and information divisions. Departmental hierarchies reflect the grading structures of civil servants although, with recent delayering and the use of project groups, not all current 14 staff grades are found in every department.

Civil servants are a huge, heterogeneous group consisting of a vast range of professions, skills and occupations. The occupational structure is classified in a number of ways. First, there is the Home Civil Service and Diplomatic Civil Service. The latter is restricted to civil servants working in the Foreign and Commonwealth Office or in overseas embassies. They are recruited separately and have their own rank structure.

Second, there is the industrial and non-industrial Civil Service. The industrials are blue-collar, skilled or unskilled manual workers. Non-industrial staff are divided into occupational groups and classes. Some are service-wide and can be found in all departments, such as the Administration Group. Others are departmental or agency specific, such as tax inspectors and prison officers. Each class or group consists of grades linked to functions, entry points and pay. At the highest level, there is an open structure, consisting of the top seven grades, where appointment is to the post and there is no formal classification by occupational group. The top three grades constitute the Senior Open Structure (SOS). Government plans are to extend the SOS, to include the top five grades, and form a new Senior Civil Service in 1996 (Cm. 2748, 1995).

The Workforce

On 1 April 1994, there were 533 350 civil servants of whom 487 435 were non-industrials. In addition, there were nearly

TABLE 3.1 Size and composition of the Civil Service, 1902–94

Thousands as at 1 April each year

Year	Non-Industrial	Industrial	Total
1902	50		
1910	55		
1914	70		
1918	221		
1919	194		
1920	161		
1921	158		
1922	133		
1923	124		
1924	115		
1925	114		
1926	110		
1927	108		
1928	106		
1939	163	184	347
1944	505	658	1164
1945	499	615	1114
1946	452	366	819
1947	457	326	784
1948	445	317	761
1949	458	326	784
1950	433	313	746
1951	425	316	740
1952	429	333	762
1953	414	341	756
1954	405	347	751
1955	386	334	719
1956	384	328	711
1957	381	314	696
1958	375	289	664
1969	470	214	684
1970	493	208	701
1971	498	202	700
1972	496	194	690
1973	511	189	700
1974	512	180	692
1975	524	177	701
1976	569	179	748
1977	571	174	746
1978	567	168	736
1979	566	166	732
1980	547	157	795
1981	540	150	690
1982	528	138	666
1983	519	130	649
1984	504	120	624

1929	109	375	1959	271	647	1985	498	101	599
1930	111	380	1960	263	643	1986	498	96	594
1931	118	387	1961	256	643	1987	507	90	598
1932	119	394	1962	253	647	1988	507	73	580
1933	118	410	1963	252	662	1989	500	69	569
1934	117	414	1964	244	658	1990	495	67	562
1935	128	420	1965	235	655	1991	490	64	554
1936	133	430	1966	232	662	1992	504	61	565
1937	142	451	1967	229	680	1993	503	51	554
1938	152	471	1968	222	693	1994	487	46	533

Source: derived from *Civil Service Statistics, 1994a*

TABLE 3.2 Civil Servants in the main occupational groups, 1994

Occupational group or grade	Total
All non-industrial grades	487 435
Open structure	
Grade 1–3	630
Grade 1	35
Grade 2	122
Grade 3	473
Grade 4–7	16 812
Grade 4	235
Grade 5	2 325
Grade 6	3 298
Grade 7	10 954
Administration group	216 881
Senior Executive Officer	9 495
AT/HEO (D)	389
Higher Executive Officer	27 997
Executive Officer	54 643
Administrative Officer	89 866
Administrative Assistant	34 491
Economist group	212
Statistician group	225
Information Officer group	843
Librarian group	448
Professional and Technology group	15 299
Science group	9 782
Secretarial group	16 167
Social Security group	44 041
Curatorial/Conservation group	141
Graphics Office group	335
Legal group	180
Research Officer group	243
Training/Instructional Officer's group	2 969
General Service groups	19 948
All other non-industrial grades	141 280
Industrial grades	49 915

Source: derived from *Civil Service statistics*, 1994a

21 000 casuals. The size and composition of the Service has changed significantly during this century, as shown in Table 3.1. The main feature of the first three-quarters of the century was long-term growth. The most rapid peacetime expansion was between 1960 and 1977 when non-industrials grew from 380 000 to 571 000. Since then, there has been a slow contraction.

The decline in the number of industrials began in the 1950s but increased rapidly after 1979 when numbers fell by 70 per cent. This was due mainly to privatization and contracting out with most of the reduction in the Ministry of Defence (MOD) (88 000) and Property Services Agency (19 000). The current figure of 46 000 industrials, 80 per cent in MOD, is likely to shrink further with the impact of market testing and continuing run-down of defence establishments.

Reduction in non-industrial grades has been uneven. Between 1979 and 1994, there was a fall of 14 per cent, from 566 000 to 487 000. This was not balanced across departments, there being big cuts in MoD, whilst the Home Office and Social Security had increases. Contraction is continuing as departments and agencies respond to market testing and further privatization is taking place.

There are widely differing numbers of staff in the groups and classes making up the Civil Service, as Table 3.2 shows. The largest group is the Administration Group with some 217 000 FTEs, followed by the Social Security Group with 44 000. All groups have a grading structure and salary scales, traditionally negotiated nationally and uniformly applied across the Service. That is now changing. Government delegated responsibility for pay and grading to a third of all executive agencies in 1994 and intends to extend delegation to all departments and agencies by 1996. This is resulting in new pay and grading structures. There is likely to be a significant reduction in civil servants in service-wide groups and an end of uniform pay and grading scales, over the next few years.

Women account for about 51 per cent of non-industrials. Most are concentrated in the lower grades, as Figure 3.1 shows, but there has been a significant increase in the

FIGURE 3.1   Gender structure of the non-industrial Civil
Service, 1994

Grade level	Total numbers, men and women (headcount)		% women
1–4	1 010		9
5	2 850		13
6	5 100		13
7	17 900		19
SEO	24 100		15
HEO	78 600		22
EO	117 200		47
AO	171 100		69
AA	87 800		70

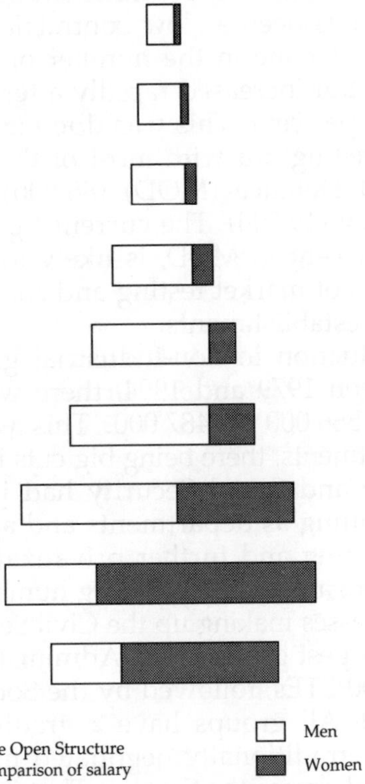

☐ Men
■ Women

[1]Includes broad equivalents to grades in the Open Structure
and Administration Group based on a comparison of salary
scales or job-weight.

Source: derived from *Civil Service Statistics*, 1994a

numbers in higher grades since 1980, because of equal
opportunities and positive action. Another trend has been
the large increase in the number of women in part-time
posts. Over 18 per cent of women non-industrials now
work part-time, a three-fold increase since 1984. Part-timers
are still concentrated in lower grades, although there have
been significant increases at grades 7 and above.

Government's equal opportunities policies cover ethnic minorities and the disabled. Both groups are generally well represented in the Civil Service, although they are concentrated in the lower levels. There were over 8000 registered disabled in 1994, 1.6 per cent of civil servants. Ethnic minorities accounted for 5.3 per cent of all posts but 7.4 per cent of lower grades and only 1.8 per cent of grades 1 to 7.

The age profile has changed over the last decade. The largest group is between 25 and 45, with those below 25 and over 50 declining. This is due to large intakes in the 1970s and lower recruitment in the 1980s and 1990s but also to recruiting a higher proportion of staff over 25 and increases in women returners.

There is always a large turnover of staff, though it fluctuates with the state of the economy and levels of unemployment. In 1993–94, over 32 000 people or 6.5 per cent of the workforce left. Of these, 10 000 were normal retirements, 4000 early retirements and over 10 000 were resignations. Over 10 per cent of those resigning had less than one year's service, and were mostly women.

The Personnel Function

From 1920 until 1968, the Treasury had overall responsibility for managing the Civil Service. Its Establishments Division, in addition to controlling manpower, set down detailed rules covering all aspects of personnel management (Mustoe, 1932; Gladden, 1966; Bridges, 1966). Many of these rules were agreed within the Whitley Councils or between the Treasury and staff associations.

Rules and regulations were brought into effect through establishment circulars, covering pay, hours, allowances and recruitment, establishment letters offering advice and 'Estacode'. Estacode, later the Civil Service Pay and Conditions of Service Code (CSPCSC), and the Establishment Officer's Guide (EOG), were used by all establishment specialists. This bureaucratic style of managing people was defended by one Head of the Service because 'it has to deal with a great variety of detailed circumstances which cannot be left to the discretion of the individual establishment branches, if the taxpayer is to be protected, and if equitable treatment of civil servants in different parts of the civil service is to be secured' (Bridges, 1966, p. 122). In each department, establishment staff dealt with all personnel matters and there was little, if any, delegation to line managers.

Post-Fulton organization

After Fulton in 1968, responsibility for managing the Civil Service passed from the Treasury to the new Civil Service Department (CSD) and a period of significant change in personnel activities occurred, especially in career development, training and management services (Garrett, 1980). Attempts were made to strengthen central management and develop the personnel role within departments. This was only partly achieved, because of the uneasy relationship between the CSD, responsible for staffing and efficiency, and the Treasury, which remained responsible for controlling public expenditure. As Fry (1985, p. 93) points out: 'if there was to be central control of civil service manpower it had to go with control of money in the Treasury, or risk duplication at the centre'.

The emphasis on reducing costs and manpower after 1979 increased tensions and, in 1981, the CSD was abolished and its responsibilities were divided between the Cabinet Office and Treasury. This bifurcation of the personnel function saw the Treasury regain control over manpower numbers, pay, allowances and pensions, whilst the Management and Personnel Office (MPO), in the Cabinet Office, absorbed the CSD's personnel management, training and recruitment functions. Further changes occurred in 1987, when the MPO was abolished and its responsibility for efficiency passed back to the Treasury, along with pay and conditions. A new Office of the Minister for the Civil Service (OMCS), still in the Cabinet

Office, assumed the residual functions of recruitment, training and staff development.

In another restructuring in 1992, OCMS was replaced and the Office of Public Service and Science (OPSS) took on its personnel functions, along with responsibility for major government initiatives – Next Steps, the Citizen's Charter and Competing for Quality. The overall effect of these changes, since 1981, has been to place the Treasury in a strong position to control expenditure on personnel, with the Cabinet Office spearheading organizational changes. Treasury control is no longer detailed. Manpower budgets ended in 1987 and personnel and pay have now been devolved to departments and agencies. The planned contraction of the Treasury, by 25 per cent, by 1997–98, (Treasury, 1995) suggests that its role will be to impose financial constraints within which personnel policies are carried out. It is likely to continue to have a strategic role in pay, although the major role in personnel policy rests with the Office of Public Service (OPS), which is the driving force behind the major changes taking place.

During the 1980s, departmental personnel divisions headed by personnel or establishment officers grew, taking on a proactive role. They continued to be directly answerable to the Permanent Secretary but were also part of a network of personnel managers, who met in committees chaired by either the OPSS or the Treasury. At departmental level, there are now a variety of personnel structures, depending upon the number of agencies and extent to which the latter are exercising personnel flexibilities. The responsibility for managing people in the Civil Service today is therefore widely dispersed and involves central departments, core functional departments, agencies, personnel specialists and line managers.

Role and activities

The personnel function was underdeveloped and over-centralized in 1966 (Fulton, 1968) and in the early 1980s remained centralized. Cassels (1983, pp. 35–6) referred to:

the extensive corpus of central rules and guidance as set out ...
in the Civil Service Pay and Conditions of Service Code (three
volumes) and the Establishment Officer's Guide (three volumes). Departments then elaborate these rules ... too much
authority is centralised, so that it is personnel divisions which
tend to take decisions – for example, on confirmation of appointments to the Service and on inefficiency cases – as well
as to give advice.

At that time there were still no professional personnel
managers. Establishment Divisions were staffed by administrators, assisted by lower level executive and clerical staff. They were assigned to the job for two or three
years, after which they moved back into mainstream policy
work. Within central departments, it was also practice to
appoint general administrators, with experience of other
departments.

Following Cassels, significant changes occurred. Each
department now has a coherent personnel strategy defining the respective responsibilities of line and personnel managers. Line managers are accountable for the
managing of staff, and increasingly personnel targets feature in their performance plans. The personnel divisions
have taken on a more advisory role and, in addition to
providing information and support, they coordinate and
monitor the work of line managers. The specialist personnel role is also more strategic, with specialists developing personnel systems and personnel plans. They still
perform some executive functions in recruitment, training and career development but the first two are increasingly being market tested.

In executive agencies, the personnel function, along with
industrial relations, has been devolved. Each agency, unless
it is very small, has responsibility for its own personnel
function. The larger ones such as the Benefits and Employment Agencies have personnel directors or human resources managers and their own policies and practices.
Although, as the Fraser report (Efficiency Unit, 1991) demonstrates, there were initially wide variations in the degrees to which core departments retained control, more

recent research (Massey, 1994) suggests that agencies now have considerable autonomy on personnel issues.

With the devolution of the personnel function to departments and agencies, there has been an increase in the numbers of specialist personnel staff with professional expertise. All staff are required to have a minimal training in personnel and many are encouraged to obtain the professional qualification of the Institute of Personnel and Development (IPD).

Cassels (1983, p. 48) recommended that the centre, then the MPO, should 'promulgate basic principles for the Service as a whole; disseminate advice, guidance and examples of good practice; and audit departmental performance selectively.' The OPSS, in addition to following Cassels' prescription, also has a major policy role. It advises government on all aspects of staffing policy and is responsible for implementing the principal initiatives designed to transform the Service and the way in which it manages staff.

There is now much greater diversity in personnel strategies and practices throughout the Service. It is more flexible and less bureaucratic. Central departments still coordinate and set down guidelines and frameworks across the range of personnel policy but departments and agencies exercise a wide degree of discretion on how they operate within framework policies. This raises questions about the future of a unitary, career Civil Service.

Recruitment and Selection

Traditionally recruitment was based on the principles of open competition and merit. In addition, entry to the three main levels, the lower, executive and higher Civil Service, has also been linked to educational qualifications and age. National competitions conducted by the Civil Service Commission (CSC) accounted for 80 per cent of recruitment. Civil servants could be called upon to work in any department or part of the country, although this was rarely enforced at the lower levels. It was more common for higher executive officers (HEOs) and the administrative class to move around the country and between departments. Educational qualifications and age limits were increasingly relaxed during the 1970s, in response to recruitment problems and to ensure equal opportunity. Mobility requirements were reduced in practice, with recruits being given more choice about location and department.

Most internal posts were filled by promotion and there was little lateral recruitment beyond initial entry. Limited competitions were held to accelerate progression from lower to higher grades and 40 per cent of the executive and administrative classes were filled from the class below. Lateral recruitment increased during the 1970s to deal with shortfalls and resignations.

Since 1982, recruitment and employment patterns have changed. As the Civil Service has contracted, recruitment has fallen. Around 52 000 staff were recruited in 1987–88, 31 000 in 1992–93 and 22 000 in 1993–94. The number of applicants fluctuates but is generally higher during periods of economic recession. The major recruitment competitions for graduate entry are always attractive with over 10 000 applicants for around 70 administrative trainee posts and 3000 for 30 places on the new European graduate entry in 1993 (Treasury, 1994a). There has also been an increase in lateral entry, particularly at higher levels, which is being actively encouraged (Efficiency Unit, 1993).

Devolved recruitment

From 1920 until the mid-1960s, recruitment, except of temporary and manual staff, was centralized and conducted by the CSC. This ensured uniformity of standards but was slow and expensive. A move away from centralization began in the late 1960s, when recruitment below executive officer (EO) was delegated to departments. In 1982, departments took over most recruitment, with the CSC retaining responsibility for only 15 per cent, including middle and senior grades at EO and above. In 1991, recruitment to posts below grade 7, except for fast-stream graduates, was transferred to departments and agencies. At the same time, the CSC was split into the Office of the Civil Service Commissioners (OCSC) and the Recruitment and Assessment Services Agency (RAS).

The present system is highly decentralized, with over 3000 recruiting units within which managers have responsibility for almost 95 per cent of recruitment. Competition has been introduced into recruitment by establishing a customer/contractor relationship. All departments, agencies and the Commissioners have three options. They can undertake their own recruitment, use private agencies or employ RAS. RAS was only involved in about 11 per cent of recruitment or 2400 vacancies in 1994. This means that nearly 90 per cent of recruitment is now undertaken by departments and agencies or by private organizations.

The future of RAS is uncertain, as it seems a likely candidate for privatization. The role of the OCSC is also likely to change as its work is currently being market tested. However, it will continue to act as guardian of the merit principle, by producing a binding recruitment code. In addition, the Commissioners will be responsible for approving all appointments from outside the Service and monitoring recruitment (Cm. 2748, 1995).

Selection practices

Selection on merit and by fair and open competition remain the fundamental principles of appointment. The only exceptions include secondments or where appointments can be justified as 'relating to the needs of the Service'. An increase in these appointments has raised concerns about whether the Service is reverting to a form of political patronage (House of Commons, 1994).

A model procedure for normal recruitment is universally applied by departments and agencies and follows good practice as set down by the IPD. In 1988 the average time was 45 days, although targets are being lowered. Recruitment to the executive classes and above usually involves a qualifying test, which eliminates from 50 to 80 per cent of initial applicants, and the use of assessment centres, where candidates are subjected to one or two days of cognitive tests, job simulations and group exercises.

Greater emphasis is now placed on recruiting staff with management and communication skills. New methods have been developed to assess management and leadership potential and these are used in all graduate entry competitions for administrative, professional and scientific trainees. Assessment centres, along with the refinement of sifting methods, are continually being developed by the Recruitment Research Unit, now in RAS.

Although the numbers of recruits are falling, there is a continuing problem of applicants failing to reach required standards or take up appointments. A low point was 1989, when only 59 per cent of vacancies were filled. This has been addressed in a variety of ways including: offering near-miss candidates posts at other levels, relaxing requirements for entry, halving the time to recruit, refining qualifying and selection tests and offering access courses.

Two further developments have been using open competitions for appointments at higher levels and executive search agencies or 'head hunters'. In 1979, the CSC conducted just 327 competitions. By 1989 it was 1001, due to an increase in the number of competitions for single posts, especially in the new executive agencies and an increasing number of targeted schemes to overcome recruitment shortfalls (Civil Service Statistics, 1979–94). In 1993, nearly 25 per cent of vacancies in the SOS were open to outside competition, rising to 30 per cent in 1994. In 1995, Permanent Secretary posts in the Central Statistical Office and the Department of Employment were filled by open competition.

Table 3.3 shows the numbers of competitions for 1986–94 at grade 5 and above. It indicates how many chief executives were recruited by open competition and how many people from outside the Service were appointed. Of 113 chief executives appointed up to April 1995, 71

TABLE 3.3 Numbers of competitions for recruitment to grade 5 and above, 1986–94

Year	Numbers of competitions[a]	Numbers of chief executives	Outside appointments
1986–87	23	0	n/k
1987–88	49	0	30
1988–90	43	6	21
1990–91	60	16	36
1991–92	63	14	39
1992–93	60	12	46
1993–94	68	11	47

a normally there is a single appointment but sometimes more than one is made.

Source: derived from Civil Service Commission Reports

TABLE 3.4 Secondments in the Civil Service, 1979–94

Year	Secondments out of Service	Secondments into Service	Total
1979	131	82	213
1980	143	67	210
1981	140	64	204
1982	152	92	244
1983	189	104	293
1984	186	116	302
1985	229	157	386
1986	280	189	469
1987	278	195	473
1988	311	194	505
1989	432	195	627
1990	n/a	n/a	n/a
1991	402	174	576
1992	406	176	582
1993	408	223	631
1994	366	315	681

Source: information provided by the Cabinet Office

had been recruited by open competition and, of those, 35 had come from outside the Service (Cabinet Office, 1995). Although the largest number of appointees are still insiders, the number of outsiders is rising.

In recruitment to many grade 3 posts and above, executive search consultants are now being used. Though the OCSC must approve the use of headhunters, this departs from the principle of open competition and may undermine equal opportunities. Another trend is the increase in the number of 'exceptional entrants'. This flexibility is to facilitate secondments and reinstatements of staff and bring in people on short-term contracts. The Whitehall and Industry Scheme launched in 1984 and the Bridge Programme in 1989 have both boosted secondments and job exchanges between the Civil Service and industry. Table 3.4 shows the numbers of secondments from 1979 to 1994.

These developments are likely to have significant effects in the future. Before 1991, there were a number of comprehensive recruitment schemes to the main grades, run by the CSC. Now recruitment is more fragmented. Most departments and agencies do their own recruiting and have started to buy-in services from specialist firms which compete with RAS. Only appointments to the Senior Management Group, grade 5 and above, require OCSC approval. Although the role of the Commissioners has been strengthened, it will be more difficult to monitor the new fragmented structure. If RAS is privatized, much recruitment will be done by private companies. This will make standardization more difficult.

Equal Opportunities

The Civil Service is an equal opportunity employer with a range of policies supporting that claim and promotes a positive image of equal opportunity and all involved in recruitment and selection are trained in equal opportunities and sexism and racism awareness. There are also Codes of Practice and Programmes of Action covering women, ethnic minorities and the disabled. Statistics on the gender and ethnic origin of applicants, candidates and appointees are recorded and there is close monitoring of procedures.

Women

An internal report in the early 1970s revealed important institutional and attitudinal barriers to gender equal opportunities (Kemp-Jones, 1971). Ten years later, little had changed, although there had been a significant increase in the number of women recruited (Joint Review Group, 1982). In 1984, a Programme of Action and an Equal Opportunities Unit (EOU) were set up and equal opportunities officers (EEOs) were appointed (Cabinet Office, 1984). Annual Progress Reviews record significant changes, although barriers to career development persist (Cabinet Office, 1988–94). A second Programme of Action was introduced in 1992.

Recruitment of women has improved over the last 10 years. They accounted for 52 per cent of entrants in 1994 and have outnumbered men for some years. Several programmes have enabled women to enter in larger numbers, including part-time work and the reinstatement programme. Between 1984 and 1993, the number of non-industrial part-timers increased from 16 000 to 48 000 and nearly 46 000 were women. Although most part-time workers are in lower grades, a significant trend has been the numbers of women part-timers in senior posts: 15 per cent of female grade 7s and 13 per cent of female grades 5 and 6 were part-timers on 1 April 1994.

Although the underrepresentation of women in the higher grades persists, numbers are increasing. There were six per cent more women in the Higher Civil Service at grades 5 and 6 and 18 per cent more at EO level in 1994 than in 1984. Female recruitment to the administrative trainee fast-stream increased from 28 per cent in 1984 to just under 50 per cent in 1994. The Civil Service is committed to Opportunity 2000 and there is a specific

FIGURE 3.2   Percentage of ethnic minorities in the administration group, 1992–94

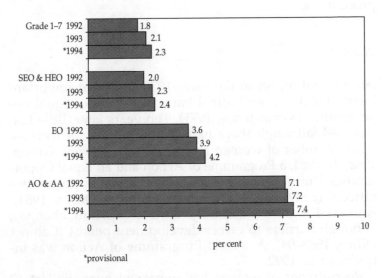

Source: derived from *Civil Service Statistics*, 1994a

benchmark set for women in the SOS, aimed at doubling their numbers to 15 per cent or more by the year 2000.

The strategies aiding women include flexible working, expansion of child-care provision and equal opportunity awareness. The most significant factor is the incorporation of accountability for equal opportunities into managers' work and their need to report on progress annually.

Ethnic minorities

The record of the Civil Service on race before the 1980s was clearly discriminatory (Behrens, 1989). A report published in 1979 identified barriers to the effective operation of the government's espoused equal opportunities policy (Civil Service Department, 1979). A Joint Working Party was set up to oversee surveys of ethnic minority groups. Monitoring began in 1982, was extended to all executive grades in 1986 and now covers all recruitment.

Although government issued a policy statement in 1983, it was not until 1990 that it embarked upon a Programme of Action. Since then recruitment of ethnic minorities has risen. In 1994, it was 5.3 per cent, above the benchmark of 4.9 per cent for the economically-active population, and there was no shortage of applicants. Changes in the representation of ethnic minorities in the Administration Group since 1992 are shown in Figure 3.2. There is an upward trend at all levels but the success rate remains lower than that for whites. Investigations indicate that it is probably linked with prior education rather than bias in qualifying tests or assessment centres (Civil Service Commission, 1992). Access training was introduced in 1991, in response to under-representation of blacks and Asians at EO level.

Promotion is generally slower for ethnic minorities than for white staff and complaints of racial discrimination led to race awareness training for those doing promotion interviews. Some large departments provide in-house training on managing ethnic relations and an element of positive action has also been introduced in staff development and training. The latest initiative by the EOU is an open learning programme This is aimed at developing and maximizing the potential of ethnic minority staff and staff with disabilities, in grades AA and AO, to improve their promotion prospects.

The disabled

Before the 1980s, the government's record on employing people with disabilities was no worse than that for other organizations but not a great deal better. In 1985, the EOU introduced a Code of Practice and each department was required to appoint a Departmental Disabled Persons Officer (DPPO) with responsibility for policy on recruitment and development of people with disabilities. Although the proportion of disabled people rose, there was evidence that they were still disadvantaged in training and promotion, because of stereotyping and prejudice. In 1994 the Code was upgraded to a Programme of Action including an action checklist and advice on how to implement it (Cm. 2729, 1994).

The aim is to raise the current 8000 registered disabled, or 1.6 per cent of all civil servants, to the three per cent statutory requirement and reduce their concentration in lower grades. Emphasis is now being placed on recruitment and staff development.

Managing equal opportunities

In 1994, there were 158 EOOs inclusive of departments, agencies and some non-departmental bodies and 110 of these were DDPOs. Most EOOs combine their work with other personnel functions and are located in personnel divisions. The EOU, within the OPS, oversees equal opportunities and encourages good practice (*Equal Opportunities Review*, 1989). It does not have power to enforce policies and responsibility for implementation rests with departments. With devolved personnel management responsibilities, the likelihood of diversity increases and, in the absence of sanctions, this is likely to lead to uneven implementation of equal opportunities and variations in outcomes.

Conditions of Service

There is still ambiguity about the legal status of civil servants. On the one hand, they are office holders and servants of the Crown and dismissable at will. On the other, they are employed by their departments and agencies. Their terms and conditions are set out by each department, on the basis of the central rules and principles set down in the Civil Service Management Code (CSMC). The CSMC replaced the CSPCSC in 1993, when responsibility for personnel and pay was delegated to departments and agencies. The employment contract consists of explicit and implied terms and its sources include statute and common law, collective agreements, civil service rules, European legislation and custom and practice. The statement of terms and conditions of service, set out by each department or agency, covers pay, leave and termination of appointment. The rules governing the principal civil service pension scheme are set out in a separate manual, which is incorporated into the employment contract.

The normal contract for civil servants is of an unlimited term but subject to specific periods of notice, although renewable fixed-term contracts have been introduced for chief executives of agencies. The case for extending fixed-term contracts to all top grades was examined in 1993 (Efficiency Unit, 1993) and rejected. Currently, government is planning to introduce individual written contracts for senior civil servants at grade 5 and above and is consulting with the unions on the form it will take. There is likely to be a mixture of fixed and other contracts in the future.

Flexible working

The Civil Service introduced flexible working in the 1970s, to offset the anticipated demographic timebomb and meet its commitment to equal opportunities. Later, in the 1980s, the focus turned to the cost advantages of alternative contracts, as the Service moved towards a core and peripheral workforce. The Mueller Report (1987) recommended a wide range of alternative working patterns, with current arrangements including: term-time working; flexible hours; career breaks; job-sharing; fixed-term appointments; home working; recurring temporary appointments; and on-call arrangements.

Through adopting these diverse modes of employment, the Civil Service is seeking to reach new labour markets, as well as catering for the increasingly diverse personal circumstances and career needs of individuals. Not least, flexible contracts enable pay costs to be kept down. The full-time contract remains the norm but the use of alternative contracts is increasing.

Rules of conduct

The CSMC sets out standards of conduct with which civil servants are expected to comply. In particular, civil servants are expected to display honesty and probity at all times and not to use their public offices for private gain. In addition, they are required to restrict their political and business activities even after retirement. All at grade 3 and above are required to obtain permission before accepting business jobs within two years of resignation or retirement. This rule has been interpreted leniently recently and this has led to demands for more rigorous enforcement (Treasury and Civil Service Committee, 1983–84).

Civil servants are subject to both the civil and criminal law but some statutes apply specifically to civil servants. These include the Prevention of Corruption Acts 1906 and 1916, Public Bodies Corrupt Practices Act 1989 and Official Secrets Act 1989. There have been several prosecutions under these Acts and an earlier Official Secrets Act 1911. It is more common, however, for civil servants to be dismissed if they are involved in fraud and corruption (Pyper, 1991; Drewry and Butcher, 1992).

There are also conventions regulating civil service behaviour. The most important is ministerial responsibility. Constitutionally, civil servants act in the name of the minister to whom thay are personally responsible. This sometimes poses dilemmas for civil servants, when they are asked to do something which is either illegal or which, in their opinion, is against the public interest. Although there is an internal right of appeal to the Head of the Service, this has been criticized. Several regulations and statements are intended to clarify the position, including the Armstrong Memorandum (1987), Osmotherley Rules (1980), now entitled Departmental Evidence and Response to Select Committees, and Questions of Procedure for Ministers (1986).

The status of the rules relating to civil servants' conduct has been challenged many times, most recently by the House of Commons Select Committee on the Civil Service (House of Commons, 1994). The Committee recommended a Civil Service Code of Ethics, setting down the fundamental principles and values of the Service, the conduct expected of civil servants and ministers and their respective rights and duties. The government accepted the Committee's proposal and produced a draft Code in 1995 summarizing the constitutional framework within which civil servants work and the values they are expected to uphold (Cm. 2748, 1995). This will complement an amended CSMC.

Restrictions on political activity

There are considerable restrictions on the citizenship rights and political activities of civil servants, which do not apply in other states in the European Union. In Europe, civil servants are free to contest elections, take seats in national and European assemblies, draw their salaries and retain their pension rights. In some cases, their jobs are held open and they can return to them should they lose their parliamentary seat. The UK restrictions vary according to the status of the civil servant and the political sensitivity of the post. The basis for restricting the political rights of civil servants stems from the principle of political neutrality, whereby civil servants are required to be loyal to the government, give honest advice and implement policies even-handedly.

An original blanket embargo has gradually been relaxed. The Civil Service is now divided into three groups: a politically-free group; a politically-restricted group; and an intermediate group. The politically-free group includes all industrial, manual and manipulative workers. The politically-restricted group, which includes grade 7s and above and fast-track recruits, are debarred from engaging in national politics but may, with permission, participate in local politics. The intermediate group, or all other civil servants, is not allowed to contest national or European elections but can stand in local elections. They can also belong to political parties, canvass, make speeches and exercise full political rights, except those dealing with policy and the public.

To protect the state from sabotage and security risks, civil servants working in departments, such as MoD, security services, Foreign Office and Cabinet Office, are subject to security vetting. Civil servants at grade 3 and above are also vetted, along with those in politically sensitive posts or with access to politically sensitive information. In 1988, over 40 000 civil servants in post had been vetted, including those belonging to proscribed political parties, such as the Communist party or the British National party. How far these restrictions deter people from entering the Service is difficult to judge. They do, however, limit the involvement of experienced civil servants in public life outside of the administration.

Pay Rewards and Performance

Traditionally, pay in the Civil Service has been determined through collective bargaining or review bodies and uniformly applied throughout the country, except for a London weighting. Annual negotiations on industrial and non-industrial pay have been conducted separately. Pay progression has been a basic principle, with incremental scales for each grade. Movement from one grade to another was by promotion. Until 1981, the principle underpinning pay determination was 'fair comparison'. The Pay Research Unit (PRU), set up in 1955 after the Priestley report, provided information on movements on outside pay and the civil service unions did their own research and fed this into the negotiating process. Cost of living, labour market factors and changes in work, along with comparability, were the variables influencing the bargaining process.

Comparability has long been debated (Fry, 1985). There clearly are problems of comparators when there are no equivalent jobs outside the Service. There is also the importance given to internal relativities in establishing fairness. The Priestley principle came increasingly under attack from the mid-1970s. It was no surprise when, in 1980, the Thatcher government decided to abandon it in its drive to reduce public expenditure. The period since then has seen significant changes in pay policy and payment systems. The Conservatives' approach has been radically different from that of their predecessors. They have pursued a more market-oriented strategy, whilst seeking to contain expenditure. Although not entirely abandoning the comparability principle, they have used it as a pragmatic device rather than as a guarantee of fairness. Their objective has been to break up centralized collective bargaining and move towards decentralized pay determination.

Top salaries

The salaries of top civil servants are determined separately by the Review Body on Senior Salaries (SSRB), formerly the Top Salaries Review Body (TSRB). The SSRB advises the Prime Minister on the remuneration of civil servants in the SOS after taking evidence from a range of bodies, including unions representing the top 600 civil servants.

Top civil servants have traditionally been paid less than those in analogous posts in the private sector, because of a notional discount reflecting job security and other reward elements in public employment. Even allowing for this lack of parity, top salaries fell behind those within the wider Civil Service and in comparable jobs outside, throughout the 1970s and 1980s. The TSRB's recommendations for substantial increases in 1980 were rejected and the situation deteriorated. This undoubtedly accounted for the high levels of resignations and difficulties in recruiting to senior posts in the 1980s. In 1992, the SSRB expressed concern about the erosion of differentials and pointed to a rise of only seven per cent for top officials since 1985, compared with rises of 40 per cent in the private sector. It recommended increases from 17 to 24 per cent but government halved them and staged them over three years.

Major changes in policy on top salaries since 1988 are linked to the creation of executive agencies, the appointment of chief executives on short-term contracts, the use of open competitions to recruit to top jobs and the introduction of performance related pay (PRP). An increasing number of top posts are filled by open competition. Although the practice is to advertise senior posts around the appropriate pay range, there is often a rider indicating that 'salary is negotiable'. Salaries offered to those recruited to the top three grades between 1992–94 tended to be 10 to 18 per cent above the top of the equivalent civil service range. In addition, many had performance bonuses of between 10 to 15 per cent of annual salary and some are also eligible for termination bonuses of between 10 to 15 per cent of annual salary. The differences between the salaries of externally appointed and internal appointments can be as much as 25 per cent. Table 3.5 shows the remuneration of the top 11 chief executives of agencies in 1994.

These differences in the treatment of external and internal appointments and the low level of top pay, compared with the private sector, fostered discontent. According to Hay Management Consultants (Cm. 2464, 1994), 46 per cent of top salary staff would leave for a better paid job outside. With plans for a slimmed-down senior Civil Service, and increases in top posts filled by open competition, there is no longer the same security and promotion opportunities associated with the higher Civil Service. This undoubtedly influenced government's acceptance of the SSRB proposals for big pay rises in 1995.

Top salaries for 1995 are shown in Table 3.6. Sir Robin Butler, Cabinet Secretary and Head of the Civil Service, received a salary of £150 000 in 1995–96, an increase of £32000 over his previous salary of £118 000. Similar increases were available for other permanent secretaries,

TABLE 3.5 Remuneration of the top 11 chief executives of agencies, 1994

Agency	Chief Executive	Remuneration
Prison Service	Derek Lewis	£160 000
Defence Research Agency	John Chisholm	£147 238
Central Statistical Office	Bill McLennan	£114 063
Highways Agency	Lawrence Haynes	£100 000
National Engineering Laboratory	William Edgar	£ 86 000
Benefits Agency	Michael Bichard	£ 83 012
Medicine Control Agency	Keith Jones	£ 82 698
Meteorological Office	Julian Hunt	£ 82 000
Agricultural Development Advisory Service	Julia Walsh	£ 80 563
Transport Research Laboratory	John Wooton	£ 72 400
NHS Estates	John Locke	£ 65 620

Source: derived from Travis, A *The Guardian*, 13 December 1994

TABLE 3.6 Salaries of top civil servants, 1995

Rank	£
Cabinet Secretary (Sir Robin Butler)	150 000
Permanent Secretaries and Second	90 000–150 000
Permanent Secretaries	90 000–150 000
Deputy Secretaries	67 000–98 000
Under Secretaries	55 000–82 000

Source: derived from Cm. 2464, 1994a

although the pay bill was capped and therefore salary increases could only be financed by staff cuts (Cm. 2764, 1995).

A further development in top salaries has been the introduction of PRP since 1987. Each civil servant, at grades 2 and 3, agrees annually with a reporting officer a personal responsibility plan containing objectives. Performance is rated on a five-point scale ranging from Box 1 (outstanding) to Box 5 (unacceptable). Only Boxes 1 and 2 obtain PRP. In 1993, over 85 per cent received PRP! Most top civil servants support PRP, although they seem to be ignorant about how it works and critical of the small amounts involved (Cm. 2464, 1994b).

In 1995 the pay system, for all grades below permanent secretary, became entirely performance based, with no automatic increases. Government also plans abolishing the central grades and replacing them with nine overlapping pay ranges, broadly linked to levels of responsibility. The objectives of this re-engineering of the pay structure are to facilitate delayering, provide better rewards for a smaller Service, give managers more flexibility over rewards, encourage mobility between departments and, according to the government, 'to establish a system which is fair and transparent in operation' (Cm. 2748, 1995, p.18). Under the new system, individual permanent secretaries will determine the management chain and control the pay progression of their staff, taking account of performance, levels of responsibility and marketability of skills.

From April 1995, a pay range for Permanent Secretaries, up to and including the Head of the Home Civil Service, was introduced. The level and extent of the range is determined with the advice of the SSRB and remuneration committee, consisting of the Heads of the Home Civil Service and the Treasury and three outside members of the SSRB. They also determine the position of individual permanent secretaries within the range.

These developments in top salaries are likely to see a growing convergence between the salaries of top civil servants and those in other public organizations and the private sector. Salaries are likely to vary amongst agencies and departments, depending upon their size and the willingness of people to take posts. Although the salaries of the top three grades continue to be controlled from the centre, agency and departmental heads exercise devolved powers over the pay of grades 4 and 5. This strengthens the trend away from standardized payments. As each agency determines its own remuneration policies, control of the cost of the senior Civil Service will be exercised through overall departmental or agency pay bills. It is also likely that the SSRB will be abolished, though outside involvement will remain through the remuneration committee.

General pay structures

Since 1979, Conservative governments have effectively operated an unofficial pay policy throughout the Civil Service. In 1980, government imposed a six per cent cash limit on all departments, making the link between pay settlements and staffing levels transparent. From 1981 to 1986, government included a 'pay factor' in its public expenditure planning, which became an imposed pay norm. From the mid-1980s, governments used a combination of cash limits and incomes policies to contain pay increases.

A confrontational approach by government was established in 1980, when it withdrew from the existing pay agreement without giving the requisite six months notice, disbanded the PRU and abolished the Standing Commission on Pay Comparability. The unions made a claim for 15 per cent, not out of line with general pay movements, but government offered seven per cent. Industrial action took place over 21 weeks, ending in the unions accepting seven per cent plus £30 and an enquiry into civil service pay. The Megaw report (1982) recommended a modified form of comparability, stating that pay comparisons should have 'a much less decisive influence than in the past' and that the governing principle should be paying civil servants enough, 'taking one year with another, to recruit, retain and motivate them to perform efficiently the duties required of them at an appropriate level of competence' (para. 91). Pay comparisons should be based on averages or 'benchmarks', with annual reviews of percentage changes supplemented by four-yearly reviews of total remuneration. But this data should only 'inform' the process. Megaw's most radical proposal was for the introduction of PRP and the replacement of incremental scales by merit ranges. Gradually, all these proposals have been implemented.

Between 1980 and 1985, civil servants' pay declined by 15 per cent in real terms and lagged behind private-sector increases by 29 per cent (Jary, 1991). This exacerbated recruitment problems and led to a staff exodus, allowing the government's planned contraction to be achieved more easily. It also divided the unions and weakened their resistance to new pay flexibilities. This enabled government to change the pay system unilaterally and introduce special and local pay additions for posts difficult to fill, or problems in keeping staff, and to provide merit pay for senior staff.

Between 1987 and 1989, the five main civil service unions agreed long-term flexible pay deals with the Treasury (Kessler, 1991a). These replaced the separate grade scales with a single spine, incorporated PRP and provided for enhancement of pay for posts having problems of recruitment and retention. There was also a form of pay comparability with the private sector, based upon the inter-quartile range. After a short period of stability the government served notice, in 1991, of terminating the agreements, and renegotiated them.

New agreements were reached which included universal PRP, permitted departments and agencies greater flexibility within the framework of national agreements and gave departments and agencies the option of departing from national agreements and devising their own payment systems. In April 1994, one-third of agencies assumed the right to determine their own pay structures and government announced that all departments and agencies would be operating along those lines by 1996.

Since 1992, government has also operated a tighter pay

policy aimed at keeping pay rises in line with or below inflation. It limited pay rises to a maximum of 1.5 per cent in 1993–94 and, in 1994–95, pay was frozen, with increases funded from productivity gains. This was extended to 1995–96 and 1996–97. In practice, with the exception of 1993–94, pay settlements have kept in line with inflation, with most increases being between 2.5 and three per cent. These continue to be negotiated annually and up to 1994–95 there were no significant variations between the agencies with delegated pay bargaining and the rest (Income Data Services, 1994a).

There is, however, a new decentralized and fragmented system of pay bargaining emerging. A number of agencies and departments have introduced new pay and grading structures, including HMSO, the Royal Mint, Employment Service Agency, Customs and Excise and Inland Revenue. Figure 3.3 shows the new structure introduced into the Inland Revenue in 1993. It replaces the 120 separate grades below the SOS with a single staff group, has five broad pay bands and a new performance management system. New pay structures emerged in 11 agencies in 1995 bringing the total at that time to 23. All these agencies make pay progression dependent on individual performance. As Corby (1994a, p. 58) writes: 'as it is government policy "to differentiate between those who are making a contribution and those who are not" ... it is unlikely that the Treasury would approve any future agency pay regime that did not contain a link between pay and performance.' Other features of the new pay and grading structures are a reduction in management levels, broad pay bands to replace separate grades and overlapping pay bands to enable rewards to be closely matched to contribution made, rather than status held.

Performance related pay

PRP, which forges a more direct link between performance and reward, was a logical development of the FMI. Almost all staff are now covered by PRP in flexible pay

FIGURE 3.3   Inland Revenue pay structure, 1994

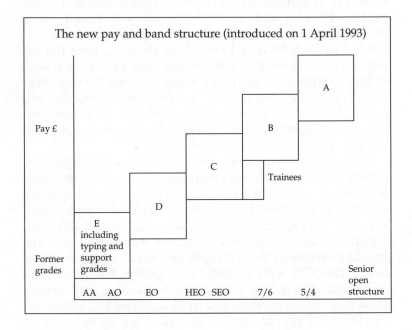

Source: derived from *Management Matters*, May 1994

agreements negotiated with the unions. The arrangements incorporate annual staff appraisals, or personal reviews, which ensure that reporting is closely linked to the achievement of objectives. PRP schemes differ in detail amongst departments and agencies but are geared so that the greatest rewards go to the highest performers.

The need to ensure that the overall pay bill was contained within the government's pay policy meant initially that there was a quota for PRP. The budget was fixed at around two per cent and payments to individuals were small. The move is towards total PRP, with high performers being given several spine point increases, whilst poor performers stand still. Reductions in pay have not yet been introduced but this could happen. Most PRP is individual, although there are examples of group bonuses covering all staff except 'unsatisfactory' performers. Bonus schemes tend to be linked to the achievement of agency targets and involve fairly small payments, either a flat rate or a fixed percentage of salary. Agencies with bonus schemes include the Vehicle Inspectorate, Central Office of Information and Companies House.

Staff appraisal

Staff appraisal has existed in the Civil Service since the 1920s. Originally a means of identifying people for promotion, it now serves a number of purposes including setting development objectives, identifying training needs and providing the basis for performance evaluation and performance rewards. Since 1991, each department and agency designs its own appraisal system, subject to two general rules. The first is that the system should identify unsatisfactory or unacceptable performance; the second is that the means of rating performance must underpin arrangements for decisions on performance pay. Non-mandatory principles of good practice are also encouraged, including openness in reporting, equal opportunity and personal reviews as a developmental, forward-looking management tool (*Management Matters*, 1993a).

Personal reviews, as appraisals are now called, are conducted by line managers annually and sometimes more frequently. Most reviews are jointly agreed and form the basis of development plans and training. They are a key element in the new performance management system, as well as the basis for PRP. The OPS has played a major role in their development: acting as a corporate adviser, disseminating information; convening meetings of personnel managers and trainers to exchange views; and running consortia of departments, agencies and outside consultants on items such as 'Objective Setting in Personal Reviews' and 'Developing Personal Review Systems' (*Management Matters*, 1993b).

Industrial Relations

Until 1979, industrial relations were highly centralized, proceduralized and standardized. The system was dominated by joint regulation and joint consultation through a well-developed Whitley system. The scope of bargaining was wide, including pay, training, equal opportunities and health and safety. Union membership was actively encouraged and union density was high throughout the Service. Terms and conditions were generally good with *de facto* job security and generous pensions. The government sought to be a model employer and encourage good practice in outside organizations.

Since 1979, industrial relations have changed, as successive governments have sought to impose a new public management. Part of their strategy has been to weaken the public-sector unions and collective bargaining and strengthen managerial prerogative and individual pay determination. Restructuring is having a radical effect upon industrial relations. It has set in motion: a more decentralized, fragmented system; diverse patterns of industrial relations; variations in payment and terms and conditions; a reduction in union membership; and a weakening of Whitleyism.

Civil service unions

Civil service unions were originally based upon grade, department, occupational group and gender (Parris, 1973). Their numbers have fallen as a result of mergers and amalgamations and there are currently seven major unions in the non-industrial Civil Service. Table 3.7 shows their membership in 1979, 1985 and 1994. The First Division Association represents senior civil servants, fast-stream entrants and specialists, such as lawyers. The National Union of Civil and Public Servants (NUCPS) represents executive and middle management staff, accountancy and computer specialists, messengers and support staff.

TABLE 3.7   Civil service unions, 1979, 1985 and 1994

Union	1979	1985	1994
Association of First Division Civil Servants/ Association of HM Inspectors of Taxes	5 825	7 609	9 595
Civil and Public Services Association	223 884	147 189	125 801
Inland Revenue Staff Federation	65 257	54 057	54 713
Institution of Professionals, Managers and Specialists	86 346	85 689	81 015
National Union of Civil and Public Servants	N/A	(SCPS) 90 397 (CSU) 36 135	107 000
Prison Officers Association/ Scottish Prison Officers Association	23 036	25 575	31 417
Total	424 812	427 558	409 541
Northern Ireland Public Service Alliance	21 370	19 483	20 506

Source: Information provided by Council of Civil Service Unions

NUCPS's wide membership arose as a result of a merger of the former Society of Civil and Public Servants (SCPS) with the Civil Service Union (CSU) in 1988. The Civil and Public Services Association (CPSA) covers clerical, secretarial and typing grades. One of the largest unions is the Institution of Professionals Managers and Specialists (IPMS). It represents specialist grades, including scientists, engineers, surveyors, architects and librarians. In addition, there are four departmental unions: the Inland Revenue Staff Federation, Prison Officers Association, Scottish Prison Officers Association and Northern Ireland Civil Service. The unions are organized into a federation, the Council of Civil Service Unions (CSSU), which is the central coordinating body designed to develop agreed policy.

Current membership of the unions is more misleading than in the past, when only civil servants were members. Today, perhaps no more than 50 per cent of the IPMS are civil servants, the rest are retired, in non-departmental agencies or in the private sector. With privatization, contracting out and redundancies, the membership of civil service unions is falling but overall density remains high and is still over 70 per cent.

One strategy adopted by the unions to combat declining membership and decentralization of bargaining has been mergers. Mergers are not new. Between 1968 and 1980, the number of civil service unions fell from 27 to nine. During the 1980s, the Association of Government Supervisors and Radio Officers was amalgamated into IPMS, followed by the amalgamation of the SCPS and CSU. One failed attempt was that to merge CPSA and NUCPS. The creation of a single civil service union would be an effective strategy to cope with the pressures on numbers and income but is unlikely to occur. A counter-trend is the links IPMS is making with specialist unions outside the Civil Service.

Union membership has been actively encouraged in the past, so density has been very high. The Treasury no longer recommends membership to new entrants but there is little evidence of any overt attempt at union de-recognition, with the exception of GCHQ. None of the executive agencies to-date has excluded unions, though there is evidence of a desire to do so and more evidence of the erosion of the rights of unions to be consulted (Corby, 1994a). Some agencies have dispensed with formal Whitley structures, whilst others have 'embarked upon a deliberate policy of reducing the role of Whitley' (p. 59). The potential for freezing out unions is in the agency framework documents, which encourage consultation with 'staff', as well as unions.

Union activities are coming under increasing management scrutiny and, in some instances, consultation rights are being ignored. Unions are also finding it difficult to cope with decentralization. The increase in the number of bargaining units, as agencies negotiate pay, is putting a strain on full-time officials. It is also changing the role of lay representatives who are now involved in negotiating local agreements, rather than discussing the application of national ones. The unions are responding by inter-union cooperation and setting up regional networks and common training for lay officers. However, a rationalization of membership and agreement on multi-union representation by a single nominated union has so far proved difficult to organize.

Procedural arrangements

Industrial relations are still conducted largely through the Whitley system. At national level, the management or official side is provided by the Treasury and the staff side by the unions. The National Whitley Council rarely meets and most negotiations are conducted in sub-committees between Treasury or OPS officials and the relevant unions. Until 1990, national negotiations covering conditions of employment, hours, holidays, superannuation, recruitment, promotion, appraisal and equal opportunities were agreed between the CCSU and the management side. But pay was negotiated largely outside the CCSU, by individual unions. National terms and conditions were applied uniformly throughout the Service. The national agreements were interpreted and applied through departmental and local Whitley committees.

Every major department has its own Whitley Council, consisting of senior civil servants, representing the official side, and representatives of departmental unions. Departments have similar constitutions but the matters discussed are specific to each. Because of the role civil servants perform in providing public services, the unions have been expected to show restraint in the ways they operate and eschew industrial action. Until the 1970s, there were no strikes and the system was held up as a model of industrial relations. Where there was a failure to agree, matters were normally referred to arbitration.

Since the 1970s, important changes in industrial relations practices have occurred. First, unions have resorted to industrial action when governments have refused to negotiate with them. Second, governments have refused to allow disputes to be referred to arbitration, preferring to stand firm and win through trials of strength. Third, governments have increasingly resorted to taking unilateral decisions, such as banning unions at GCHQ and abolishing the PRU, or have offered only token consultation with Whitley representatives. Fourth, from the end of the 1980s, government has sought to dismantle traditional centralized Whitleyism, by devolving responsibility for pay and personnel matters to agencies. By 1996, all departments and agencies will control their own employment policies and industrial relations. This dismantling of national Whitley will also make any service-wide industrial action unlawful, especially, as seems likely, if agencies become *de jure* employers.

Joint consultation

An original objective of Whitleyism was to provide means of involving employees in management through joint consultation, particularly at departmental level. This includes: informing employee representatives or obtaining information from them; discussing matters of common concern enabling employees to influence decisions; and problem solving. This last type of consultation is not easily distinguished in practice from collective bargaining (Farnham and Pimlott, 1995).

There is a long tradition, since 1945, of using all these forms of consultation, with management responding quickly to staff complaints and requests for consultation. It was most developed on issues such as training and welfare. Some departments had Joint Production Councils which involved staff in improving efficiency (Callaghan, 1953).

Joint consultation is being reduced, but largely by stealth. When consultation occurs, it is increasingly of the pseudotype, where management use Whitley forums to explain changes and gain support and acceptance of proposed actions. Practice varies, however, both amongst and within departments and agencies. It depends on the strength of union representation and management attitudes. There is evidence suggesting that where top management is recruited from the private sector, there is more antipathy than where posts are filled from within. In some cases, consultation continues to flourish and enables staff to take the initiative in raising problems. In others, alternative forms of communication have supplemented, if not replaced, the formal Whitley structures. Increasing use is being made of informal meetings and there is a clear trend towards more unilateral action by managers.

Staff involvement

A major change in the relationship between management and staff has been direct communication with individual employees. Throughout the 1980s, more open styles of management have been developed and new strategies for gaining the commitment of staff to organizational change have been adopted. Employees are informed about the goals and objectives of the organization, its achievements, plans for the future, policies and activities of people in it, by issuing departmental or agency mission statements and annual reports on progress. Staff also receive copies of policies on personal development and career planning. Notice boards, letters to employees, bulletins, briefing notes, newsletters and house journals are all used as media for written communication. Staff handbooks and employee reports provide further ways of communicating policy and practices. Another innovation has been videos and films which ensure consistency in the information being presented.

Interactive communication is achieved through meetings and briefing groups, whilst some departments have experimented with quality circles. These structures sidestep Whitley committees and can be seen as a way of subverting them. They involve more people and can assist in the communication process. Increasing use is also being made of attitude surveys. These enable management to investigate staff views on issues relevant to them and get feedback.

Training and Development

The Civil Service spends some six per cent of its salary bill on training. Responsibility for training and staff development rests with departments and agencies. They decide what training is needed, the form it takes and who provides it. They can: provide it themselves, through their own training divisions; buy in consultants; use the Civil Service College; or use universities and further education colleges. In recent years, the balance of provision has changed, with departments accounting for about 70 per cent of training days, the Civil Service College for about five per cent and external agencies 25 per cent.

Training is designed to ensure that people have the knowledge, skills and competences to carry out their work and achieve the objectives of the organization. People need to be inducted into organizational culture and develop and update job skills. New skills are required as they move into supervisory and managerial posts. The rate of change in the Service, the introduction of IT and, in particular, the imposition of a new culture in the last 15 years have put great pressure on all areas of training. But it is developments in management education and training that have been most marked.

Management development

The MPO (1984) identified the need for a more structured approach to management and career development. It called for departments to develop a training strategy and to identify their training needs, in terms of knowledge and skills required in: strategic policy-making and implementation; managing people, money and other resources; and in specialist work like personnel, accountancy and data processing. Training and career development were to be linked.

Four priority areas were identified: financial management; professional qualifications; training potential managers; and training for those selected for the Open Structure. Emphasis was also placed on the need for staff to have training in computers and IT.

Management training is where most developments have occurred. An extensive portfolio of training programmes has been developed by the Civil Service College, including foundation training for administrative trainees, training for HEOs and courses for scientists and professionals. In addition, departments organize courses for those identified for promotion to middle-level posts. The intention is that anybody entering the top Civil Service will have sound training.

Initiatives in senior management development began in 1984. A Top Management Training Programme was introduced and became a pre-requisite for promotion to deputy secretary. This six-week programme brings together managers from public and private sectors to explore common problems and strategies for dealing with them. A Senior Development Programme, launched in 1985, combines on-the-job and off-the-job training, for principals and above. There is also a Management Development Programme for junior staff.

The Civil Service College

The College, set up in 1970, provides major training courses in administration and management. It became an agency in 1989 and has sought to establish itself as the top public-sector training centre. Its main role is to help develop managerial and professional skills and promote best practice. The current role of the College was spelt out in the white paper *Continuity and Change* (Cm. 2627, 1994, p. 32):

the Civil Service College has a clear remit to meet the training needs of departments and agencies, particularly at more senior levels, and helps the cross fertilisation of ideas between departments and between the Civil Service and the wider economy.

The College is now organized into seven business groups which are responsible for training, advisory and consultancy services. Each has a particular focus and targeted clients. The Consulting Group specializes in strategic management, measuring and rewarding performance, training and development strategies and successful in-house bidding. The Senior Programme Group provides courses for grade 7s and comparable staff from other organizations which facilitates networking. The Management and Personal Development Group focuses on developing personal competences and courses for women and ethnic minorities.

The Policy, Government and Europe Group offers a wide range of courses in public policy and European and International Affairs, whilst the Professional Training and Development Group focuses on those working in personnel, auditing, computing and other professional areas. The Group on Commercial Management Practice runs courses in improving quality and services to the customer, market testing, purchasing, project management, TQM and the Transfer of Undertakings Protection of Employment Regulations (TUPE, 1981). The Group on Developing Specialists runs courses in the management skills and competences required by scientists and other professionals. The College also responds to changes in government policies and requests for tailor-made modules. The latest to be developed are Pay Delegation, Benchmarking and Process Re-engineering.

In 1994, the College offered nearly 500 courses and over 8000 civil servants, one-third of the top seven grades, attended. The number of students trained by the College on customer's sites also rose from 3600 to 10 700 over the same period. The College has to meet quality and volume targets set down by the OPS and is required to cover its running costs. It regularly exceeds the targets set each year, mainly by introducing new courses and by developing consultancy and tailored training. Quality is assessed by participant evaluation, which has been in excess of the 80 per cent targets and rising since 1990 (Cabinet Office, 1994). The College will continue as an agency until 1997 but is a strong candidate for privatization.

Training for competences

Influenced by the Management Charter Initiative (MCI) in 1987, the Civil Service has been at the forefront of developments in competency-based training. The OPS, working with consultants, departments and agencies, has identified the core factors making for effective performance at each level of the Open Structure. Profiles of qualities and skills required of those filling posts at each level are used to match candidates to jobs and for career development and training purposes. Succession planning now involves a check list against which the training needs of potential top managers can be assessed.

All courses offered by the College are linked to core criteria. Figure 3.4 shows the core competences identified for the SOS and corresponding courses to develop the necessary skills. A similar profile has been developed by the College and Price Waterhouse to match grade 7. Most departments now run competency training programmes for Grades 5 to 7 and many agencies have management development programmes, underpinned by competence frameworks, personal development plans, planned postings and targeted training.

The MCI framework is being widely adopted by departments and line managers are becoming involved in training and development. Agencies and departments are also looking to raise the standards of competence of lower staff by using NVQs. The Benefits Agency launched a programme in 1993 aiming to raise the standards of competence of all its staff and offering them the chance to

FIGURE 3.4   Core competences and training programmes for the senior open structure, 1994

DIRECTION

Leadership

- Creates and conveys a clean vision
- Initiates and drives through change
- Is visible, approachable and earns respect
- Inspires and shows loyalty
- Builds a high performing team
- Acts decisively having assessed the risks
- Takes final responsibility for the actions of the team
- Demonstrates the high standards of integrity, honesty and fairness expected in public service

Course

Strategic leadership

Developing Strategic Behaviour

Personal Power & Influencing Skills

An Introduction to Public Accountability for Chief Executives

Strategic Thinking Planning

- Identifies strategic aims, anticipating future demands, opportunities and constraints
- Demonstrates sensitivity to Ministers needs and to wider political issues
- Sees relationships between complex interdependent factors
- Makes choices between options which take into account their long term impact
- Translates strategic aims into practical and achievable plans
- Takes decisions on time, even in uncertain circumstances

MANAGEMENT AND COMMUNICATION

Management of People

- Establishes and communicates clear standards and expectations
- Gives recognition and helps all staff develop full potential
- Addresses poor performance
- Builds trust, good morale and co-operation within team
- Delegates effectively, making best use of skills and resources within the team
- Seeks face to face contact and responds to feedback from staff
- Manages the change process perceptively

Stepping up in Senior management

Management Skills for Senior Managers

Introduction to Management for Senior Staff: Staff Management

Managing Conflict Effectively

Coaching for breakthrough Performance

Business Mentoring for Senior Managers

Being a mentor

Communication

- Negotiates effectively and can handle hostility
- Is concise and persuasive orally and in writing
- Listens to what is said and is corrective to others' reactions
- Demonstrates presentational and media skill
- Chooses the methods of communication most likely to secure effective results
- Is comfortable and effective in a representational role (with EC languages where needed)

PERSONAL CONTRIBUTION

Personal Effectiveness

- Shows resilience, stamina and reliability under heavy pressure
- Takes a firm stance when circumstances warrant it
- Is aware of personal strengths and weaknesses and their impact on others
- Offers objective advice to Ministers without fear or favour
- Pursues adopted strategies with energy and commitment
- Adapts quickly and flexibly to new demands and change
- Manages own time well to meet competing priorities

Young Node

Senior Management in a Changing Organisation

Managing priorities & Time

Managing stress

Learning Sets

Intellect, Creativity and Judgement

- Uses intellect to offer insights and break new ground
- Generates original ideas with practical application
- Homes in on key issues and principles
- Analyses ambiguous data and concepts rigorously
- Defends logic of own position robustly but responds positively to reasoned alternaives
- Encourages creative thinking in others

	DIRECTION	
Course	*Delivery of Results*	Course
Strategy & Planning	• Defines results taking account of customer and other stakeholders's needs	Organisational Change
Managing Decisions		Strategies for Service Excellence
Option & Investment Appraisal	• Delivers results on time, on budget and to agreed quality standards	Objective Setting & Performance Measurement
Strategic Control	• Demonstrates high level project and contract management skills	Project Management
Planning & Business Management	• Ensures that others organise their work to achieve objectives	Project Management for Policy Staff
	• Knows when to step in and when not to	
	• Encourages feedback on performance and learns for the future	

	MANAGEMENT AND COMMUNICATION	
	Management of Financial and Other Resources	
Senior Negotiating Skills	• Negotiates for the resources to do the job, in the light of wider priorites	Introduction to Management for Senior Staff: Resource Management
Managing Meetings	• Commits and realigns resources to meet key priorities	The Government Accounting Framework
Managing Difficult Meetings		
Effective Presentation for Senior Staff	• Secures value for tax payers' money	The public Expenditure Framework
Effective Briefing for Senior Specialists	• Leads initiatives for new and more efficient use of resources	Management Accounting
Effective Speech Writing		Commercial Accounting
Media Skills	• Ensures management information systems are used to monitor/control resources	Government Purchasing & Market Testing
Appearing Before Select Committee	• Manages contracts and relationships with suppliers effectively	The financial Environment
Appearing Before the Public Accounts Committee		
Drafting Briefing & PQ Skills		

	PERSONAL CONTRIBUTION	
Management	*Management*	
Creative Problem Solving	• Earns credibility through depth of knowledge/expertise	Strategic Planning Seminars
Using Research	• Knows how to find and use other sources of expertise (including IT)	Human Resources Seminars
Making Data Work Harder	• Understands parliamentary and political processes and how to operate within them	The public Sector Reform Agenda
	• Applies best practice from other public/private sector organisations	Specialists & Generalists Working Together
	• Understands how policy impacts on operations, staff and customers	Breakfast Briefings
		Senior Finance Seminars
		IT briefings
		The Senior Induction Programme
		Europe

work towards national qualifications. The DVLA and the Employment Service Agency have also introduced work-based training programmes.

Human resources development and investors in people

In line with the central strategy for improving the efficiency of the Service, departments and agencies are encouraged to formulate policies on human resources development (HRD) (Cabinet Office, 1993). One department developing a plan of action is the Employment Department. Its HRD objectives are: to make the development of people one of its corporate objectives; to include HRD in operational planning; and to give everyone the opportunity to agree personal development objectives. HRD is now widespread throughout the Service, with line managers responsible for implementing policy.

All government departments and agencies are also signed up for the award of Investors in People (IIP). IIP is a means of improving people's performance by a planned approach to setting and communicating corporate goals and developing people to meet the goals, so that they are motivated to meet organizational requirements. IIP is based upon a national standard or benchmark against which the organization is assessed by local Training and Enterprise Councils. An IIP has to make a public commitment to develop all employees, review training and development needs, train and develop employees from recruitment throughout their employment and evaluate training and development. By June 1994, eight agencies had obtained the award.

Career development and succession planning

In 1993, the Efficiency Unit examined career management

for key jobs at Grade 3. Only four departments were using skills and competency profiles to identify top management potential. Some departments used assessment centres and panels to identify talent but most used management development programmes (Efficiency Unit, 1993).

The report recommended that departments and agencies should be more open about their personnel policies and encourage individuals to take more responsibility for their own career development. They should design schemes enabling individuals with potential to gain experience of front-line service delivery and of interchange with other sectors, including the private sector. From grade 7 upwards, there should be annual reviews of staff development, ensuring that staff gain breadth and depth of experience and develop the competences identified for each level of responsibility. Most of the proposals are being implemented to ensure an adequate supply of internal candidates for top management posts over the next decade.

Conclusion and Evaluation

The Civil Service has experienced a 'quiet revolution' over the last 15 years. Traditional people management policies and practices (TPM) have given way to new systems of people management, incorporating both continuity and change. The unitary, integrated structure of departments, controlled through hierarchy, rules and regulations, by an elite of administrative mandarins, has been replaced by a federal structure of central and core departments, surrounded by a constellation of agencies run by chief executives, appointed for their managerial abilities. Nearly 80 per cent of civil servants now work within semi-autonomous agencies, interwoven with the private sector as a result of contracting out.

In this post-bureaucratic structure, each agency has powers to recruit its own staff and determine their pay and conditions. People management has been devolved and this is leading to greater diversity of personnel policies and practices. There is already evidence of movements away from nationally negotiated pay scales and many other characterics of TPM are being changed. The old system had a number of features: it was isolated from political jobbery; based on the principle of merit with open, competitive recruitment; provided life-long careers in return for commitment to the public-service ethic; had standard pay rewards rather than pay related to performance; used rules and regulations to limit discretion and ensure standard and equal treatment of the public; and was directed by an elite corps of administrators, rather than by managers hired on the open market (Hood, 1994). This elite were notably paternalistic in their attitudes towards subordinate staff. These characteristics are now under threat.

Today, the smaller federal Civil Service operates along the lines of a 'holding company', with core departments in Whitehall strategically managing a collection of 'public businesses'. This model reflects the paradigm of the new public management which rests upon the key ideas that: public services should be run like private businesses; competition guarantees efficiency; rivalry cuts costs and pushes up standards; the job of managers is to control performance and get results; and people are motivated by performance rewards, particularly money. There is a new culture and language of managerialism which is the medium for communication. Civil servants no longer supply standard services to the undifferentiated public but focus on individual customer needs, value for money and quality services. This emphasis on quality and responsiveness calls for new types of behaviour and staff are now selected for managerial skills and competences and are being enculturated into the new values.

The emphasis on costs and value for money is resulting in a segmentation into core and peripheral staff, with a variety of modes of employment. There are also new management systems which control financial and human resources, using advanced computer technology and informatization, on the one hand, and HRM techniques, on the other. Paradoxically, there is now both more effective centralization and greater decentralization in the Civil Service. Agencies and individuals are being controlled at arms-length through performance indicators, target setting and staff appraisals. This new performance management system can appear more oppressive than the former professional bureaucracies, which effectively provided a great deal of personal autonomy. For most civil servants, the work process is now far more directed. Rewards are based on performance, which is constantly geared to increased efficiency. With suppressed pay increases, this has resulted in substantial gains in productivity.

The new public management clearly challenges the traditional Civil Service but it provides opportunities for those who take on new managerial roles. There is some evidence that it is welcomed by many rank-and-file staff, although there are some pockets of resistance amongst trade unionists and, not least, amongst senior civil servants in the central departments. The latter's strategy has been to implement enthusiastically those elements, such as the transfer of operational units to agency status, which they welcome, whilst protecting their own traditional role. The latest government white paper, written by Whitehall mandarins, reaffirms a commitment to maintaining a smaller permanent Civil Service 'based on the values of integrity, political impartiality, objectivity, selection and promotion on merit and accountability through Ministers to Parliament' (Cm. 2748, 1995, p. 3). A new Code of Ethics, incorporating these values, whilst no guarantee of standards, is a political statement offering some protection to traditional mandarins. The top tier of the Civil Service looks likely to survive intact.

Government commitment to the new public management, however is destined to continue, as the white paper, *The Civil Service: Taking Forward Continuity and Change* (1995), points out. It sets out proposals for improving performance and reducing costs by 10 per cent, in real terms, over the next three years. All departments have to produce annual efficiency plans, using privatization,

contracting out, market testing and the application of Next
Step principles, together with techniques such as
benchmarking and business process engineering. This is
likely to result in a further contraction of jobs. Since 1992,
eight civil service agencies have been privatized and a
further six have been announced. Over 30 000 posts have
gone through privatization and competing for quality
programmes. The Deregulation and Contracting Out Act
1994 is likely to lead to further job losses, as the scope
for transfers to outside companies is extended. In future,
agencies will decide what to market test and how to provide services.

Re-engineering of departmental structures is likely to
reduce hierarchies and devolve all executive activities to
agencies. Small policy departments will be separated from
the operational agencies delivering services. Within both,
there is likely to be distinctions between core and other
activities, with the latter being most vulnerable to privatization and contracting out. Personnel and training services
in departments and agencies may be provided by a variety of public and private organizations in the future.

The new senior Civil Service will be smaller, better paid,
better trained than previously, with written contracts and
more competition from outsiders, for a smaller number
of top posts. But it will continue to be the permanent
arm of government and the link between the political and
administrative spheres. There are likely to be a number
of different 'civil services', reminiscent of the pre-Northcote-
Trevelyan system in the nineteenth century.

What aspects of TPM have survived? The people management system is still centrally controlled, albeit differently from the past. There is now an arms-length strategy,
incorporating cash limits, targets and PIs – in place of
detailed rules and regulations. Framework policies rather
than directives now characterize many areas of people
management. Managers, in charge of agencies and cost
centres, have discretion over the use of resources, within
quality, output and performance targets, and are required
to report regularly on their achievements. There has been
an increase in accountability and transparency.

The Civil Service is still committed to being a good employer 'providing terms and conditions in line with the most responsible large employers and good enough to recruit and retain and motivate a committed and efficient Service with the highest standards of probity; ensuring equal opportunity . . . maintaining a predominantly career Civil Service and the training and development of staff' (Cm. 2748, 1995, p. 10).

Industrial relations are in transition but the traditional collectivist structures are still in place, union representation is still important and joint consultation and collective bargaining continue to involve employees in decision-making. The national Whitley System is being weakened, however, and is unlikely to survive the devolution of personnel and pay functions to departments and agencies. Yet pluralism is still strong and departmental and agency Whitleyism is still in place. The individualization of relationships between management and employees, and the development of direct means of communication, are parallelling rather than replacing representative channels. A hybrid model of employment relations seems to be emerging. It incorporates the collectivist and pluralist structures of traditional industrial relations with the new individualistic and unitarist structures introduced since the 1980s.

With the ending of national agreements there are openings for wider differentials, depression of pay for lower grades and regional pay. It is not a general recipe for higher salaries and rewards, since the Treasury continues to set the financial criteria and targets for agencies and these are likely to act as surrogates for cash limits and pay norms.

It is evident that TPM is being challenged by a 'new people management' (NPM) system in the Civil Service. The NPM, which is emerging as the demands placed on the state change and are redefined, consists of many elements of the old system, associated with the model employer and the pluralist, collectivist tradition. But these are being combined with business approaches to the managing of people, which are economistic and rationalistic in emphasis. At their best, they motivate and reward people for their contributions to the organization, facilitate staff development and career opportunities and are people-centred and personalized. They are therefore in advance of the old system. However, there are also human costs involved in the changes taking place, in terms of job insecurity, loss of professional autonomy, increased managerial control and a new competitive culture resulting in individual winners and losers. There also appears to be a diminished sense of job satisfaction and quality of working life, as performance management demands constantly rising standards of work, effort and productivity, within continually constrained resources.

CHAPTER 4

The National Health Service

Susan Corby

The National Health Service (NHS) was established in 1948 to deliver health care according to clinical need and irrespective of an individual's ability to pay for it. Essentially, it is funded by central government out of general taxation and is free at the point of use, but government is not the employer. District health authorities (DHAs) and family health service authorities (FHSAs), which are merging, and health service trusts are the employers of over one million staff working in the NHS, although most general practitioners, dentists and opticians, are self-employed.

There were reorganizations of the structure of the NHS in 1974 and 1982 (Harrison *et al.*, 1992, p. 21). Then the Conservative government, as part of its drive to improve efficiency in the public services, broadly implemented the recommendations of the Griffiths report (1983). Following the Griffiths reforms, the NHS in England was headed by the Secretary of State for Health, who chaired a Supervisory Board whose members included the Minister for Health, permanent secretary, chief medical officer and a non-executive member. It had strategic responsibility for NHS resources and objectives. A full-time, multi-professional NHS Management Board was accountable to it and responsible for overseeing implementation of the strategy. This was chaired by the Minister for Health and included the NHS chief executive. Although the composition of the Management Board varied, roughly one-third of its members had a commercial background, one quarter came from the NHS and the remainder from the Civil Service (Harrison *et al.*, 1992, p. 46). Fourteen regional health authorities (RHAs), in turn, controlled 190 DHAs and 90 FHSAs. In addition, there were eight special health authorities (SHAs), such as London postgraduate teaching hospitals, which reported directly to the NHS Management Executive (Seifert, 1992, p. 174). A general manager headed every RHA, DHA and SHA, taking overall responsibility and replacing what had previously amounted to consensus decision-making by a team, on which the clinical professions were represented.

There were similar arrangements for Scotland and Wales. The Secretary of State for Scotland and the Scottish Office and the Secretary of State for Wales and the Welsh Office performed essentially the same functions as the Health Secretary and the Department of Health in England. Scotland had 15 health boards which combined DHAs and FHSAs and Wales had nine DHAs and eight FHSAs. There were no RHAs in either Scotland or Wales (Welsh Office, 1994; Scottish Office, 1993).

Recent Reforms and Structural Change

In 1990, the government set in train more fundamental changes to the structure of the NHS, under the National Health Service and Community Care Act. The Act's key feature is the separation of the purchasing of health care from its provision. The DHA, or general practitioner (GP) fundholder, makes annual, non-legally enforceable contracts to buy services from providers, on a block basis, or a cost and volume or cost per case basis. On 1 April 1994, in addition to the 190 DHAs, there were nearly 9000 GP fundholders in England serving over one-third of the population (Department of Health, 1994a).

Purchasers buy most services from NHS trusts, although the private sector is increasingly an important provider. Trusts are formed from the units providing health care in the NHS. They vary in function and include: acute hospital, ambulance, community, mental health or combined trusts. They vary in size from under 500 to over 5000 employees. By 1 April 1994, there were 419 trusts in England, 96 per cent of all provider units (Department of Health (DoH), 1994b). In Scotland, there were 39 trusts, or 70 per cent of provider units, and in Wales, 24 trusts, or 75 per cent of provider units, on 1 April 1994, according to the Scottish Office and Welsh Office.

Trusts are directly accountable to the Secretary of State, unlike the few remaining units which are directly managed by DHAs. Moreover, they are governed by a board of normally 11 people, a chairman plus equal numbers of executive and non-executive directors appointed directly or indirectly by the Secretary of State. There are similar provisions in respect of DHAs (NHS Management Executive (NHSME), 1990).

The 1990 Act also changes power relationships in the NHS. Before the Act, there was a clear chain of command running from the Secretary of State to the Health Department, and then to RHAs and DHAs (health boards in Scotland), with the provider units as part of DHAs. The Act, however, devolves decision-making. Not only does it give purchasers more power, for instance DHAs can choose with whom to contract, but trusts also have a degree of autonomy on financial matters and considerable autonomy on personnel and employment matters. For instance, trusts are the employers, whereas before the 1990 changes most hospital staff were employed by DHAs, with consultants employed by RHAs. Also, as discussed below, trusts can set their own terms and conditions of employment, devise industrial relations procedures irrespective of national arrangements and apply these to new or promoted staff.

The centre, too, has been streamlined, as part of the new structure. The Supervisory Board and Management Board have been replaced by a Policy Board, chaired by the Secretary of State for Health, and includes business people as well as the chief executive of the NHS. Under the Policy Board is the NHS Management Executive (NHSME), now called the NHS Executive. Comprising over 800 civil servants, it is both an integral part of the DoH and head office of the NHS. Also, as a result of the changes outlined above, further modifications to the NHS structure are being made. In 1993, the role of RHAs was reduced and their number fell from 14 to eight. Legislation is in hand to abolish RHAs and replace them with regional offices of the NHS Executive, with a monitoring function only. The legislation will also enable DHAs and FHSAs to merge and will facilitate mergers between DHAs, so putting developments in practice on a statutory basis. For Wales, too, legislation will provide for mergers between DHAs and FHSAs and reduce their number from 17 to five (Welsh Office, 1994).

By these changes, the government has made the NHS more like the private sector. First, it has introduced people from the private sector into the NHS at all levels, from the NHS Policy Board to trusts boards (Gilligan, 1994). Second, by inserting quasi-contracts into the NHS, government has introduced proxies for the market mechanism and processes akin to those found in the private sector. Third, it has introduced structures similar to those found in many large private-sector companies, thus substituting a quasi-autonomous multi-divisional structure (M-form organization) for a unitary one (U-form organization) (Williamson, 1975).

This decentralized structure is not unproblematic. There are countervailing pressures and the trusts' theoretical autonomy on personnel matters is constrained in practice in four main ways. First and foremost, it is constrained by political initiatives under which trusts are strongly encouraged to achieve ministerial ends and directed on how to do so. The government essentially funds the NHS and, although the Secretary of State can no longer command units, government is the paymaster. Moreover, the NHS Executive faces in two directions. On the one hand, it has a political role, supporting the Secretary of

State, and is part of the DoH. But, on the other hand, it also has a managerial role, ensuring the implementation, for instance, of health targets, financial parameters and personnel objectives. Thus, for example, it monitors compliance on equal opportunities; gives leadership by holding workshops on performance pay; and provides guidance on local pay bargaining. In short, the NHS Executive, with its chief executive, may be modelled on the private sector but it has both government policy responsibilities and is accountable for operating a public health service.

Second, the trusts' new-found autonomy on personnel matters is limited in practice by the collectivist and pluralist traditions dating back to the NHS's inception. Allied to this is the NHS's well-embedded pay determination arrangements under which national terms and conditions for each functional group are set in one of two ways. Over half of NHS staff, namely doctors and dentists, nurses, midwives, health visitors and the professions allied to medicine (PAMs), have their pay determined by government on recommendations of pay review bodies. Their other terms and conditions are essentially determined by collective bargaining in the Whitley machinery. Nearly all the remaining NHS staff, such as administrative and clerical workers, ancillaries, ambulance staff and scientists, have all their terms and conditions agreed in the Whitley system. This consists of one general and 10 functional councils. The main exceptions are general and senior managers and healthcare assistants, who are not covered by national arrangements, and maintenance staff, whose unions negotiate directly with the Health Departments.

Compared with private-sector collective agreements, those in the NHS have been far more detailed. This remains the case, even though over the last decade NHS agreements have become looser by incorporating, for instance, flexible pay points to allow managerial discretion, or taking the form of so-called enabling agreements setting broad parameters for local negotiations. Whatever form they take, however, these national arrangements at best sit uneasily with trust autonomy on personnel matters.

Third, the autonomy of trusts is constrained by TUPE Regulations 1981. Under its provisions, staff previously working in a unit which has become a trust, or part of one, can continue to receive nationally negotiated terms and conditions, and/or pay rates arising from pay review body awards, for as long as they choose to do so. This is provided they stay in the same job and are not promoted. Furthermore, all collective agreements with the old employer, generally a DHA, including those covering union recognition, transfer to the new employer, the trust, in respect of existing staff.

Fourth, trust autonomy is constrained because the employer is not the only focus for staff loyalty or the sole source of role definition. The majority of staff in the NHS are professional workers. Professional training, standards of entry, the nature and remit of their work are laid down by professional bodies, not the employer. These include the General Medical Council for doctors, the UK Central Council for nurses and the Council for Professions Supplementary to Medicine for physiotherapists, radiographers and other professions allied to medicine. It is no coincidence that so far trusts have removed job barriers only in non-professional areas (Corby, 1992). This dual focus of loyalty for the majority of NHS staff is a dimension in people management that marks the NHS from some other public services, such as the Civil Service and local government.

The Personnel Function: Some Emerging Issues

The NHS is a labour intensive organization. Its total labour force has not changed significantly over the period 1981 to 1993, as shown in Table 4.1. In England, Wales and Scotland, total numbers employed in the NHS were 1.2 million in 1981 and 1.1 million in 1993. The numbers of doctors and dentists and PAMs have risen, although nursing and midwifery staff numbers fell in England and Scotland between 1989 and 1993. But this may be partly

explained by the removal of students from the figures.
The numbers in some non-professional groups, however,
have altered greatly. In particular, the number of ancillaries has more than halved since 1983, reflecting competitive tendering for laundry, cleaning and catering
services. Some contracts went outside the NHS but, even
where in-house tenders were successful, this was often
because hours and jobs were cut (Mailly *et al.*, 1989). Seifert
(1992) estimates that 82 per cent of tenders were won in-
house.

More recently, as a result of decisions by the European
Court of Justice (*Dr Sophie Redmond Stichting v. Bartol and
others* [1992] IRLR 366) and the Court of Appeal (*Dines
and others v. (1) Initial Health Care Services and (2) Pall
Mall Services Group Ltd* [1994] IRLR 336), the number of
successful external bids looks set to dwindle, with knock-
on effects for the terms and conditions of in-house staff.
This is because outside contracts have been won essentially since contractors have taken on NHS workers, but
with wage rates lower than those in the NHS. Court decisions, however, have held that this is unlawful under
TUPE Regulations.

The number of general and senior managers in England and Wales has risen dramatically in the last few
years, from less than 5000 in 1989 to over 21 000 in 1993.
The numbers for Scotland have only recently been kept.
Some commentators argue that this partly is a result of a
reclassification of those who previously had managerial
roles, such as chief laboratory technicians or directors of
midwifery services. Others argue that the rise in the
number of managers is an inevitable result of the internal market (Brindle, 1994a).

The structure of the personnel function

Until the establishment of trusts, the main locus of the
personnel function was at the centre, in the Health
Departments, where standardized rules and procedures
were determined. Personnel managers at local level largely

TABLE 4.1   NHS workforce, 1981–93

	1981	*1983*	*1986*	*1989*	*1993*
NHS: England					
General and senior managers					
Nos	—	—	510	4 630	20 320
Wte	—	—	510	4 610	20 010
Doctors and dentists					
Nos	51 520	52 970	53 970	56 730	59 720
Wte	39 420	40 690	41 880	44 090	48 740
Nursing and midwifery					
Nos	445 890	452 380	459 080	466 740	445 160
Wte	388 010	394 680	397 240	398 050	361 460
PAMs					
Nos	—	—	41 580	45 160	48 950
Wte	—	—	33 590	36 710	39 770
Admin. and clerical					
Nos	128 180	129 620	131 390	141 570	162 840
Wte	108 800	109 960	110 840	116 840	132 650
Ancillary					
Nos	221 450	215 330	167 580	141 540	108 440
Wte	172 180	166 180	124 270	102 360	77 770
Total – all staff groups					
Nos	**970 190**	**979 050**	**946 820**	**927 990**	**941 030**
Wte	**819 070**	**825 420**	**794 730**	**787 200**	**766 710**
NHS: Wales					
General and senior managers					
Nos	—	—	—	190	1 190
Wte	—	—	—	190	1 160
Doctors and dentists					
Nos	2 590	2 670	2 790	2 870	3 260
Wte	2 310	2 400	2 470	2 600	2 950
Nursing and midwifery					
Nos	29 730	30 330	31 680	33 240	3 440
Wte	25 360	25 980	27 190	28 040	26 455
PAMs					
Nos	2 070	2 270	2 550	2 870	3 330
Wte	1 700	1 890	2 090	2 410	2 810
Admin. and clerical					
Nos	7 320	7 500	7 860	8 630	10 510
Wte	6 400	6 530	6 970	7 480	8 920

TABLE 4.1 *Cont.*

Ancillary					
Nos	15 110	14 940	13 690	11 900	10 000
Wte	11 840	11 560	10 210	8 650	7 060
Total – all staff groups					
Nos	**62 830**	**63 840**	**64 590**	**66 500**	**69 850**
Wte	**53 270**	**54 170**	**55 370**	**55 830**	**55 940**

NHS: Scotland

Doctors and dentists					
Nos	6 820	7 960	7 850	8 160	8 460
Wte	6 410	6 660	6 550	6 870	7 310
Nursing and midwifery					
Nos	70 940	72 230	72 990	74 950	64 520
Wte	61 130	62 400	62 870	64 450	53 390
PAMs					
Nos	—	—	4 970	6 500	6 477
Wte	—	—	4 160	4 680	5 370
Admin. and clerical					
Nos	15 190	15 820	16 360	17 420	20 070
Wte	13 630	14 090	14 450	15 220	17 390
Ancillary					
Nos	34 790	34 740	32 680	25 960	20 580
Wte	27 350	26 970	24 570	18 660	13 290
Total – all staff groups					
Nos	**142 810**	**146 440**	**146 570**	**143 720**	**133 210**
Wte	**122 640**	**124 800**	**124 040**	**121 060**	**109 200**

Notes

1. Abbreviations – Wte = whole time equivalents, nos = numbers, PAMs = professions allied to medicine.
2. All figures rounded to the nearest 10.
3. Figures as at 30 September each year.
4. The figures for nursing and midwifery in 1993 no longer include student nurses.
5. The figures are collated by three separate statistical units and therefore may not be strictly comparable. Nevertheless, the author has tried to provide a common basis for the three countries' figures, e.g. by excluding general medical practitioners and general dental practitioners, as they are self-employed.
6. Scotland does not have figures for general and senior managers for the years between 1981–1989 inclusive.
7. Figures for PAMs for 1983 and 1986 are not available for England and Scotland as they were included in 'professional and technical' and cannot be broken down.

interpreted and implemented these rules and procedures. Pay rates, for example, were determined nationally and the roles of DHA and unit personnel managers' were essentially administrative ones. In addition, RHAs had a personnel function and, for instance, developed region-wide computerized personnel systems, as well as organizing training.

There is now no personnel function at regional level and, in line with trust autonomy on personnel matters, the personnel function at unit level has changed from an administrative to a strategic and operational one. There is now only a very limited personnel function in DHAs, that is at purchaser level, since they employ very few staff. Some DHAs have actually contracted out their personnel function, although this is rare even among the smallest trusts.

There is still a continuing personnel function at the centre. Thus the NHS Executive, and the NHS Management Executive in Scotland, which is staffed by civil servants, mediates between trusts and ministers and deals with other parts of the Department and other government departments. The NHS Executive deals with the Treasury on pay, represents the NHS on employment issues and manages industrial relations at national level. At the same time, it supports and encourages trusts to adopt government initiatives. At the time of writing, these include the move to local pay flexibility, performance pay and the achievement of goals on equal opportunities.

There is no common model for organizing the personnel function in trusts. Some trusts have personnel specialists attached to clinical directorates, but with a personnel or 'human resources' director taking an overall view. Some trusts centralize the personnel function and others operate a half-way house. Bach (1995) points out that devolution, i.e. the first model, has benefits. There is a clear separation between the operational personnel role and the strategic one. Also, with proximity to divisional managers, personnel specialists can make a greater contribution to the divisions. Yet devolution of the personnel function creates new conflicts amongst divisions and between divisions and the centre. At one trust, there were differences in the manner in which divisions handled discipline and these differences were exploited by the unions.

There is no requirement for the head of the personnel function to be one of the five executive directors with an automatic seat on the trust board, though, symbolically, there is such a requirement for the chief executive and directors of nursing and finance and the medical director. In fact, a survey by the NHSME (1993a) found that in 60 per cent of respondent trusts, the senior personnel manager was an executive member of the board and this compares well with the private sector and trading parts of the public sector, where the equivalent figure is 40 per cent (Millward *et al.*, 1992).

Guest and Peccei (1992), studying personnel management in the NHS, found that the effectiveness of the personnel function, for which they apply a number of tests, tends to be highest where personnel has a significant influence over major organizational decisions. This, in turn, was found to be related to the representation of personnel on trust boards. Where the personnel director does not have a seat on the board, some trust personnel directors have told the author that they are much closer to the business planning process than in pre-trust days. Bach (1995, p. 112), however, doubts this, saying: 'the personnel function has a peripheral position within trusts and limited credibility.' He argues that this, in part, is because the NHS Executive imposes external constraints for instance on local pay bargaining.

There is no systematic analysis of the employment background of personnel directors. Nevertheless, evidence suggests that most have been appointed from personnel departments inside the NHS. Significantly, though, neither the NHS Executive's current Human Resources Director nor the previous one had a background in personnel. It is becoming more common, however, to appoint personnel staff below director level from among those with personnel experience outside the NHS.

As to the relationship between the personnel department and the line, Guest and Peccei (1994) found personnel managers clearly dominated in the areas of equal opportunities, industrial relations and manpower planning information. The areas where non-personnel managers dominated most clearly were productivity, quality and flexibility. Using the same data, Guest and Peccei (1994) also found that 38 per cent of NHS personnel staff possessed or were studying to obtain a professional qualification, but the number of personnel staff with professional qualifications or degrees of any kind did not make any difference to personnel effectiveness.

There is evidence that there are some serious tensions between personnel specialists and doctors. Personnel officers are often intimidated by consultants whom they see as a law unto themselves, or the 'Eiger mountain we have to conquer' according to Maddock and Parkin (1994, p. 56). Undoubtedly doctors have been successful in safeguarding their autonomy. It is the doctor, for instance, who diagnoses, prescribes treatment and discharges. This has implications for staff numbers and workforce composition of not only doctors but also nurses and the professions allied to medicine. Thus managerial plans, including human resources plans, are subverted (Harrison *et al.*, 1992). In an attempt to alleviate such tensions, doctors have been made clinical directors, bringing them into the managerial process. Nevertheless, tensions continue to surface and doctors often dominate, as for instance at Brighton Healthcare and Burnley Healthcare. In both these trusts, there were votes of no confidence by the consultants in a trust board member, with the result that at the former, in September 1994, the chairman was ousted and at the latter, in November 1994, the chief executive and medical director were forced to depart (Brindle, 1994a; Bunyan, 1994).

Personnel policies and employment strategies

Over 70 per cent of trusts' costs are attributable to labour costs, so *prima facie* one would expect the development of long term employment strategies by employers. Yet as we have seen, the structural changes under the 1990 Act have led to a quasi-market system with trusts receiving annual contracts from purchasers. This leads to an uncertainty that units did not have in the last decade and militates against planning for longer than 12 months ahead, putting a premium on *ad hoc* decision-taking and opportunism. Thus one trust in Manchester had to deal suddenly with redundancies in autumn 1994 as a result of the loss of a contract, whilst another in Mersey, which won a contract formerly held by a neighbouring trust, had to deal with the integration of transferred staff.

Nevertheless, as well as the new structure leading to short termism, decentralization of the new structure also leads to diversity. So, whereas most trusts are adopting an opportunistic and *ad hoc* approach, a few have deliberately tried to adopt a steady-state employment strategy and a few have seen it as an opportunity for the adoption of a raft of new employment strategies, underpinned by a philosophy of individualism, in contrast to the NHS's traditional pluralism (Corby and Higham, unpublished). Thus a chief executive of a mental health trust pointed out to the researchers that inevitably the adoption of trust status involved restructuring the unit's relationship with the DHA but, where possible, he wanted to limit the turbulence. Accordingly, the trust's employment strategies and personnel policies are centred on maintaining stability. This entails, at least initially, preserving the Whitley arrangements for new employees, as staff associate security and continuity with Whitley. It also entails making changes gradually. This approach, he thinks, is most likely to win staff co-operation.

In contrast, a number of ambulance trusts (Corby, 1992) and a few community trusts, notably Homewood (Lilley and Wilson, 1994), are already making maximum use of their autonomy to break with employee relations traditions. They have established new systems of pay determination, made changes to workforce composition and introduced individual performance pay.

A key consideration is whether the trust has a personnel strategy and, more importantly, whether it is published and approved by the trust board. According to the NHSME survey (1993a), 79 per cent of trusts had a personnel strategy, 53 per cent had a published strategy, whilst 65 per cent had a strategy approved by the trust board. Guest and Peccei (1992, p. 9), taking a different approach, looked at 17 areas of personnel work and asked whether there was 'a written policy, agreed by the executive management team'. Whilst 96 per cent of respondents had a written policy agreed by the management team on equal opportunities, only four per cent had one on productivity of staff, with the average per unit being just over seven of the 17 policy areas. They found that the effectiveness of personnel management was associated with the extent to which personnel policies were written down and agreed by members of the management team.

It is difficult to assess trends or forecast developments in respect of employment strategies at this juncture. The key environmental pressure on trusts is governmental policy but many trusts take the view that a number of employment strategies will take a few years to develop. By that time, there will have been a general election and perhaps a change of political priorities and yet another reorganization of the NHS.

Staffing and Employment Resourcing in Trusts

In the trusts, staffing and employment resourcing issues continue to be of central importance in people management. Three key ones considered here are: contracts of employment; local pay; and equality issues.

Contracts of employment

The volatility engendered by annual contracts between purchasers and providers has had a significant effect on the type of employment contract offered by trusts. Previously most staff were employed on indefinite contracts, with job security being a feature of NHS employment. This was first undermined by the terms and conditions of general managers who, since 1985, have been employed on fixed-term contracts. More recently, there is some evidence that increasingly a range of staff, including nurses and PAMs, are being employed on fixed-term contracts. Staff employed on fixed-term contracts of one year or more can lawfully be required to sign away their unfair dismissal rights on the expiry of the contract or, where such contracts are for two years or more, their rights to redundancy pay. Thus if a purchaser does not renew a contract with a provider, the trust may avoid redundancy costs and the inevitable deterioration of staff morale which would have occurred if redundancies had been declared. Nevertheless, staff on indefinite contracts are sometimes made redundant. Examples include redundancies at Guy's and Lewisham Trust and at Bradford Hospitals Trust (House of Commons, 1992) and at Wellhouse Trust (Brindle, 1993).

Another way that trusts are trying to protect themselves against uncertainties in the reformed NHS is by using temporary staff. Some trusts, for example, employ temporary administrative and clerical staff at the end of the financial year, when there is an expansion of work, as financial accounts have to be prepared and business plans drawn up. Trusts are also using nurse 'banks'. Under a bank system nurses, having proclaimed a willingness in principle to work at the trust, then agree with the employer to work particular shifts. This is what the hotel industry terms 'regular casuals'. A bank allows the employer to vary staff to accommodate demand and/or non-availability of core staff, through sickness or holidays. Although nurse banks have operated in the NHS for decades, they are now being expanded and a few trusts are setting up PAM banks. Furthermore, managers have changed terms and conditions to increase the temporal flexibility of staff. At one trust, for instance, instead of nurse contracts sometimes specifying particular nights or days for working, nurses are now contracted to work any shift, subject to a maximum number per week (*PM Plus*, 1994).

In addition, there are initiatives in multi-skilling in non-professional areas and increases in the proportion of support staff to professionals. Dyson (1991), in a paper which was widely circulated amongst NHS managers, argues that such strategies enable the staff concerned to achieve improved remuneration and trusts to achieve substantial reductions in labour costs. In other words, they enable the circle to be squared. This is an important consideration at the time of writing, when government is freezing public-sector pay budgets. There is evidence that such labour-use strategies are being pursued. For example, ancillary workers are combining the traditional duties of porters, catering and cleaning staff, whilst health care assistants, in nursing areas, perform some of the tasks traditionally carried out by nurses, such as making beds, feeding and escorting patients. A recent NHS Management Executive survey (NHSME, 1993a) points out that ambulance trusts have been particularly pro-active in changing skill mixes, with the introduction of a health transport/attendant grade and changes to shift systems.

Local pay

There is strong government encouragement for trusts to adopt local pay regimes. For instance, the NHS Chief Executive, Alan Langlands (1994), wrote to trust chief executives in England, asking them to have local pay machinery in place by February 1995. The NHS Executive followed this up by visits to trusts, mounting workshops and subsidizing them. In the Welsh NHS, there have been similar developments, though, at the time of writing, not Scotland. Where trusts have employees on trust contracts, they mostly mirror national arrangements on pay and conditions and make only minor changes. For instance, they have departed from Whitley terms on removal expenses to give managers more discretion or they have incorporated the two NHS statutory days of holiday into annual leave entitlement. Because of TUPE Regulations, major changes to terms and conditions of employment are expensive, an important consideration in the context of the internal market and the government's freeze on public-sector pay budgets. Also most trusts are not experiencing labour market pressures and thus do not have business reasons for improving pay beyond the levels determined nationally.

Only a small minority of trusts, 11 out of 419, had introduced comprehensive local pay deals by October 1994 (Wood, 1994). Research (Corby and Higham, unpublished) suggests that those trusts which have introduced comprehensive pay regimes have been in a financially robust position. Nevertheless, even where trusts have a comprehensive pay regime, employees may choose to remain with national arrangements. In 1994, for instance, 15 per cent of employees at St Helens and Knowsley Community Trust were on that trust's pay spine; 60 per cent at Homewood; but 98 per cent at Northumbria Ambulance Trust, according to figures provided by these trusts.

Where there are local pay arrangements, they normally involve a single pay spine, determined on the basis of job evaluation, ranging from cleaners to consultants. There are no 'off the shelf' job evaluation schemes which command general support, however, and attempts to develop a dedicated job evaluation scheme at Central Manchester Trust have already taken over three years and were not completed at the time of writing. Arguably, a single pay spine reinforces loyalty to the trust and helps in the development of a new organizational culture, whereas the national arrangements, with pay determined according to functional groups, serves to reinforce professional differences. Moreover, single pay spines are also consistent with other personnel objectives, such as breaking down job demarcations and introducing single table bargaining. However, the power of the doctors *vis à vis* senior managers has already been mentioned. Significantly, the majority of trusts with such pay spines are either ambulance trusts, with no doctors, or mental health or community trusts, where the proportion of doctors in the workforce is significantly lower than in general acute trusts. In addition, a minority of trusts, about five per cent of them, have made significant changes to the reward system of a single occupational group, such as ancillary staff.

The position on local pay, however, is extremely fluid. The government exhorts trusts to adopt local pay regimes. Although the Human Resources Director of the NHS in England, Ken Jarrold, says he does not expect every trust 'to be all singing all dancing on pay' by 1995 (Huddart, 1994a), the number with local pay schemes looks set to increase.

Alternatively, trusts may adopt top-up arrangements. Government and the unions, albeit reluctantly, concluded enabling agreements, as part of the 1994 pay deals, for NHS employees whose pay is determined by Whitley. The agreements allow trusts to make local payments 'based on the performance of the organization' to those who have their pay determined by Whitley. But there is a proviso: 'agreement with staff and their trade unions and extensive communication with those affected are essential'. Similarly, the pay review body reports of 1995 for nurses, midwives and health visitors and the professions allied to medicine provided for local top-up payments. They awarded one per cent nationally, with a further 0.5 to two per cent to be awarded locally sparking off a union campaign to defend national pay determination. Doctors and dentists, however, were treated differently by their pay review body, whose 1995 award was 2.5 per cent nationally (Bolger, 1995), underlining their special position in the NHS. At the time of writing, it is not clear to what extent top-up payments will provide an impetus to the reality of local bargaining as opposed to local bargaining in name only. There is evidence that most trusts applied local payments uniformy, in full and without changes to conditions or allowances. Furthermore, the Government has agreed to constrain severely local bargaining for staff covered by pay review bodies until 1998. Trusts are not permitted to change allowances or conditions and there is a safety net for pay rates. Under a complex procedure, any locally agreed rates which fall below the going rate are nationally uprated annually.

The NHS Executive, meanwhile, is also strongly encouraging trusts to adopt performance management, giving some trusts money for pilot projects. It claims that performance systems can change the organization's culture to make it more customer aware and improve line management style (NHSME, 1992a). In response, trusts are in the process of extending performance appraisal to all staff and linking appraisal with the standards set in the purchasers' contracts. A variety of systems of performance appraisal is being used, so it is impossible to generalize. A further complication is that there is sometimes a tension between standards based on total quality management and those based on resource management. Professionals tend to prioritize quality, whilst business managers tend to prioritize cost and activity (Koch, 1992). Whatever system is adopted, performance appraisal is covering increasing numbers of employees in the NHS, with some trusts inevitably further along the road than others.

So far, there have been few moves to link performance appraisal with performance pay. Indeed, a survey in 1994 found that the extent of PRP in the NHS was 'very limited' (Incomes Data Services, 1994a, p. 27) and mainly covered senior managers, whose pay has incorporated an element of performance pay under national arrangements since 1989. Where trusts have local pay spines, some make progress dependent on individual performance, not length of service as under the national arrangements. Others, such as South Tees, make progress dependent on the performance of the trust as a whole (p. 8). A few trusts, which do not have comprehensive pay regimes, have established individual performance pay for discrete groups of staff on trust terms, particularly ancillaries, whose traditional bonus schemes based on output have been replaced by more qualitative measures (Health Service

Report, 1994). In contrast, a Mersey trust has scrapped bonuses and PRP completely, and the directors of personnel at Dorset Community Trust (Merrick, 1995) and at Guy's and St Thomas's Trust (*People Management*, 1995), have publicly expressed doubts about individual PRP. Interestingly, the Human Resources Director of the NHS in England, Ken Jarrold, said to trust personnel directors: 'We don't insist on individual performance related pay for everyone ... You decide on the system appropriate to your organisations' (Huddart, 1994b).

Although local pay and performance pay are analytically different concepts, they are intertwined in practice at trust level and in government and union statements. For instance, the Whitley agreement pay deals in 1994, which allow for local payments, talk about 'schemes based on the performance of the organisation'. The staff organizations, in turn, likewise equate local pay with performance pay in their publicity (British Medical Association, 1994). In 1994, for instance, the BMA called on junior doctors to lobby MPs, claiming that local pay bargaining and PRP are undesirable for doctors and patients.

Irrespective of any local pay arrangements, there are more opportunities for promotion than in pre-trust days. For instance, nurse managers or PAM managers are becoming generalist managers, while managers who have not come from a profession are taking on responsibilities for areas including professionals, despite tensions with and resentment especially from doctors. The position on recruitment, however, has not changed since pre-trust days. For the majority of potential NHS employees, the numbers of job seekers and their qualifications are largely set by the professional bodies, not by employers.

Equality issues

A recurring theme throughout this chapter has been the impact of the new NHS structure on employment practices and, in particular, the tension between central control and trust autonomy on people management matters.

Perhaps this tension is nowhere more sharply reflected than in the NHS's programme on equality for women. Women comprise 79 per cent of those working in the NHS but are concentrated in lower-paid occupations, nurses not doctors, ancillaries not managers. Many work part-time, especially in predominantly female occupations such as nursing. Women are also disproportionately concentrated in the lower grades of the occupational hierarchy. For instance, Hutt (1985) found that whereas only 10 per cent of nurses were male, they filled 40 per cent of senior nurse posts.

In 1991, two reports were issued, identifying a number of barriers to women's progress in the NHS. The first report, by Goss and Brown (1991), highlighted the limited availability of part-time and flexible working arrangements at senior levels, the limited availability of appropriate child care provision, the convention in many jobs that long hours are required and the widespread use of patronage and head hunting for senior posts. The second report, by the Equal Opportunities Commission (1991), pointed out that most health authorities did not implement their equal opportunity policies effectively or plan or evaluate progress. It recommended a national corporate plan with equality targets and the establishment of an NHS equality unit.

Against this background, in October 1991, the Secretary of State for Health signed up to Opportunity 2000 on behalf of the NHS in England. Opportunity 2000 is a business and government supported, voluntary campaign to increase the quality and quantity of women's participation in the workforce by the year 2000. In the NHS, where the problem was the quality, not the quantity of women's jobs, a women's unit was established which initially set eight Opportunity 2000 goals, of which four are numerical, to be achieved by the end of 1994 as a milestone towards 2000 (NHSME, 1992b). Examples of numerical targets are goals of women comprising 30 per cent of general managers and 20 per cent of consultants by 1994. Examples of non-numerical goals centre on initiatives for recruiting or retaining nurses or the provision of development centres for women aspiring to management positions. After progress on those goals has been assessed, further goals will be set.

Research suggests that the overall position is patchy and some goals are not being achieved (Corby, 1994b; 1995). This failure stems partly from the NHS structure. Trust autonomy on personnel matters does not sit easily with a comprehensive NHS-wide equality programme, strategically directed from the centre. Thus the NHS women's unit can only cajole, support and provide funding for innovative projects. It cannot order and control, although it asks each trust to produce annual statistics and a local action plan. Significantly, the only goal that has been surpassed is that women should comprise 35 per cent of members of health authorities and trusts, as here alone there is central control. The Health Secretary appoints the chairman and up to three out of five non-executive directors of each trust (NHSME, 1990).

Moreover, the need for cost effectiveness in the quasi-market provides infertile ground for an equality programme which inevitably carries costs. There are resource implications in starting a creche, producing and publicizing an action plan and administering a career break scheme. Yet there is little financial reason for trusts to embrace measures to aid staff retention when labour turnover is low. This is not to say that reasons for lack of progress only relate to NHS structure. In some trusts, there have been failures in implementation. For instance, some managers fail to publicize the programme, whilst others discourage staff from making use of flexible work provisions, such as career breaks or job sharing, which would help them combine work and parenthood, because of staffing repercussions. Despite weaknesses, however, the Opportunity 2000 campaign has given a high profile to women's equality in the NHS in England. An Opportunity 2000 campaign in the NHS in Wales was launched in mid-1994 (*Personnel Management*, 1994) but there is not one in Scotland at the time of writing.

Turning to equality of opportunities for ethnic minorities, in 1986, the DoH and the King's Fund jointly estab-

lished a task force. Its final report (King's Fund Task Force, 1991) found that only limited progress had been made in tackling equal opportunities for ethnic minority staff. Consequently, in 1993, the Secretary of State launched a programme of action for the NHS in England, with the aim of achieving an equitable representation of ethnic minority groups at all levels. Eight goals were set and every trust was asked to draw up a local action plan to be incorporated into the business plan (NHSME, 1993b). Meanwhile the DoH is carrying out ethnic monitoring of the entire NHS workforce in England, as part of its annual census. Nevertheless, as with gender equality, the extent to which the centre can direct trusts, given their autonomy, is limited. Moreover, the ethnic minority equality programme has received far less publicity than the programme for women. Indeed, according to a staff representative, at one large general acute trust in Manchester, an area with a sizeable ethnic community, neither the chief executive, nor the human resources director, professed knowledge of the programme one year after its launch.

In terms of equality of opportunities for disabled staff in the NHS, the NHS Executive had not developed a strategy by 1994. Perhaps unsurprisingly, an Equal Opportunities Review survey (1994, p. 29) found: 'trusts are giving considerably higher priority ... to the under-representation of women than that of ethnic minorities or disabled people'.

The New Industrial Relations

As noted above, under TUPE Regulations, collective agreements with the former employer, normally DHAs, transfer to the new employer, the trust. However, DHAs did not set the main terms and conditions which are set at national level, so trusts have a clean slate in respect of any arrangements for determining trust pay. Research (Corby, 1992) suggests that many trusts have established

arrangements for determining pay and benefits, although
the majority have rarely made use of them to produce
substantive outcomes. In fact, most of the new arrangements embody the NHS's pluralist traditions. Only four
trusts are known to have decided not to recognize unions
for collective bargaining purposes. These four have been
able to adopt this approach essentially because the staff
organizations, on account of factors at the workplace, have
been unable to mount any effective opposition to management. Allied to this, existing staff in these trusts have
chosen to go on to trust terms, because a significant pay
rise has been offered, with unilateral regulation of pay
by management as part of the package.

The unions and staff organizations

A significant feature of the NHS is the plethora of occupational groups management has to deal with and the
even greater multiplicity of staff organizations, of which
over 20 have certificates of independence. Essentially, staff
organizations can be divided into two categories: trade
unions and professional associations. Trade unions recruit
from both inside and outside health care and are all affiliated to the TUC. The professional associations, in contrast, are specific to the health sector and are rarely TUC
affiliates. The largest TUC affiliate is UNISON and the
largest non-TUC affiliate is the Royal College of Nursing (Farnham and Giles, 1995b).

Although there tend to be a large number of recognized unions and staff associations in public services,
compared with the private sector, the multiplicity of bodies
representing NHS staff, with their overlapping jurisdic-
tions, is unique. For instance, general acute hospital trusts
normally have in the order of 16 active unions within
them and mental health hospitals have eight, whilst midwives can be represented by four independent staff organizations. Inevitably this leads to fragmentation and is
a factor that managers and personnel managers have to
take into account in dealing with staff collectively.

TABLE 4.2 Membership of key unions in the NHS, 1988 and 1992

Membership numbers	1988	1992
UNISON*	1 608 022	1 486 984
MSF	653 000	552 000
Royal College of Nursing	281 918	299 157
British Medical Association	82 359	88 107
Chartered Society of Physiotherapists	34 376	37 558
Royal College of Midwives	33 487	36 327
Society of Radiographers	12 047	12 931
Total union membership	10 387 238	8 928 902

* UNISON, was formed in 1993 as a result of a merger between three unions: National and Local Government Officers' Association, the National Union of Public Employees, Confederation of Health Service Employees. Accordingly its figures are based on the membership figures of ifs constituent unions.

Source: derived from Certification Office, 1989 and 1993

Managers also need to take into account the fact that union density in the NHS is high. Although in recent years union membership has been falling in the UK as a whole, and labour force figures show a decline in union density in hospitals from 67 per cent in 1989 to 61 per cent in 1993, density in the NHS remains relatively high (Bird and Corcoran, 1994). Also the professional associations in the NHS have been bucking the trend and increasing their membership, as shown in Table 4.2.

Local bargaining machinery

In a small number of trusts, management, conscious of the weight of tradition in industrial and employee relations, has recognized all the unions active in the unit and negotiates with them all. The pattern in these trusts is that if they are large organizations there is bargaining by functional group, as in the Whitley system, whereas in smaller trusts there is one body – a single-table bargaining unit.

In the overwhelming majority of trusts, however, there is what is called a 'prime union' system. All the staff organizations are recognized for collective bargaining, which is consonant with the NHS's employee relations traditions, but a smaller number have seats on a single-table negotiating executive, though the name of the body varies with the trust. So not all staff organizations are at the main bargaining table. In the main, the staff side determines amongst itself who should fill the seats and thus have the key negotiating roles, along with any mandating and reporting back arrangements. This saves managers from the approbrium of decisions which are unlikely to please all (Corby, 1992).

A prime union system, which is not normally found elsewhere in the public or private sectors, has a number of advantages for NHS management. First, key negotiations are carried out by a streamlined body, an important consideration in view of the multiplicity of unions. Second, as all the staff organizations are recognized for bargaining purposes, managers can negotiate with organizations which are not on the main body about minor matters affecting a discrete group of staff. Third, as all the unions are recognized, none can complain. Fourth, the main negotiating body provides for single-table bargaining and this fits management's longer term objectives for a single pay spine, the breaking down of job demarcations and harmonization of conditions of employment. Currently, conditions amongst and within functional groups vary considerably under the national arrangements.

Research by Corby and Higham suggests that the unions affiliated to the TUC and the non-affiliated staff organizations are uniting together in dealings with management. This contrasts with a decade ago, when there were examples of TUC-affiliated unions refusing to sit down with non-affiliates (Seifert, 1992). Arguably, inter-union cooperation is opportunistic and the British Medical Association (BMA) and UNISON, for instance, or the Royal College of Midwives and MSF, do not have shared visions but they do face common problems.

The negotiating roles of full-time officials in trusts vary considerably and, unlike many private-sector agreements, trust agreements often specify the nature of the involvement of the full-time officer in negotiations. Some trusts allot them seats on the main negotiating body. Others say they can attend and speak but not vote, whilst others limit the numbers of full-time officials. Whatever the *de jure* position, evidence (Corby and Higham, unpublished) shows that full-time officials are playing a key part in supporting their local lay representatives who, in the past, did not have to deal with terms and conditions of employment.

Only a very few trusts mention arbitration as a method of dispute resolution, whether of a conventional or pendulum kind, and in all cases it is dependent on a joint reference. This may be because managers do not want pay determination decisions going outside the confines of their unit. After all, many managers have long criticized Whitley, because it is outside unit control (Warlow, 1989).

Other procedures

Before the 1990 changes, there were formal joint committees at DHA level and sometimes at unit level. Such committees, although termed JCCs, were in practice forums for both consultation and negotiation on a limited range of matters, such as shift patterns and ancillary bonus schemes. With trusts becoming the employers, formal consultative bodies have been established at this level. In most, but not all cases, management, to prevent blurring the distinction, have set up separate consultative and negotiating bodies. This, of course, ties in with the prime union model, as all the recognized unions have a seat on the consultative committee, though not on the key negotiating body.

Just as negotiating procedures have been redrawn because of the formation of trusts, so too have procedures that can be exercised individually, such as grievance and disciplinary procedures. By the end of the 1980s, the vast majority of employing authorities had negotiated their own local procedures with their JCCs. When those procedures were exhausted, it was open to all NHS employees, through their recognized staff organizations, to take their case beyond the local boundaries to regional level and, in the case of individual grievances, to national level.

These procedures have been recast for a number of reasons. First, for most staff, the employing authority is no longer the DHA but the trust. Second, the Whitley provision relating to individual grievances (s. 32) was abolished from the end of March 1992. Accordingly, no NHS employee can now take a grievance beyond the employer. As to discipline, the RHA always had discretion whether or not to entertain an appeal from beyond employer level. Anyway, RHAs are abolished so the new procedures end at trust level. Instead of a hearing by a sub-committee of the DHA, a matter is now determined by a sub-committee of the trust board. This mirrors the fragmentation of the NHS, as there is no longer a chain running from local to national level on matters connected with employment. Exceptionally, hospital doctors and dentists can still appeal directly to the Health Secretary on grounds of redundancy, professional – not personal – misconduct and professional incompetence (Ward, 1995).

What essentially amounts to the bypassing of Whitley can also be seen in trust initiatives to foster employee involvement in ways not covered by Whitley. These include team briefing, which according to the NHSME survey (1993a, p. 11) is 'the preferred method of intra-unit communication', followed by in-house newsletters. According to Storey (1992, p. 271), unit general managers are also experimenting with team building and quality circles and embracing the concepts and language of culture change. Yet he says the 'weight of the extant systems were such that the new initiatives were pushed to the fringes'.

Training and Staff Development

The current pattern of training and staff development mirrors organizational changes in the NHS. Until the early 1980s, training and staff development grew in an uncoordinated way. For example, the DoH's estates division carried out training for managers as did other departmental divisions. As part of its drive to improve efficiency, government formed the NHS Training Authority (NHSTA) in 1984 to coordinate training in England and Wales (NHSTA, 1985). Interestingly, it was formed as a special health authority, responsible directly to the Secretary of State and with a governing body drawn from the NHS nationally, regionally and locally, the professions and staff side.

The NHSTA played a key role in certain areas, such as management education and development, ambulance training, training for professionals in their non-professional duties such as finance. It also developed individual performance review systems to assess training needs. It carried out training, owning training centres and improved training technology, such as computer assisted learning. At the same time, it also conducted projects for the Secretary of State on NHS audits including analysing training needs, developing standards and establishing a training programme to be delivered by training centres, validated by such bodies as the Chartered Institute of Public Finance and Accountancy.

The NHSTA, with some 200 staff, was at the pinnacle of a hierarchical structure. It worked with and through the RHAs which, in turn, had their coordinators and training departments. Linked to them were the DHAs, which also had their own training staff who liaised with trainers in hospitals. With the establishment of the first trusts, the structure of the NHSTA changed. Instead of a special health authority, it became a directorate reporting to the human resources director of the NHS. However, to draw it more tightly into the NHS Executive, it underwent a further change in 1994. It became the NHS Training

Division (NHSTD) with some 100 staff.

These structural changes were accompanied by changes in its function. The NHSTD hived off its training centres and so no longer provides training. Instead, it is concerned with standard setting. For example, it has developed National Vocational Qualifications (NVQs) for support workers, operating department assistants and physiological measurement technicians, setting standards for workplace assessors and accrediting training centres. It encourages trusts to go for the Investors In People award. It also acts as a resource, such as producing open learning packages and, as before, carries out commissions and oversees the national management training scheme and the financial management training scheme, appointing the awarding bodies. At the same time, it plays a leading role in organizing training for NHS Executive initiatives, such as local pay.

Whereas the NHSTD has already lost a significant part of its role, RHAs are set to lose their training function completely. At the time of writing, however, they commission others, such as colleges of nursing, to provide professional education and training for all staff groups except doctors and dentists, on the basis of figures provided by trusts, though this too is likely to be devolved to trusts soon. As to DHAs, they are not large employers now and have lost most of their training function.

Indeed the focus of training and staff development, which formerly flowed from the centre, now flows from trusts, and Guest and Peccei (1992) found that the top priority for trust personnel staff was training and development. A typical trust spends about two per cent of its budget on training, not counting the professional education and training currently arranged through RHAs. In some trusts, the training budget is held centrally, whilst in others part of the budget is held centrally and part is devolved. Within these budgetary limits, trusts analyse their training needs. For professional staff, they place contracts with training providers, generally local colleges, for statutory professional update training. For ancillaries and health care assistants, trusts decide what competences are needed on the basis of their skill mix plans and then determine who should undergo training. In fact, most trusts have staff who have completed, or are undertaking, NVQs. The majority are health care assistants at level two (NHSME, 1993a).

There is much discussion in the NHS currently about the need for management development but, according to some trust personnel directors, there is more talk than action. Whether or not that view is representative, there is considerable variation. The NHS Executive found that only 41 per cent of trusts use assessment or development centres (NHSME, 1993a). It also found that some trusts have in-house accredited management certificates, some send staff on university courses, such as Diplomas in Management Studies or Masters in Business Administration (MBAs), and some use the NHS management scheme. Some trusts concentrate on management skills for managers, whilst others are concentrating on management skills for clinical directors and other professionals. Nevertheless, whilst the mode and extent of management development vary, there is growing importance attached to financial management. Marketing is also a new feature of NHS management education. There is evidence too that there is more in-house training than before. Trust human resources directors see it as less costly and more relevant and it provides a management development opportunity for trust staff, although outsiders are used as well as insiders to provide the training.

It is likely that trusts will do more training and development themselves and the NHSTD will reduce to around 30 staff, with a strategic function enmeshed in the NHS Executive. Other current NHSTD initiatives may continue, provided they can be financed by income generation. It is too early to say whether training provision will become more effective under these arrangements, though the measurement of training effectiveness is bedevilled with problems. Some trust personnel directors argue that training of the workforce must be embedded in workforce planning and analysis of needs, which only trusts can do effectively. Anyway, the centre will continue to oversee management training, whilst the strong professions will also set standards. Some in the NHS Executive fear that training may no longer be seen as crucial, or that training may be duplicated, as it was before the NHSTA provided coordination. Whatever the validity of these views, the devolution of training to trusts is consonant with their new personnel responsibilities relating to the management of people.

Conclusion and Evaluation

Many NHS personnel people now have a job title which incorporates the term 'human resources' or HR in it. But one has to go behind the HR label. There is evidence that people management in the NHS still corresponds more with TPM than human resources management (HRM). This, of course, begs the question of the nature of the differences between the two and there has been much debate about this (Guest, 1987; 1990). One distinction that has been made between HRM and personnel management is that the former is more strategic and integrated with business policy than is the latter. There is some evidence that trust personnel managers are now much more involved in business plans than formerly and over half sit on trust boards. Yet because of the annual purchasing process, there is a premium on short termism. As one HR director of a community trust said: 'we are trying to be strategic, but in practice we find ourselves reacting to the purchaser'. She instanced the loss of a family planning contract which meant that she suddenly had to decide which three family planning sessions had to end.

Sometimes HRM is measured by the extent to which the content of its policy and practice is different from personnel management. There are examples of new communications strategies associated with HRM, such as team briefing, but this does not necessarily signal a change of approach. Indeed, Guest and Peccei (1992, p. 13) in their study of NHS personnel managers found that 'policy goals associated with traditional personnel management are still accorded slightly higher priority than those linked to the more contemporary human resource management.' This may be because HRM is linked with individualism and personnel management is linked with collectivism, which is still important in the NHS since union density remains high. The unions themselves, particularly the BMA, are powerful not least because many of them, through their professional role, work with the professional bodies to limit entry and maintain training standards and success-fully intertwine their professional and industrial relations roles. The BMA's campaign against performance pay is an example of this (BMA, 1994).

Furthermore, collectivism in the NHS has not been seriously undermined by the government. For instance, Whitley and the pay review bodies remain, though the messages about their continuation emanating from the centre are mixed (Bach and Winchester, 1994). At local level too, collectivism prevails on the whole. Only a handful of trusts have decided not to recognize unions for collec-tive bargaining purposes and the letter from the chief executive of the NHS to trust chief executives (Langlands, 1994) talks about stimulating local pay *bargaining* (author's emphasis). Moreover, recent research (Corby, 1992; Corby and Higham, unpublished) finds that trust managers are proceeding cautiously and that unions have suc-ceeded in deflecting management from a unilateral to a collectivist approach. At one trust, for instance, the staff side were able to secure negotiations about a local pay deal, although originally management had only wanted to consult the unions. At another, the staff side were able to secure negotiations over trust contracts, although management had originally said that these would be determined unilaterally.

The larger staff organizations, though not necessarily the smaller ones, also seem to be surmounting the problems caused by the trend of moving key industrial relations decisions away from the centre to the locality, where traditionally public-sector unions have been weak. They are providing training, information and full-time officer support to lay representatives to build up their confidence and capabilities. So lay representatives are well placed to negotiate either local pay deals or local top-up arrangements.

Nevertheless, the collectivist approach is not going unchallenged by management. There is evidence that local pay determination tends in practice to be linked with individual or group performance pay, which, in turn, depends on managerial assessments. Thus it is counter to the notion of joint agreement over a rate for the job. If performance pay becomes the norm rather than the exception, as at present, collectivism may be seriously threatened.

Collectivism is not the only feature of the NHS which is being challenged by the new developments in people management. The whole nature of employment is too. First, employment in the NHS is becoming less secure. In particular, the system of annual purchasing of healthcare has introduced volatility into NHS employment which, in turn, has led to redundancies, fixed-term contracts of employment, temporary work and the use of nurses' banks. Second, there is evidence of deterioration in the quality of working life and increased workload. For instance, a nurse looked after 19.3 patients in 1989–90 but this had risen to 21.4 patients in 1992–93 (Brindle, 1994b). The aim of the NHS and Community Care Act 1990 is, of course, to improve quality of service, not the quality of life of those working in the NHS. However, the jury is still out on quality of service (Robinson and LeGrand, 1994).

In recent years, the NHS has become more like the private sector in a number of respects: trust and health authority boards modelled on company boards; quasi-contracts similar to the market process; and decentralized structures akin to those found in many large companies. At the same time, terms and conditions for employees in the NHS and the private sector are converging, such as the erosion of job security and the growing emphasis on performance management and performance pay. In addition, whereas conditions for NHS staff were once at the leading edge, this does not always apply now. For instance, annual leave in the private sector has increased, particularly in engineering, and career-break schemes were developed in the clearing banks, not the NHS. Moreover, like large parts of the private sector, the NHS is active in the area of equal opportunities for women and has embraced the Opportunity 2000 campaign but is doing little to advance equal opportunities for disabled staff.

Nevertheless, these similarities between the NHS and the private sector do not outweigh the differences and the NHS exhibits many features found only in the public services. These include: pay determination by pay review bodies; a relatively high level of unionization, over 60 per cent compared with 23 per cent in the private sector (Bird and Corcoran, 1994); a multiplicity of unions in the NHS, with from eight to 16 per establishment, compared with a mean of 1.7 recognized unions in the private sector (Millward *et al.*, 1992); and a tradition of detailed joint regulation of employment issues.

Moreover, for the vast majority of NHS staff, the national level is the most important one for pay determination. This contrasts starkly with the private sector. The Workplace Industrial Relations Survey 1990 shows that national level bargaining was the most important level of pay determination for only a small minority in the private sector: five per cent and 24 per cent for non-manual employees in private services and private manufacturing respectively (Millward *et al.*, 1992).

The key distinction between the NHS and the private sector is the political context but, up to 1990, party political controversy revolved around aspects of the NHS, such as levels of funding, 'paybeds' and the pay of employees. With the 1990 Act, the NHS moved to the forefront of the party political agenda and controversy has centred on the ethos, nature and fundamental structure of the NHS.

If the Conservative party wins the next general election, we shall probably see the developments set in train by the 1990 Act carried further. For instance, national arrangements for determining terms and conditions are likely either to be scrapped or wither away and, at the same time, local pay determination could become the norm. We are also likely to see more skill mix changes and more temporal flexibility as the internal market becomes more deeply rooted.

In contrast, if the Labour party wins the next general election, there could be changes to the NHS, as evidenced in its documents, *Health 2000 and Renewing the NHS* (Labour Party, 1994; 1995). Instead and of annual purchasing contracts, the Labour party proposes service agreements on a three-year rolling basis with GP fundholding being phased out in place of new commissioning agencies. This would reduce volatility and provide more fertile ground for longer term employment planning, with knock-on effects for employment patterns. The Labour party also favours the expansion of the regional tier which would limit local autonomy, as would its plans to retain the pay review bodies and a national framework for collective bargaining. Moreover, its plans for a national minimum wage, and its commitment to end CCT, would have implications for the terms and conditions of NHS staff, as would its collectivist ethos and its commitment to equal opportunities, including its proposal for targets for employing people with disabilities. It also proposes to make changes in the criteria for the appointment of non-executive directors of the trusts to increase accountability to local communities. The thinking of NHS managers may continue to be informed by their experiences in the first half of the 1990s. But the outcome of the next general election could shape the future direction of the NHS, and its approaches to people management, for the rest of the decade and beyond.

CHAPTER 5

Local Government

Geoff White and Barry Hutchinson

Local government forms the largest single component of public-sector employment with over 2.6 million employees, including 700 000 white-collar administrative, professional, technical and clerical (APT&C) staff (Audit Commission, 1995). Local government provides a wide range of services, including education, social services, housing, leisure, fire and, until 1995, police services. Whilst the specific powers and duties of local government are decided and conferred by Parliament, actual administration and discretion in the use of statutory powers is left to locally elected councils.

Local government is similar to other public services in its traditional espousal of model employer policies, such as Whitleyism, and an acceptance of union recognition and employee consultation (Farnham, 1993). It also shares a number of features of TPM: complex collective bargaining structures, based on highly stratified, occupational groupings; a multiplicity of trade unions; highly structured national pay systems and conditions of service; index-linked national pensions; and a national structure for training and developing staff, including professional qualifications specific to the sector. Pay comparability mechanisms have played less of a role in local government than in other services, although both the police and fire services have had their pay indexed to movements in national earnings and, from 1990, school teachers in England and Wales have had a review body, the School Teachers Review Body, to determine their salaries (see Chapter 6).

In several important respects, however, local government is different from other public services. Most importantly, the democratic process ensures that local government's political masters are elected separately from central government. Indeed, the majority of local councils in Britain are currently under the leadership of Labour, Liberal Democrat or coalition majorities. Since 1979, Conservative governments have taken greater control of local council expenditure and forced changes in policy but the countervailing authority of locally-elected councillors has ensured that some independence of manoeuvre has been maintained.

This has been especially vital in the area of collective bargaining, where central government has no direct role, except in the cases of the police, fire services and teachers. Each local authority has been a separate employer, with a high degree of freedom to interpret national guidelines on pay, gradings and local conditions of employment. Government has therefore been limited to either exhorting from the sidelines or imposing indirect financial penalties for authorities breaching government pay guidelines. This independence has also meant that the professional personnel function is more developed than in some public services and a national body of personnel directors – the Society of Chief Personnel Officers (SOCPO) – has existed since 1975. Recently, this independence has been extended by some councils departing from national collective agreement guidelines and establishing their own pay and grading systems.

Structure and Finance

Local authorities have their origins in nineteenth-century social reforms. These created local government systems for towns and counties through the Municipal Corporations Act 1835 and the Local Government Act 1888 respectively. A further Act created urban and rural districts in 1894.

Until the 1960s, each council consisted of a multiplicity of committees and departments which defied coordination and planning. The Maud Committee, which investigated the management of local government in 1967, identified the major obstacle to a coherent management structure as compartmentalized and departmentalized management, based on professional specialisms. This contrasts sharply with the generalist approach to management in the Civil Service. The Maud report (1967) recommended a systematic approach to management, with clear objective setting for officers and regular reviews of progress. Furthermore, the Town Clerk was to become a chief executive, to whom all departments would report.

The present structure of local government derives largely from the reorganization in 1974 and the internal structure of local authorities stems from the Bains report (1972). Bains proposed a central coordinating management role for chief executives and the creation of multi-disciplinary management teams. A further recommendation was the development of a professional personnel function.

There are around 500 local authorities in the UK. In England and Wales, these are divided into 39 counties, 296 non-metropolitan districts, 36 metropolitan districts, 32 London Boroughs and the City of London Authority. In Wales, there are eight counties and 37 districts. In Scotland, which has its own system under the control of the Scottish Office, there are nine regions, 53 districts and three island areas. Northern Ireland has 26 district councils, with some major services administered by separate statutory bodies responsible to central government.

A Local Government Commission (LGC) is currently considering the future structure of non-Metropolitan local government in England. Structures in Scotland and Wales have also recently been reviewed. In March 1995, the Commission reported but many of its proposals were rejected by the government. Only 15 new unitary authorities and 12 two-tier counties were approved and the LGC was asked to reconsider its other proposals, under a new chairman. The Commission is expected to report again by 1996.

Total standard spending by local government in 1994–95 was set by central government at some £43 billion. The largest share of this goes on education and housing, and pay accounts for some 70 per cent of expenditure. In 1993, the total pay bill of local government in Great Britain was £36.8 billion, including National Insurance and pension costs. Central government grant provides about 80 per cent of tax-based local government current expenditure.

A major change in local government, since 1979, has been the increasing centralization of financial controls by Whitehall. Whilst these had begun to emerge in the mid-1970s, when the Labour government introduced cash limits, councils were still free to raise local rates and were relatively free to use their revenues as they saw fit. However, since 1979, local political autonomy has been weakened, with changes on two fronts: first, through centralization of financial control and, second, by legislation. The latter has imposed: CCT of services; privatization of public transport; abolition of the GLC and Metropolitan counties in 1986; and local management of schools (Duncan and Goodwin, 1988). Democratically-elected local councils are no longer able to decide their own expenditure on the basis of perceived social needs. Instead, central government determines the financial boundaries for spending and 'overspending councils' are penalized through capping of their council tax demands and loss of block grant.

Standard Spending Assessments (SSAs) are designed to 'reflect the amount local authorities need to spend to provide a standard level of service consistent with the Secretary of State's view of affordability'. They are not 'intended to reward or penalise the differences between authorities in levels of efficiency or to match local political choice of service levels' (Audit Commission, 1995, p. 9). Councils retain the right to set a budget and decide how many staff to employ and how much to pay them, although they may be constrained by nationally agreed terms and conditions. SSAs clearly affect the staffing levels of authorities. According to the Audit Commission: 'more than 80 per cent of the difference between London Boroughs in the number of staff they employ per 1,000 population can be explained by the difference in their SSA per head' (p. 8).

New legislation and increased financial control have clearly limited the power of local authorities to define their own spending priorities, including staffing, whilst the difference between planned expenditure and actual outturns has created major problems for local authorities. Although councils retain the freedom to bargain collectively over pay and conditions, government is able to penalize authorities for exceeding pay guidelines, by failing to provide extra cash. The 'size and allocation of central government grant and the constraints on money raising by authorities place severe limits on authorities' ability to pay' (Local Government Management Board (LGMB), 1993a, p. 19).

The Workforce

Staff employed by individual authorities varies from 200 to 100 000 people. The largest employers are Metropolitan districts, London Boroughs and county or 'shire' councils. These are responsible for major services such as education, social services, planning, roads, environmental health and leisure, although in county areas, local districts are responsible for housing, environmental health and leisure services. In London and other metropolitan authorities, separate boards provide for fire services and transport. Since 1 April 1995, 43 statutory police authorities in England and Wales are responsible for police services, although they still precept on local authorities (see Chapter 7). Table 5.1 shows the distribution of employment in the English and Welsh local authorities, by type of authority, for 1994.

Local government employs a wide range of staff – including refuse collectors, environmental health officers, architects, building labourers, street cleaners, school teachers,

TABLE 5.1   Distribution of local government employment in England and Wales by type of local authority, 1994

Type of authority	Number of authorities	Number of employees
Non-Metropolitan Counties	47	1 035 503
Non-Metropolitan Districts	333	253 812
Metropolitan Districts	36	525 281
London Boroughs	32	266 843

Source: derived from LGMB, 1994

caretakers, social workers and home helps. Employment by headcount stood at 2.6 million in mid-1994, with education accounting for 1.2 million, social services 408 000, the police 207 000 and construction services 87 000 (Hughes, 1995). Employment peaked in 1988 at over three million, following steady growth throughout the 1970s and 1980s. The decline since 1988 is due largely to the effects of CCT and the removal of functions from local government. The latter include the transfer of the former polytechnics – now the new universities – and further education colleges to independent status through incorporation and the opting out of local government control by schools with grant maintained status (see Chapter 6). Further reductions followed from the transferral of staff to the new police authorities in 1995 (see Chapter 7). The main contraction has been in manual jobs with most white-collar areas continuing to grow.

The main changes in employment between 1979 and 1994 are shown in Table 5.2. Growth areas were the police, up from 176 000 to 207 000 and social services from 344 000 to 408 000. In comparison, construction fell from 156 000 to 87 000, mainly due to CCT, whilst education fell from 1.5 million to 1.2 million over the same period.

There is also evidence that the workforce is ageing. A survey of older and mature workers in 1992 shows that 61 per cent of manual and craft workers were over 40 and 31 per cent were over 50. Over 51 per cent of APT&C

TABLE 5.2   Changes in local government employment (FTEs), 1979–94

Service	1979	1994	Per cent
Education			
Teaching –	693 057	493 681	–28.8
Other –	715 850	591 518	–17.4
Construction	135 027	73 661	–45.4
Transport	22 622	1 511	–93.3
Social services	303 846	355 548	+17.0
Libraries/museums	41 199	43 811	+6.3
Recreation	92 678	93 904	+1.5
Environmental health	23 522	21 175	–10.0
Refuse	50 267	22 268	–55.7
Housing	56 305	76 550	+35.9
Planning	22 466	22 863	+1.8
Central Services			
Chief executive	2 326	4 491	+93.1
Finance	44 796	58 453	+30.4
Secretarial	47 342	39 987	–16.4
Legal	6 383	7 490	+17.3
Engineering	89 335	64 486	–27.8
Architecture	25 277	14 283	–43.5
Estates	8 099	7 092	–12.4
Personnel	4 048	6 533	+61.4
Management services	5 821	2 000	–65.6
Computer services	8 739	11 780	+35.0
Consumer protection	4 075	4 456	+9.4
Other administration	11 685	12 100	+3.5
Technical services	4 713	4 281	–9.2
Fire Service			
Regular –	35 292	35 676	+1.1
Others –	6 504	7 316	+12.5
Other Services	32 397	25 271	–20.9
General Services			
Total	2 493 701	2 104 403	–15.6
Agency Staff	640	2 118	+230.9
Magistrates Courts	8 822	11 782	+33.5
Probation Officers	5 070	8 018	+58.1
Others	5 097	10 666	+109.7

TABLE 5.2   *Cont.*

Police			
All ranks	111 905	127 503	+13.9
Traffic wardens	4 510	4 921	+9.1
Cadets	2 893	111	−96.2
Civilians	37 959	53 373	+40.6
All law and order	176 246	216 374	+22.8

Source: information provided by LGMB Joint Staffing Watch

staff were over 40 years old (LGMB, 1992a).

Changes in employment can be linked to legislation and new financial accountablity and control systems (Duncan and Goodwin, 1988). Prior to 1979, some councils ran their own public transport systems but the Transport Act 1985 forced councils to put their services out to tender and create new passenger transport companies. Similarly, the provision of council housing, traditionally a major local government activity, has been reduced. The Housing Act 1980 gives council tenants the right to buy their properties, whilst the Housing Act 1986 gives council tenants and estates the right to 'pick a landlord'. Such voluntary transfer of council housing to Housing Associations has so far taken place in 31 local authorities (LGMB, 1994b). Whilst restrictions on new council house building, coupled with the right-to-buy policy, has reduced local authority housing stock.

The Local Government Housing and Land Act 1980 forced local authorities to put new construction and maintenance work out to private tender, whilst the Local Government Act (LGA) 1988 extends CCT to all other manual services. Locally managed schools can also contract out and may choose not to use council services (Ward *et al.*, 1988). The Local Government Act 1992 extended CCT to additional manual services and white-collar services including IT, legal and financial services, housing management and personnel services. Some local authority personnel departments have already been privatized (Thatcher, 1994).

TABLE 5.3   Local government success in winning contracts, 1984–94

Activity	DSO per cent of contracts won	DSO per cent of value won
Building cleaning	40.5	74.2
Refuse collection	67.6	69.7
Other cleaning	66.3	77.4
Vehicle maintenance	75.1	85.5
Catering (education and welfare)	86.0	95.3
Catering (other)	69.8	82.2
Ground maintenance	58.9	76.1
Sports and leisure management	85.8	92.3
Average	61.8	82.0

Source: derived from LGMB, 1994b

Overall, local authority Direct Service Organizations (DSOs) have been relatively successful in winning contracts against private competition, as shown in Table 5.3. However, successful bids usually involve radical restructuring, along private business lines, and significant changes in working patterns and terms and conditions of employment (Ward *et al.*, 1988; Colling, 1993; Labour Research Department, 1990).

Recent legal decisions of the European Court of Justice have thrown the government's CCT legislation into disarray. TUPE Regulations 1981 protect employees' rights to existing terms and conditions on the transfer of a business to another owner. Government interpreted these regulations as not applying to transfers from the public to the private sector, because of an exclusion clause for non-commercial ventures. This interpretation was successfully challenged in both the British and European Courts and led to the exclusion being removed by the Trade Union Reform and Employment Rights Act 1993 (Williams, 1993).

The Personnel Function

Prior to 1974, the professional personnel function was relatively underdeveloped. This was due to the tradition of specialist management in local government, centralized collective bargaining and the small size of most council workforces (Kessler, 1991b). Any attempt to impose wholly integrated personnel policies at local authority level was likely to be resisted by service managers. As Kessler suggests: 'the relatively undeveloped nature of the personnel function was reflected in the commonly used title for a personnel specialist of the "Establishment Officer".' This indicated a responsibility limited to staffing needs and a role confined to the control and monitoring of those needs (Kessler, 1991b, p. 9).

The new structures created in 1974 resulted in larger employment units and the need for more sophisticated personnel management systems. Moreover, the Bains report (1972) gave a major boost to the personnel function with its emphasis on a corporate management approach. Almost foreshadowing the human resources management (HRM) approach of the 1990s, Bains saw a major strategic role for the personnel function, with representation at the highest corporate levels. The report stressed the importance of manpower planning and the need to redirect the focus of training away from slavish adherence to professional qualifications.

A survey of local government personnel departments in 1982 found that: corporate personnel committees were either free-standing or within the remit of the policy and resources committee; independent personnel departments or personnel sections were part of the chief executive's department; and chief personnel officers were usually members of the management team (Walsh, 1982). As Table 5.2 demonstrates, between 1979 and 1984, there was an increase of 61 per cent in the numbers employed in personnel work, although some of this growth reflects absorptions of management services staff. There was little decentralization of people management to line managers

(Kessler, 1991b). Instead, there was a strong centralizing tendency, with the personnel department acting as 'watchdog' of corporate rules. Central personnel was often all-powerful. It operated in the role of a 'Regulator' and was interventionary at a tactical rather than strategic level (Storey, 1992). Storey describes the personnel practitioners as 'managers of discontent', because of their intermediary role in industrial relations.

By 1988, things had started to change. The traditional centralized and regulatory model of people management was being challenged and a new model was being proposed (Fowler, 1988b). The Local Government Training Board (LGTB) exhorted personnel specialists to become more customer-oriented, more responsive and more cost effective. They should assist in managing change, through developing more flexible job and organizational structures, management systems and conditions of service (LGTB, 1988). A survey in 1990 found that 63 per cent of authorities had either introduced or planned to introduce more devolution of personnel decisions to line managers (Kessler, 1990). Issues such as the administration of agreements, selection of staff, staffing levels, deployment of labour, overtime, grading variations and staff appraisal are now much more likely to be done by line managers than in the past. Personnel managers increasingly provide a more strategic direction (LGMB, 1994a).

The decentralization of personnel management is being driven by financial constraints and CCT. Operational criteria are becoming much more closely linked to commercial and business considerations. Line managers have become more important, as managerial decision-making is fragmented and devolved. The requirement to establish dedicated and semi-autonomous business or trading units, under CCT, has created a new internal contracting system. Business units are now the 'customers' of the central personnel department and personnel services are now bought and sold. Managers in business units are more likely to scrutinize their overhead costs, and reduce their requirements from the personnel department, than in the past. Some of the traditional clients for professional personnel management have also disappeared, such as schools and FE colleges.

A third factor in the growth of line manager control has been increasing emphasis on performance management, quality and customer care. Line managers have been given much more authority to improve services and control staff. Nevertheless, the existence of national agreements covering the main terms and conditions of employment has helped to retain a strong corporate personnel presence. Decentralization has, however, led to changes in the structure of personnel departments. Kessler (1991b) found that a third of personnel departments had been recently restructured or were about to be. In some cases, an autonomous personnel department had been amalgamated with other services, whilst in others the personnel function had been decentralized. In a few cases, the central personnel function had been completely abolished, such as in the London Borough of Greenwich, where personnel officers report to service managers rather than to a central personnel function. This changes their role from being a watchdog of corporate policy and procedures to one of advisor to service managers.

There appear to be two new roles emerging in personnel management. One is the 'facilitator' or 'enabler' role, the other the 'corporatist' role (Kessler, 1991b). Enablers primarily provide advisory support to line managers, whilst corporatists retain a strong central role in policy making. The political control of local councils means that the corporate dimension remains strong, despite the fragmentation of service provision. Many councils continue to have personnel committees at the highest levels and, even where DSOs have their own management boards, major personnel issues are still dealt with at council level. These developments have been uneven and much depends upon local circumstances. Tensions are also identified in the new managerial relationships. These include: the dual responsibilities of departmental personnel managers to their immediate service managers and the centre; tensions between departmental personnel managers and line managers over what constitutes good human resources practices; the new contractual relationships between business units and central personnel units; and the continuing strong presence of trade unions and collective bargaining which place constraints on management decisions.

Employment Resourcing and Performance Management

Personnel policies and employment strategies in local government changed significantly in the 1980s. These were related to the financial and political pressures identified above. The most significant effect of these pressures was the change in the culture of local government. The model of benevolent but bureaucratic paternalism, prevalent before the 1980s and championed by all political parties, gave way to the radical policies of the New Right, which began to challenge the very concept of local authorities as direct providers of services. As Nicholas Ridley, the Secretary of State for the Environment, stated in 1988: 'authorities will need to operate in a more pluralist way than in the past, alongside a wide variety of public, private and voluntary agencies. It will be their task to stimulate and assist these other agencies to play their part instead of, or as well as, making provision themselves' (Brooke, 1989, p. 14). Indeed, the most radical proposal was that elected councils should meet just once a year to allocate contracts for the various services – the so-called 'enabling council'.

In contrast, the left promoted the virtues of public provision, along with support for direct labour services (DLS) focused on customer care (Incomes Data Services/Institute of Personnel Management (IDS/IPM), 1989). The left's new agenda included both decentralization of service planning and greater democratization of control over services. The former offered a consumerist solution, whilst the latter addressed the need to be accountable to under-represented groups in society. This was reflected in the emphasis on equal opportunities in employment, provision of services to the community and the creation of Race and Women's Committees, in many left-led inner city councils. The emphasis was clearly on customer rights, as opposed to improving customer relations *via* customer-care programmes (Smith, 1986).

Whatever the political direction of change, there was a new impetus to reduce the collective power of employees and shift the focus from 'producerism' (Smith, 1986) – where the basic priority in service provision was the employees' interests – to a 'customer orientated' focus. This attack on the perceived vested interests of employees is at its most direct in Conservative councils. However, Labour and Liberal Democrat councils are not immune from conflictual relationships with their employees, especially white-collar professionals, in their pursuit of new working practices.

Whatever form the shift to new community-oriented authorities takes, it has implications for people management. Where authorities set out to achieve a new organizational culture focused on quality services to the public, a more sophisticated approach to the managing of employees is required. A study of the personnel management implications of customer-care initiatives (IDS/IPM, 1989, p. 11) found that employers 'recognised the importance of securing this change in attitude among their staff'. This was 'seen by most in terms of fundamental change in the corporate culture of their organisation . . . a task achieved through promotion of the "core values" and mission statements' (IDS/IPM, 1989). The councils studied had taken the need for employee involvement to mean a policy of staff care and support. Birmingham City Council, for example, had instigated an extensive staff programme dealing with aggression which recognized that vulnerable front-line employees, who have to deal with potentially difficult clients, are more likely to adopt the council's consumer approach 'if they can feel the council is looking after them too' (IDS/IPM, 1989, p. 11). Another example was Wrekin District Council, which promotes its customer-care policy on the basis of being a model employer.

Equal opportunities

Local government has been at the forefront of good practice in equality of opportunity in employment. In 1987, a new job evaluation scheme was introduced, based on equal value considerations and included caring skills as well as more traditional male skills. This led to significant improvements in grading for many female, often part-time, manual employees (Lodge, 1987). Job sharing is also more common than in other public or private organizations, with large numbers of shared posts in Camden, Hackney, Leeds, Leicester and Sheffield and in Hampshire and Kent County Councils (Industrial Relations Services, 1989).

Recruitment and selection procedures have been affected by equal opportunities policies. Some Labour councils endeavoured to use 'contract compliance' procedures, to ensure that contractors followed good equal opportunities practices (IPM, 1987). This was blocked by the LGA 1988, which expressly forebade councils placing such requirements on contractors.

Some local authorities have been identified with promoting equality for excluded or disadvantaged groups for whom no legislation exists, including homosexuals, lesbians, older workers, and the long-term unemployed. Other authorities have take a vigorous stand over their obligation to achieve the three per cent quota of registered disabled employees. Good practice is often in Labour-held councils in areas of high ethnic minority populations, such as Birmingham, where no-one is allowed to interview without having attended special interviewer training courses. Manchester has set up an Equal Opportunities Unit, which monitors employment targets for women, ethnic minorities and the disabled.

A survey in the early 1990s confirmed commitment to equality of opportunity in employment, with 82 per cent of respondents having such policies (LGMB, 1993b). Implementation was achieved through careful recruitment, selection and training, although there were few examples of equality targets. The main reason cited by respondents for adopting equal opportunities policies was that it was part of a 'good employer policy'.

In spite of equal opportunity policies, and some good practice, a survey of 41 councils published by the CRE (1995) revealed that two-thirds were failing to reflect the ethnic composition of the local working population and one-in-four were unable to provide an analysis of their workforce by ethnic origin. The CRE warned that councils are failing to meet their legal duties to promote racial equality in all council activities (*Financial Times*, 1995). Moreover, only 22 out of 500 councils have signed up to Opportunity 2000 to improve employment opportunities for women.

There are undoubtedly varying commitments to equal opportunities among local authorities and internal divisions can arise. The push for positive action often stems from personnel officers but may not be in line with views of elected members. Tensions can also arise when semi-autonomous decentralized units interpret policy in different ways. Changes to quasi-independent business units, under CCT, mean that authority-wide equal opportunities policies may be more difficult to enforce.

Recruitment and selection

In many respects, local government recruitment and selection methods are little different from those in the private sector. For manual workers and lower grade white-collar staff, recruitment methods remain basic, although equal opportunities policies and the legal requirements to vet applicants for certain jobs, such as those in residential care homes, mean that some selection processes are sophisticated. For senior professional, technical and management staff, selection methods are more elaborate, although there is evidence that local government is perhaps more traditional in its methods than the private sector (Williams, 1992).

Although there is more job mobility than in the past, it remains common for professional, technical and management staff to pursue their careers within local government. Indeed, for many white-collar staff, their academic and professional qualifications generally limit their careers to local government. Local government is the major employer of social workers, environmental health officers and school teachers. However, for many staff with transferable skills, local government may not be a lifetime career – a fact which becomes evident whenever labour supply tightens.

Unlike the Civil Service, there has never been a national system of recruitment into local government. Each council is an independent employer and recruits its own staff. Manual and clerical staff are generally recruited by line managers in conjunction with personnel officers. For higher level jobs, selection is through panel interviews, involving both members and council officers. For top positions, such as chief executives, recruitment consultants may be engaged to carry out selection.

Recruitment and retention problems in the late 1980s prompted local authorities to review traditional methods. A significant number targeted specific groups, such as ethnic minorities, the disabled, older workers and less qualified people. Many established closer links with schools and colleges. According to a report: 'general council image promotion is now common and should have spin offs for recruitment, as should other . . . policies such as the promotion of equal opportunities and a wide range of "good employer" policies' (LACSAB/LGTB, 1990a, p. 3). The problems experienced in the tight labour market of the late 1980s had eased by 1991, although staff in key professional groups were still in short supply (LGMB, 1992b).

The combined effects of tight cash limits and exposure of further areas to CCT is having an impact on recruitment and selection in the 1990s. In a survey of 86 councils in 1994 (IDS, 1994a), over half reported net job losses, totalling some 23 000 over the year. Whilst 64 councils reported no problems in recruitment and retention, some had experienced problems with particular groups including social services, environmental health officers and computer staff. Most councils cited CCT and government's public-sector pay policy as major reasons for job losses and non-filling of vacancies.

Recent surveys of management selection in local government in England and Wales suggest that tradition remains a powerful influence on selection methods (Williams, 1992; LGMB, 1992b). Local authorities still use application forms and panel interviews rather than more reliable and valid methods such as CVs, biodata, psychological tests and assessment centres. This traditionalism is partly explained by the continuing involvement of members in recruitment and the presence of personnel to monitor procedures.

Performance management and performance related pay

In 1985, when the local authority employers' body carried out a consultation exercise on PRP, most councils were unenthusiastic about introducing it. By 1989, over 100 authorities were either operating or planning schemes (IDS, 1989), although in most cases such schemes applied only to senior staff. IDS identified three reasons why schemes were being introduced: a response to CCT; a response to recruitment and retention problems; and part of the shift to a performance management culture.

A survey of 300 Councils carried out by LACSAB (Spence, 1990) concluded that performance management had been introduced because of legislation, consumer demands, demands for increased accountability, tighter cash limits and recruitment and retention problems. Performance management and PRP were viewed positively by local government managers as effective management tools for improving performance, although only 20 to 30 per cent of authorities in the survey were using performance indicators (PIs) to monitor performance. The PIs covered quality of service, service output, employee performance and employee attitudes.

A further survey in 1993 (LGMB, 1994c) found that almost 60 per cent of responding authorities had introduced a formal PMS or were planning to introduce one, although only one-in-ten schemes included manual

workers. PRP had been adopted in a quarter of authorities, a figure close to the 1989 IDS figure, with a further
two per cent planning to introduce it. Only two authorities had PRP for manual workers but about 40 per cent
covered most non-manual grades, with the greatest cover-
age amongst chief officers and deputies. In general, PMSs
appear to be more widespread than PRP.

Authorities now acknowledge that the mad scramble
to introduce PRP in isolation in the 1980s was a mistake.
Whether PRP was introduced for reasons of recruitment
and retention, or as the latest personnel 'fad', it is now
accepted, if it has a place in local government, that it can
only work as part of a properly integrated PMS. Since
1990, only 10 authorities have introduced new PRP schemes,
whilst five have abandoned them. PRP is found predominantly in the south-east and applies mainly to senior
managers. This supports the claim that PRP has been a
pragmatic response to recruitment and retention problems.

Reward packages

National terms and conditions have existed in local government since the second world war but collective agreements have always allowed local interpretation. Ingham
(1985) found, for white-collar staff, extensive evidence of
councils paying basic rates above national levels; holiday
allowances superior to the national one; shorter hours of
work than those stipulated in the national agreement; and
supplements above national levels. For manual workers
there was less variation, although 21 per cent of authorities provided above national holiday allowances and 25
per cent paid other supplements.

The late 1980s saw a significant increase in benefits flexibility. Labour market pressures, in the south, led to a pro-
fusion of 'pay supplements' targeted at employee groups
in short supply, such as computer staffs, accountants,
architects and teachers (IDS, 1988; LACSAB, 1987a). Many
councils also began providing benefits previously found
only in the private sector, such as mortgage subsidies,

leased cars, free life insurance and private medical cover.

A survey in 1989 (LACSAB/LGTB, 1990b) found greater use of flexible entry to scales, relating career progression to ability; selective pay enhancements; accelerated progression through grades; and longer salary scales to suit new recruits. Other changes included extended salary scales and flatter grade structures. A common theme was linking pay to ability and performance and market rates for particular occupations.

The pace of change in pay policies has been fastest in those parts of the country where labour shortages first appeared, such as London and the south-east. With the reduction in labour market pressures in the early 1990s, and the reimposition of central government pay limits from 1993, many of the extra benefits have been withdrawn (Bryson *et al.*, 1993; IDS, 1994a).

Changes in labour utilization

Local government has always operated a flexible workforce. For many years, around two-thirds of its manual labour force has been part-timers, whilst the use of contractors, especially in construction, was commonplace. The 24-hour nature of some services, such as police and fire services, social services and emergency maintenance, has dictated that many employees work shifts, unsocial hours and irregular working patterns. As Kessler (1991b, p. 19) notes, models of the 'flexible firm', such as Atkinson and Meager (1986) propose, with core and peripheral workforces, are therefore problematic, if not inappropriate to local government.

Nevertheless, pressures exerted by the introduction of CCT, financial stringency and new customer-care strategies have led to considerable changes in labour utilization, especially amongst manual workers. Manual employment has declined due both to private contractors winning contracts and to downsizing by DSOs, in order to win contracts. CCT has led not only to major reductions in employment but also to less favourable working conditions and a major intensification of work. Whilst basic rates of pay have been nationally determined, there have been reductions in bonuses and holiday entitlements and increases in working hours. Some authorities now have annualized hours to allow for peaks and troughs in demand and seasonal variations in daylight hours. Overtime has also been significantly reduced (Ward *et al.*, 1988; Colling, 1993).

Strategies to alleviate staff shortages now include: job redesign; re-deployment of staff, such as upgrading and conversion of manual workers to staff status; and resource planning, such as conducting skills audits (LACSAB/LGTB, 1990b). This affected planning and finance staff, administrative/clerical grades and staff in DSOs.

A concern in the late 1980s that the demographic decline in school leavers might create recruitment problems also led to changes in working patterns. The main measures introduced were: job shares; part-time working; flexible working hours; special leave; career break schemes; creche or nursery provision; and financial contributions to childminding.

Personnel information systems

Personnel managers have not traditionally been at the forefront of computer applications. It was finance departments that were the pathfinders of IT applications in local government and personal computers did not appear in personnel offices until the early 1980s. However, in the following years, computerized personnel information systems (CPIS) have become commonplace.

Adoption was highest in the shire counties, metropolitan districts and London boroughs. The necessity to network and interface with payroll systems resulted in the use of either existing mainframes or mini-computers. In parallel with decentralization generally, more control is being exercised at departmental level. Personnel departments no longer control access to personnel information which is vital to the survival of service areas, especially those exposed to CCT, whilst line managers require personnel data in increasing quantities to construct and monitor the performance of in-house contracts.

Restriction in the use of CPIS to operational and/or tactical levels is one that is mirrored in the private sector. There is no doubt that computers have enabled personnel staff to free themselves from the tedium of maintaining inefficient manual record systems. The production of information for committee reports, and the generation of standard letters, is now straightforward but the strategic use of personnel information is less in evidence.

Industrial Relations

Industrial relations in local government were relatively trouble free until the late 1960s. In 1968 the Donovan Commission had little to say about the public sector, other than to praise its model system of industrial relations. However, rapid growth of union membership and increasing friction over governmental controls on public-sector pay led to increases in industrial action (Laffin, 1989). In the 1970s, there were disputes involving social workers, school teachers, firefighters, manual and non-manual employees, culminating in the so-called 'Winter of Discontent' in 1978–79. These were mainly national disputes over pay, and industrial action locally remained less common (Ingham, 1985).

Although local government employers have recognized unions and engaged in collective bargaining for over 60 years, the framework of Whitley machinery and national terms and conditions was only finally completed after the second world war. A central local government employers' organization, LACSAB, was established in 1948. However, 'the national system of industrial relations in local government has always had a fragile base' (Kessler, 1991b, p. 7), with the 500 or so independent employers retaining the right to decide on most employment issues. This observation is reinforced by the local government

TABLE 5.4 **Main local government bargaining groups, 1993**

Group	Settlement date	Nos	Paybill £m	Area
APT&C	July	735 000	8796	E&W
Police	September	148 000	4200	UK
Manuals	September	697 000	3472	E&W
Fire (FTs)	November	42 000	752	UK

Source: derived from LGMB, 1994

employers' body, which states that 'each local authority is responsible for managing its own pay and employment, to suit its own local conditions and its own policies on service provision, finance and management' (LGMB, 1993a, p. 6).

The machinery created in 1946 continues to this day, with around 15 negotiating groups. The largest bargaining groups in England and Wales in 1993 are shown in Table 5.4. Attempts to move to a single agreement for the manual NJC and APT&C group have yet to succeed, although both groups negotiated through a single-table bargaining arrangement for the first time in 1994 (IDS, 1994b).

Employer organizations

The local authorities are represented by the LGMB, whilst in Scotland there is a parallel Scottish Local Authorities Secretariat. The LGMB was created in 1991, after the merger of three local government bodies – LACSAB, the LGTB and the Local Authorities Management Services and Computer Committee. The LGMB is governed by a board representing the various local government associations – the Association of County Councils, Association of Metropolitan Authorities and Association of District Councils. There are also regional negotiating bodies, the provincial councils, which are employers' associations in their own right.

The trade unions

There are a large number of recognized trade unions, although their numbers fell during the 1980s and early 1990s. The major unions representing manual workers are the General Municipal and Boilermakers (GMB), Transport and General Workers Union (TGWU) and UNISON. Amongst manual workers UNISON probably has most members but these are predominantly female and part-timers. The TGWU and GMB tend to have more full-time employees in membership. The white-collar staffs are represented mainly by UNISON, whilst craft groups are covered by the Amalgamated Engineering and Electrical Union (AEEU), Union of Construction Allied Trades and Technicians (UCATT), Manufacturing Science and Finance (MSF) and GMB and TGWU. Chief executives have their own association, while the Chief Officers are represented by Managerial and Professional Officers, a non-TUC association, and UNISON. The fire service has its own trade unions, the main one being the Fire Brigades Union (FBU).

Union membership remains high, compared with the private sector. According to the WIRS 1990 (Millward *et al.*, 1992), union density in local government is 70 per cent, compared with 48 per cent in all industries. Virtually all establishments in local government have union members – 95 per cent compared with 64 per cent in all industries – whilst some 94 per cent of establishments recognize unions compared with 54 per cent in all industries.

The major development in local government trade unionism, since 1979, was the creation of UNISON in 1993 after a merger between NALGO, the National Union of Public Employees (NUPE) and the Confederation of Health Service Employees (COHSE) (Certification Officer, 1994). UNISON is now the largest union in the UK with 1.6 million members and by far the largest union in local government with 860 000 members. Two-thirds of UNISON's membership is in local government. This merger of NALGO with one of the three unions for manual workers, NUPE, provides the potential for harmonizing the two major local authority agreements, for white-collar staff and manual workers.

Changes in collective bargaining

Writing at the start of the 1980s, Walsh (1981) noted that increasing financial control of local government had increased the pressures to centralize collective bargaining. 'The need for contact with central government means that the role of the central representative institutions of local authorities, and the central union bureaucracies, is enhanced.' Moreover, 'the limited amount of money available for pay rises under cash limits, and the operation of incomes policy, leaves little money available for local negotiation on pay' (Walsh, 1981, p. 49). This led to conflict between the centre and periphery amongst employers and unions and within the employers' central bodies. In the unions, the rank-and-file wanted decentralized bargaining, whilst full-time officers wanted centralized negotiations. Walsh commented that: 'the formal situation, in which local authorities are independent employers, who voluntarily cede certain rights to national and regional representative institutions, no longer matches reality' (Walsh, 1981, p. 53).

By the early 1990s, however, the power of the centre was waning. Local bargaining was present in a range of authorities. This decentralization was driven by several factors and the reasons differed between the manual and non-manual workforces. For manuals, the major catalyst was the introduction of CCT, whilst for non-manuals, not challenged by tendering of services at that time, the catalysts were labour market pressures and party political factors.

Fragmentation of the manual workers' agreement

CCT began with the LGPLA 1980 which required authorities to put building and building maintenance contracts out to tender. When CCT was extended to other council services, the response from councils depended on the political control of the authority. Some Conservative councils were ardent supporters of contracting-out and had already closed their DLOs, whilst others tried to protect direct services by restructuring them as separate business units, able to compete with private contractors. As the requirements of CCT were increasingly tightened, and attempts at 'contract compliance' outlawed (IPM, 1987), councils chose to renegotiate the terms and conditions of manual workers to allow more flexibility of response to private tenders (Ward *et al.*, 1988; Colling, 1993). Base pay rates remained determined nationally but other conditions, such as bonus schemes, holidays and sick pay, were often reduced to levels offered by private contractors. CCT has meant not only a reduction in the number of manual workers in local government but also decreasing influence of the nationally agreed terms and conditions, which are now seen as a framework for local negotiations.

Non-manual employees

The major factors influencing decentralization of bargaining for non-manual staff have been labour market pressures and political decisions. Conservative governments have sought to reduce the power of public-sector unions and breaking the influence of national agreements was seen as a key to achieving this. However, this was more difficult to achieve in local government than elsewhere. The ending of cash-limited pay settlements in 1986, and the switch to a flexible policy of pay targeting, designed by government to encourage decentralized bargaining and meet labour market pressures, began to erode the power of the centralized institutions (White, 1993). Whilst most councils remained wedded to national bargaining, there was a clear shift towards local bargaining in the late 1980s. Labour market problems in the south-east led to an explosion of 'market supplements' and special benefits to attract and retain key groups of staff such as accountants, lawyers, surveyors and computer staffs.

Surveys in 1987 (LACSAB, 1987b) and 1988 (IDS, 1988) revealed the spread and diversity of such innovations in pay and benefits. In addition, an increasing number of councils were introducing individual PRP for senior staff (IDS, 1989). LACSAB, aware that national arrangements were under threat, issued a consultative document (LACSAB, 1988) and organized a conference in April 1988. A consensus emerged that all councils wanted greater flexibility within a framework APT&C agreement, with district councils and councils in the south-east wanting more local negotiations, whilst Metropolitan authorities and those in the north wanted to keep most terms and conditions national (LACSAB, 1988). This split largely reflected the political complexions of the two groups, with Conservatives strong in the south-east and rural districts and Labour in the north and conurbations.

Following the consultation exercise, LACSAB attempted to negotiate a new 'slimmed down' national agreement with APT&C staff in 1989 which would have set a national floor of minimum rates upon which each authority would negotiate locally, according to local labour market conditions. This proposal was strongly opposed by NALGO and led to its first national strike over pay. During the strike, the employers were split and several councils decided to break with the national agreement and settle. This gave them the opportunity to introduce changes addressing issues of recruitment and retention and new pay systems (Bryson *et al.*, 1993). By 1993, 34 councils had opted out of the national agreement. The majority were small district councils but there were three large county councils – Kent, Buckinghamshire, Surrey – and one London Borough, Harrow, did also. A list is shown in Table 5.5.

Griffiths (1990, pp. 103–4), head of personnel at Kent County Council, indicates that the factors responsible for Kent's opt-out were: the erosion of 'the public monopoly of services'; CCT; increased emphasis on customer care; the need to relate pay to performance; the shift from 'professionalism' to 'managerialism'; the shift from central direction to more devolved management; and, most important of all, changes in the funding of local government.

TABLE 5.5   Authorities adopting local collective bargaining for APT&C staff

	Date	Size APT&C	Political control
Ashford Borough Council	1989	400	C
Aylesbury Vale District Council	1989	500	C
Brentwood District Council	1989	550	C
Buckinghamshire District Council	1990	7 000	C
Canterbury City Council	1989	650	H
Dartford Borough Council	1989	450	C
Dover District Council	1989	430	C
East Hampshire District Council	1991	565	C
Epsom and Ewell Borough Council	1991	270	I
Guildford Borough Council	1989	550	H
Harrow London Borough Council	1993	5 000	C
Hertsmere Borough Council	1989	550	H
Hove Borough Council	1988	350	C
Huntingdonshire District Council	1989	400	C
Kent County Council	1990	11 500	C
Maidstone Borough Council	1990	610	H
Mendip District Council	1989	300	H
Milton Keynes Borough Council	1990	750	H
Mole Valley District Council	1989	250	H
New Forest District Council	1990	800	C
Rother District Council	1990	313	C
Runnymede Borough Council	1987	300	C
Shepway District Council	1988	430	LD
South Bucks District Council	1992	183	C
South Northamptonshire District Council	1990	300	C
South Oxfordshire District Council	1991	420	C
Surrey County Council	1993	7 400	C
Surrey Health Borough Council	1988	400	C
Swale Borough Council	1990	350	H
Tandridge District Council	1988	440	H
Test Valley District Council	1992	526	C
Thanet District Council	1991	520	H
Tonbridge and Malling Borough Council	1991	388	C
Waverley Borough Council	1989	350	LD
Wealden District Council	1990	460	C
Woking Borough Council	1989	450	H

C = Conservative LD = Liberal Democrat H - Hung, no overall control
I = Independent (political control is at the time of opting out)

Source: derived from Bryson, 1993

Four pressures seem instrumental in decisions to secede: ability to pay; performance; market forces and labour supply; and comparability. Whilst the decision to shift to local bargaining seems primarily officer-led, in a number of cases opt-outs were initiated by the local Conservative group on councils, which actively supported government policy for decentralized bargaining (Bryson *et al.*, 1993). In the main, opted-out councils tend to be Conservative controlled at secession.

Most authorities which have withdrawn from national bargaining were advised by external consultants. In a number of councils, the new pay determination system was based on index-linking to management consultants' annual pay surveys, such as Hay, and, in one case, to inflation. This led to salary drift in the short term as 'the new local contracts of employment offered to staff following withdrawal from national bargaining were packaged in such a way that most employees affected stood to gain financially from accepting new terms and conditions' (Bryson *et al.*, 1993, p. 569). Half the authorities which have withdrawn did not negotiate the proposed changes with the unions, although none have derecognized them.

Other examples of new industrial relations practices in opted-out councils include no-strike pendulum arbitration at Brentwood and Swale and single-table bargaining at Ashford and Tandridge. Almost all the councils ended automatic incremental progression and introduced PRP.

A major objective in the opted-out authorities was to secure control over labour costs. CCT provided the opportunity to create devolved budgets so that service managers gained a measure of control over their labour costs. The introduction of PRP gave managers a degree of control over the pay of individuals in their teams. These, however, 'were only side products of the measures that needed to be taken to solve the most critical problem – their ability to recruit and retain staff' (Bryson *et al.*, 1993, p. 572). The reimposition of central government pay controls in 1993 created problems for these new pay systems. The onset of recession also removed labour market pressures which had driven the opt-outs (IDS, 1991).

Establishment-level union organization

Union organization at national level is still strong but important changes are happening at authority level. A layer of lay union representatives was developed in the 1970s and 1980s, in response to de-centralization and the expanding scope for local decision-making by line managers (Kessler, 1993). The new financial framework and development of proxy market forces have created an environment in which there is increasing scope for local union organization to develop.

Despite the shift to local negotiations, however, Kessler (1991b) found that establishment-level trade unionism is relatively weak. The dispersed nature of the workforce, its segmentation into occupational groupings and the large number of part-time employees have always been obstacles to effective workplace unionism, although not to union membership. It was not until the late 1960s that shop stewards were recognized by local authorities and, even then, such a development was not a rank-and-file one but a creation of the national union, to democratize it and bring officials closer to the membership (Fryer, 1989). Farnham (1978, p. 32) describes how, in the 1970s, NALGO members often felt isolated from their full-time officials who showed 'too great an identity of interest and sentiment with the employers'.

Staff Development

The traditional emphasis in local government training has been on professional qualifications for white-collar staff. In contrast with industrial training in private manufacturing, there was little in the way of training for manual workers, except in construction where there was a highly developed apprenticeship system. Both the Mallaby (1967) and Bains (1972) reports concluded that training was underdeveloped and viewed as a cost rather than an investment. There was a heavy reliance on outside professional bodies and educational institutions to provide training, with internal training very limited. In management development, there was very little training at all.

This was surprising because local government had a long commitment to training. It was written into the APT&C agreement from its inception and clear directions were given to what types of training and development should be provided. The Local Government Examination Board (LGEB) was established in 1946 to administer qualifications for clerical and administrative staff, followed, later, by apprenticeship and training schemes for manual workers. After the establishment of Industrial Training Boards, under the Industrial Training Act 1964, the LGEB was absorbed into a new, more strategic LGTB, which existed until its absorption into the LGMB in 1991. The LGTB, whilst not a statutory body, followed the same principles of seeking increased efficiency by ensuring that training was provided and its costs spread through levies on employers. There was no uniformity, however, and some authorities, like the GLC, became heavily involved in training, whilst others preferred to poach skilled, qualified staff from other authorities.

An important feature of the Bains report (1972) was its proposal to shift training and development away from professional training towards management training. In the 1980s, the importance attached to management training increased and first the LGTB and later the LGMB developed courses and distance learning materials for each level of management from supervisory to top level. Whilst its role is less prominent than the LGTB, the LGMB continues to act as the central body for training initiatives. Another body working closely with the LGMB is the Institute of Local Government Studies (INLOGOV), at the University of Birmingham. Founded in 1964, it quickly established a reputation in research and in providing a wide range of seminars, either at the university or in-house.

Towards the end of the 1980s, councils indicated that they wanted to move away from a national structure for training towards a more local focus but, by 1992, it was recognized that there was a need for national coordination of training for senior managers. The LGMB now offers a competency-based modular programme for chief executives, chief officers and managers identified as potential chief officers. At present, the programme is not linked to any recognized qualification but there is scope for it to be accredited towards a master's degree. The programme is self-directed, leading to a personal self-development plan, with attendance required for only seven days over the year. Additionally, the Board runs a leadership programme for women managers, which is also modular.

Provincial councils also provide courses and tailor-made programmes to meet specific council requirements. There is a general move in local government, as elsewhere in the public sector, to gain accreditation for all training, either within the NVQ framework or MCI.

Towards the end of the 1980s, growing interest in strategic management provided fertile ground for an integrated approach to training and development. The LGTB (1987) emphasised the importance of loosening the grip of professionalism to achieve a more corporate perspective of local government. This was followed by a report stressing the need for training to be embedded within a strategic framework (LGTB, 1988). Individual development needs were to form part of departmental objectives which, in turn, would be supportive of the authority's corporate values and goals. Kessler (1990) notes that strategic consideration was given to training in all the authorities covered in the 1990 SOCPO survey.

A significant factor underpinning the new approach came from the customer-care policies adopted by many councils. Local authorities were urged to 'get closer to the public' (LGTB, 1987) and the shift from 'producerism' to 'consumerism' redefined the focus of training. The new imperative demanded a change from uncoordinated training initiatives, that were essentially inwardly focused, to a wholesale re-examination of how employees needed to be developed to reflect the new local government climate of the 1990s. Additionally, CCT created new management development needs such as preparing tenders, evaluating external bids and meeting the requirements for monitoring. CCT forced managers and politicians to reassess the levels of service that were expected within budgetary limits and sharpen the skills of contract monitoring. Training needs extended beyond skills development to 'cultural refocusing', with the requirement to split the client and contractor functions in those affected by CCT.

In common with the private sector, local authorities have recognized the importance of managing change. The theory of change management, and its associated skills, increasingly features within training programmes at a variety of levels. There are many examples of higher education programmes being delivered either in-house or *via* traditional modes. These range from specialist Certificates and Diplomas in Management, now increasingly linked to NVQs, through to MBAs.

Despite the budgetary restrictions imposed upon local government, commitment to management development and training by employers remains strong. Where local government has not kept pace with the private sector is in recognizing the strategic opportunities offered by a competency-based approach to staff development. Such initiatives, whether based upon the generic standards of the MCI or, more commonly, a bespoke set of competences, have been widely reported. Competency-based approaches tend to have supporters and detractors. It could be argued that local authorities are unwilling at this stage to dispense with traditional methods of recruitment and selection, career development and remuneration. However, the LGMB is currently developing NVQs for firefighters and social care assistants.

Rainbird (1994) suggests that, whilst there is no evidence of a single model for organizing training, constraints on local authorities are resulting in a greater degree of integration of training with business strategy. The training function is increasingly taking the form of an in-house agency run as a cost centre. Decentralization of training is also growing, based upon the desire to integrate departmental training with local service delivery objectives. In the past, departments were often presented with a menu of training courses from centralized training divisions and required to nominate staff to attend. Not surprisingly, departments are welcoming the opportunity to develop their own training plans and manage training budgets.

Authorities have benefited from the development of Service Level Agreements (SLAs) in working towards the implementation of CCT. In anticipation of CCT, some authorities have created a purchaser/provider split, with training set up as a cost centre within the provider unit. It does not appear that training is being contracted out in advance of CCT but this is an area where competition will be fierce, with authorities typically spending up to three per cent of payroll on training and development activities. However, CCT will be less problematic for authorities which have historically purchased training from the private sector, whilst concentrating themselves on identifying training needs.

In February 1995 the Joint Initiative for Community Care published the results of a 'mapping exercise', the aim of which was to identify what action Social Services Departments were taking in relation to applying CCT to personnel management and the provision of staff development and training in particular (Bell, 1995). Surprisingly, few authorities appeared to have undertaken any detailed preparatory work. But, of those who had begun to formulate plans, the indications were that CCT had provided a substantial impetus to the separation of the commissioning and contracting of staff development and training. A significant finding was a trend in London Boroughs and metropolitan districts towards centralizing the personnel function, including employee development, within the authority as a whole. This appears to contradict Rainbird's research and could be seen as an increasingly pragmatic response to the pressures brought about by CCT. One of the main issues concerning Social Services Departments is that CCT and personnel centralization may dilute the effectiveness of training. The strategic integration of employee development at departmental level will inevitably be less effective. As the report indicates, the irony is that CCT assumes a model of employee development from which most authorities are beginning to move away. The report states: 'it is a model for the 1980s, not for the forth-coming new century' (Bell, 1995, p. 20). Also, although the report focuses upon Social Services Departments, its conclusion makes depressing reading for authorities in general: 'it must seem as if the future of staff develop-ment and training depends upon the roll of the dice and the spin of the wheel!' (Bell, 1995, p. 25).

The increasing adoption of PMS has given added im-petus to the introduction of staff appraisal, where train-ing needs can be identified to facilitate the achievement of individual targets closely linked to wider service de-livery targets. This, in turn, requires that line managers become more involved in identifying training needs of staff. A guide to performance management published by the LGMB (1993) indicates that some councils are including training and development checklists for consideration at appraisal interviews, such as at Cambridgeshire County Council and Adur District Council.

Conclusion and Evaluation

The 1980s witnessed significant changes in people man-agement in local government but a strong element of continuity remains. A clear shift towards a more proactive form of managing people can be detected, with an increase in the role of line managers and decentralization of the personnel function to business units. But it is still a mat-ter of conjecture how far local government has moved in the direction of a strategic human resources management model. Numbers of personnel management staff increased by 59 per cent between 1979 and 1994. Even allowing for the fact that some of this increase compensated for the decline in management services staff, the figures suggest an enlargement of the professional personnel role in local government rather than any appreciable shift of personnel duties to line managers.

Local government, like any other sector, is subject to the latest personnel management fads. Some initiatives, such as PRP, have simply been copied uncritically from the private sector. Others have followed the advice of management consultants, irrespective of their appropriateness for public-service teams of professionals. The financial imperative, which has driven councils to seek savings in employment costs and increases in productivity amongst the remaining workforce, has created a more business-centred approach. The creation of internal markets of providers and purchasers, whilst not established by statute, as in the case of the NHS, has none the less been driven by central government policy such as CCT legislation. This legislation has forced authorities to set up arms-length, in-house contractors to bid for work against private competitors.

The major changes in people management to-date have been amongst the manual workforce, where CCT has hit hardest. The Local Government Act 1992 now brings in white-collar staff, so far protected from the effects of competition. Under this legislation, even a proportion of personnel work will be subject to tender. One effect of CCT on the manual workforce has been substantial job losses, with the remaining workforce having their national conditions of service changed. Whilst a national agreement on pay, hours and conditions continues, it is increasingly a framework within which local DSOs create their own agreements. There is clear evidence of an intensification of work by manual workers, with a lengthening of working hours and more flexible working patterns.

Trade union presence remains strong. Indeed, it is one of the strongest unionized sectors within the economy, although there are disparities in union density in different parts of the country and amongst different groups. This high density means that local government remains fundamentally pluralist in its industrial and employee relations. Even in those councils which have opted out of national bargaining, there have been few examples of union derecognition and, where it has occurred, it has been where membership was virtually non-existent. Union opposition to CCT has often been tempered by a pragmatic realism. Faced with the threats created by CCT, there has been a remarkable degree of cooperation between management and unions in many authorities, especially in Labour-led councils, to ensure that DSOs are capable of winning contracts. Despite isolated local disputes the manual workforce has been relatively quiescent since the late 1980s, and industrial conflict low.

Conflict between white-collar trade unionists and their employers, in contrast, has become more common, especially amongst the so-called radical professionals such as social workers and teachers. To some extent this has been a by-product of increasing unionization. But discontent has also been created by legislative and operational changes faced by social services staff and teaching staff, such as Care in the Community and the National Curriculum. In addition, CCT for services provided by manual workers and the introduction of LMS have led to pressures to cut central services and costs. This has resulted in increased industrial action over pay and local disputes. Recently, the APT&C union side has concentrated on low-pay issues and settlements have tended to benefit lower grade staff (Audit Commission, 1995). This weighting of the pay award towards the lower-paid has led to discontent amongst more senior staff who, in some cases, have left UNISON to join the non-TUC Managerial and Professional Officers.

Whilst the number of manual workers has declined, it is the reverse with white-collar staff. The number of non-manual staff increased by 90 000, or by 15 per cent, between 1987 and 1993 (Audit Commission, 1995). About half of this was due to central government initiatives, such as the community charge ('poll tax') and increased numbers of schools-based administrative staff. In addition, CCT may have created extra senior posts, whilst some manual workers have been reclassified as white-collar staff, such as leisure centre attendants and residential care workers. The largest increase in non-manual staff has been of managers, with an over 60 per cent increase in posts of Principal Officer (PO) and above. Although the overall pay bill for local government went up by 60 per cent between 1987 and 1993, it increased by

85 per cent for non-manual workers. This is largely explained by the increase in more highly-paid staff at PO
and above. It also reflects grade and salary drift in the
late 1980s, as councils struggled to recruit and retain staff
in the tight labour market conditions of that period.

The Audit Commission has identified a number of challenges facing local government in the 1990s. These include increasing fragmentation of services, dealing with
real cuts in spending and evolving adequate management
structures. Problems identified include: low staff productivity; top-heavy management structures; poor link-
age of staff skills with workload; pay levels out of line
with market rates and job size; mismanagement of pay
progression; and poor pay bill management, due to inadequate information and lack of an integrated management of pay.

National collective bargaining remains the norm for most
councils, despite governmental exhortation and cajoling
to move to local bargaining. Some councils have opted-
out, although mainly for recruitment and retention reasons and often at some cost. For employers remaining within
national bargaining, agreements have become more flexible
and open to local interpretation. Moves to leave national
agreements slowed considerably in the early 1990s, due
to a slack labour market and public-sector pay policy.
Both served to undermine the advantages of secession.
The Audit Commission (1995, p. 10) argues that 'national
agreements contribute to good pay management' by providing a framework which 'can restrain pay leap-frog-
ging and thus help to prevent pay inflation in skill shortage
areas from extending to the whole workforce'. Whilst
arguing that it would be difficult and expensive to dup-
licate national collective bargaining at local level, the
Commission says that such agreements must become more
flexible to reflect the uncertain employment conditions
of the 1990s. However, contrary to the often stated views
of central government, the Commission says that opting-
out of national agreements can be costly in the short term
and 'does not guarantee that authorities will manage pay
in a structured and rational manner' (p. 11).

Local political control has maintained a grip on personnel policies at the centre in many authorities, which has seen the continuation of some model employer policies, particularly commitment to equal opportunities and union recognition. In many ways, local government has been the public service least affected by the shift from a traditional public-sector management style to a new public management, identified in the Civil Service and NHS. This is largely explained by the continued independence of local government from central government, despite 16 years of attempts by Conservative governments to weaken local government. Elected members continue to exert a strong influence over the management of people and this tends to reflect, though not always, the political perspectives of those members. Indeed, it is the continuing involvement of members in the details of decisions over staff numbers, pay grades and individual posts below chief officer level which the Audit Commission views as problematic. Commenting on those councils which operate policies on 'low pay', the Commission states that: 'when working with capped budgets, if such authorities pay higher salaries than is necessary, they restrict the number of staff they can employ and the level of service they can provide' (Audit Commission, 1995, p. 22). However, it is the political will to behave as a model employer which motivates many councillors to provide such minima.

There is no doubt that the immediate prospects for people management are challenging. The continuing squeeze on public expenditure, including pay limits and reductions in staffing, is coinciding with a fragmentation of local government services. This is undermining the notion of a national or even a local government service. The holistic approach to management advocated by Bains (1972), which took root to some extent in the late 1970s, has begun to wither as individual business units compete with one another. Increasingly, councils are viewing their employment practices as their concern alone and this view is encouraged by bodies such as the Audit Commission, which argues for more local determination of employment matters.

Moves towards an enabling role by councils will mean that services will become increasingly impermanent, with contracts awarded for specified periods and no guarantee of renewal. Concepts of job security, lifetime commitment to council-service and career development are becoming more difficult to provide, as employment becomes more precarious. Whilst some councils see employee commitment as the key to service quality, the reality of growing numbers of casual and contract staff makes this harder to achieve. Clearly, the future of people management depends to a large extent on its ability to retain and extend its independence from central government and a change of government at Westminster could clearly make a difference.

The Labour party's commitment to wider local democracy, and the establishment of regional assemblies, might lead to a resurgence of local government institutions in the longer term. However, control of public expenditure will remain a high priority, whichever party is in power. This will undoubtedly be the key influence shaping human resources management policies in local government for the foreseeable future.

CHAPTER 6

Education

David Farnham and Lesley Giles

Since 1979, public education services have undergone considerable change and reform, imposed by successive Conservative governments. These reforms reflect wider public-service policies, centred on the belief that if the quality of education is to be improved, then private-sector management techniques and commercial criteria need to be imported into schools, further education establishments and universities. In line with other public services since 1980, education has felt the full force of privatization, restructuring, decentralization and CCT. These initiatives, rooted in the values of enterprise and market competition, have aimed at enhancing efficiency and value for money, securing tighter controls over public spending and promoting improvements in educational standards. All have impacted on the ways in which in education people are managed.

Whilst the majority of schools still remain within the local authority sector, the former polytechnics – now 'new' universities – colleges of higher education (CHEs) and colleges of further education (CFEs) have been designated as higher education and further education corporations (HECs and FECs). Although most of their funding is provided by the Higher Education and Further Education Funding Councils (HEFC and FEFC), these bodies are technically in the private sector and are no longer the responsibility of elected local education authorities (LEAs). The traditional or 'old' universities have Royal Charters but they too have had to respond to higher education initiatives. No part of the education system has escaped the impact of government policy since 1980.

Educational Policy

Legislation has played a prominent role in these educational reforms. Six major statutes have been enacted since 1980: the Education Acts of 1980 and 1986, Education Reform Act 1988 (ERA 1988), Education (Schools) Act 1992, Further and Higher Education Act 1992 (FHEA 1992) and Education Act 1993. These legislative reforms have resulted in fundamental changes in the structure, organization and management of education. Through legislation, government has sought to: increase the efficiency of schools, colleges and universities; obtain value for money; raise the quality of teaching; make educational institutions more responsive to parents, students and industry; reduce the power of teachers and their unions; and concentrate power in boards of governors and education managers. Developments in pursuit of these policy objectives include: new systems of financial management, with devolved budgets and PIs; a national curriculum along with standardized assessments and testing, monitored by an independent schools inspectorate and the Audit Commission; and strengthened boards of governors. These changes have introduced: performance management with appraisal systems; school and college-based training; management development programmes; flexible reward systems, including PRP; and internal markets with competition amongst institutions for pupils, students and money.

Government has also sought to undermine the collective power of teachers by weakening their traditional links with Whitehall and LEAs (Coates, 1972). Also, the powers of LEAs have been reduced and instead of being educational providers, their role is a more limited purchaser/ enabling one. The rationale for these changes is that traditional education was claimed to be unresponsive to the needs of the country and consistently failed, throughout the postwar period, to contribute to economic success and social improvement. It was also dominated by the teaching profession (McVicar, 1993; Sinclair *et al.*, 1993b; and Tomlinson, 1993).

With the introduction of Local Management of Schools (LMS) and Grant Maintained Status (GMS) in England and Wales, under the ERA 1988, management responsibility has been devolved from LEAs to schools. Governing bodies have been given more control over staffing and expenditure and head teachers have become like managing directors of small businesses. Although LEAs remain the legal employer of most school staff, their role has been substantially weakened and is now largely an advisory one. Where schools choose GMS and opt out, LEAs have no authority. With the implementation of its own schemes of Devolved School Management (DSM) since 1994, and the introduction of self-governing schools – the Scottish counterpart to GMS, it seems Scotland is adopting similar forms of reorganization in its schools. LEAs no longer have a role in further (FE) and higher education (HE). Under the ERA 1988 and FHEA 1992, all FE and HE institutions have become independent corporations managed by appointed boards of governors.

This weakening of the power and influence of democratically-elected LEAs has been parallelled by the weakening of the role of teacher and lecturer unions. The school teaching unions have been undermined by the loss of national negotiating rights under the Teachers' Pay and Conditions Act 1987 (TPCA 1987). Furthermore, they are facing increasing problems, in adapting to an ever more fragmented and divided educational sector. They have less influence in decision-making, because of the anti-corporatist approach of government and the new managerialism introduced into schools, colleges and universities. As a result, both the teacher unions and LEAs are being forced to adjust and to reorganize themselves to ensure that they retain some influence and involvement in education policymaking. Within the school sector, union resistance to both the core curriculum and testing has achieved some success in modifying government policy. The partnership of the postwar settlement amongst central government, LEAs and teachers has lapsed.

To meet the government's statutory requirements, schools, colleges and universities have been forced to introduce changes in management, by adopting a variety of management techniques in pursuing economy, efficiency, effectiveness and quality. Educational establishments have mission statements, business plans, devolved budgets, PIs and more managerial staff. The reforms have had a profound effect on TPM in all educational institutions. Although people management issues did not figure explicitly in the planning of educational reforms (Keep, 1993), they have been prominent elements in their implementation (Seifert and Ironside, 1993). As educational institutions are encouraged to operate more autonomously in employment matters, new approaches to people management are replacing the traditional system, which was formerly conducted at national and LEA levels.

People Management in Schools

In 1994, there were 129 LEAs in England, Wales and Scotland employing over 1.2 million people in almost 30 000 maintained schools. In addition, there were 820 GMS schools employing some 10 000 teachers (Pearson, 1994; School Teachers Review Body (STRB), 1994; Scottish Office Central Statistics (SOCS), 1994). The overall expenditure was estimated at £18 billion, with £11 billion spent on employing about 480 000 teachers.

The workforce and the unions

Schools are highly labour intensive. Apart from teachers, schools employ administrative, technical and manual staff, child psychologists, educational advisers and peripatetics such as swimming and music instructors. In 1994, there were around 23 000 nursery and primary schools and 4500 secondary schools (STRB, 1994, SOCS, 1994). There are approximately eight teachers per primary school and 51 per secondary school (Ironside *et al.*, 1993). Teachers also work in special schools, unattached units, on supply or as peripatetic staff. Women account for about 80 per cent of primary teachers and 60 per cent of secondary teachers. However, they represent less than half of primary heads and about a fifth of secondary heads. Ethnic minority groups are also under-represented in comparison with their numbers in the total population, comprising less than two per cent of the profession (Commission for Racial Equality, 1988).

The non-teaching workforce is very diverse. There are school-based staff, directly employed by schools and LEAs, and there are those in school services which the local authorities are now required to put out to tender. The former group includes administrative, clerical and technical staff, nursery assistants and manual staff. The latter group, in services now subject to CCT, include cleaners, catering and maintenance staff. They may now be employed by independent private contractors or, if tenders are awarded in-house, by local authority DSOs. Many non-teaching staff are women employed on part-time and term-time contracts.

Schools have always been highly unionized, with union density at around 80 per cent (Beatson and Butcher, 1993). Along with nurses, teaching remains the most highly unionized of all the qualified professions (Sinclair *et al.*, 1993b). Within the school workforce, there are 10 teaching unions. Since the creation of UNISON in 1993, non-teaching staff have been represented predominantly by three main unions: UNISON, the Transport and General Workers Union (TGWU) and General Municipal and Boilermakers (GMB).

The two largest classroom teaching unions are the National Union of Teachers (NUT) and National Association of Schoolmasters and Union of Women Teachers (NAS/UWT). These have memberships of about 244 000 and 213 000 respectively and are both TUC affiliates (Certification Office, 1995). The Association of Teachers and Lecturers (ATL), formerly the Assistant Masters and Mistresses Association, with a membership of 169 000, is not in the TUC and tends to represent teachers in ex-grammar schools and the private sector. The remaining smaller unions, the Professional Association of Teachers (PAT), National Association of Head Teachers (NAHT), Secondary Heads Association (SHA), Scottish Secondary Teachers Association, Association of Head teachers in Scotland and National Association of Teachers of Wales have reported memberships of about 41 000, 39 000, 8000, 7000, 1000 and 3000 respectively. The largest teaching union in Scotland is the Educational Institute of Scotland, with over 49 000 members.

Each teacher union has different traditions, policies and political orientations. These differences reflect the origins, histories and long-standing divisions in the teaching workforce. 'Inter-union conflict between teachers' unions is deeply rooted in differing conceptions of status, professionalism, and the legitimacy of industrial action' (Winchester, 1983, p. 162). Such divisions have undoubtedly impacted on teacher union membership and effectiveness.

There was growth in union membership, particularly in the secondary sector, in the postwar period. Since 1980, however, there has been a considerable redistribution of members amongst the unions. Between 1979 and 1992, the NUT suffered the effects of damaging internal political rows and a series of largely ineffective industrial disputes, with its membership falling by more than 70 000 (Farnham and Giles, 1995a; Seifert 1989; Seifert and Ironside, 1993; Sinclair *et al.*, 1993b). In contrast, the smaller, moderate non-TUC unions experienced membership growth, with the biggest increase of 54 000 members exhibited by the ATL. Union densities remain relatively high in teaching but unions are experiencing challenges to their organization, as government persists with its school management reforms.

Traditional people management and the LEAs

For much of the postwar period, schools were managed under a tripartite system, involving central government through the Department of Education and Science (DES) – now the Department for Education (DFE) – the LEAs and teaching profession, represented by the teacher unions. In Scotland, government was represented by the Scottish Office Education Department (SOED). The DES and SOED set educational policy and determined strategic issues, such as national staffing requirements, entry qualifications to the profession, numbers recruited on initial teacher training and the national educational budget. Policy was administered and implemented by LEAs, with schools involved in operational school management.

The LEAs, particularly in England and Wales, had considerable authority. They had a statutory obligation to execute educational policy and provide compulsory schooling up to the age of 15 and, after 1973, 16. Each LEA was required to provide sufficient places, teachers and non-teaching staff, buildings, equipment and ancillary services to meet the educational needs of its area. LEAs were the major educational providers, with responsibility for most schools in their areas, including nursery, primary, middle, secondary and special education. Schools managed by LEAs and publicly-financed were termed 'maintained' schools in England and Wales and public schools in Scotland. These maintained schools included schools established by LEAs and voluntary schools.

LEAs allocated budgets to schools, managed reorganizations, mergers and closures and assumed primary responsibility for staffing and people management issues. LEAs were the employers of all staff in the maintained sector. They determined the numbers and levels of staff, controlled appointments and promotion, redeployed staff to meet fluctuating school rolls and provided training and staff development. LEAs also implemented pay and conditions of service, negotiated at national and local levels.

The people management functions of the LEA were carried out by education officers in education departments.

Decisions were taken by committees of elected councillors and co-opted members, advised by LEA officials. Local rules and procedures, mainly interpreting national policies and guidelines, were developed to standardize practices, secure a stable industrial relations climate and achieve effective educational provision. The system was highly centralized and bureaucratic, with education officers taking most personnel decisions to ensure the consistent implementation of national, regional and local staffing policies.

Within the tripartite system, teacher unions played a prominent role particularly in determining pay and conditions of service, at both national and LEA levels. They also assumed a major role in the resolution of individual and collective disputes locally. Teachers participated in determining the curriculum, through national examination boards and within schools. The day-to-day running of schools was the responsibility of head teachers and their deputies, with governors occasionally assisting in school management decisions. Heads and governors traditionally had little authority in people management, with LEA officers usually intervening in personnel matters as soon as they arose.

People management under schemes of devolved school management

During the 1980s and 1990s, the TPM system has been transformed. In Scotland, there have been moves to decentralize managerial authority and people management. This process started with the School Boards (Scotland) Act 1988 and was extended, in 1992, through the consultation paper, *Devolved School Management: Guidelines for Progress* (SOED, 1992). The guidelines clearly devolve financial and managerial responsibility from education authorities to head teachers, with a consultative role for 'School Boards'. All primary and secondary schools are expected to have implemented DSM schemes between 1994 and 1996. Under these schemes, head teachers and School

Boards are to assume control over staffing and at least 80 per cent of the school's education budget is to be devolved to schools. In addition, under the Self Governing Schools (Scotland) Act 1989, Scottish schools can now also opt out of LEA control. However, by 1994, only one school had done so.

In England and Wales, the changes are more advanced. The ERA 1988 introduced LMS and GMS and removed responsibility for most people management from LEAs. Schools applying for GMS were given the opportunity to opt out from LEA control and receive their funding directly from the DFE. Schools choosing to remain under LEAs moved to LMS status over a four-year period, from 1990 to 1994, with the largest schools being the first to change. Under LMS, LEAs delegate most of the educational budget directly to schools, with governors and heads having direct responsibility for school expenditure. Governors and head teachers also have greater responsibility for staffing and people management.

LMS budgets are allocated according to a system of 'formula funding', based largely on types and numbers of pupils. At least 95 per cent of the educational budget is devolved directly to schools (Sinclair *et al.*, 1993a), with the rest retained by the LEA, for the provision of central services. Delegation of the budget to schools means that governors and heads have gained substantial controls over staff at the expense of LEAs. Although governing bodies are still bound by some national and local collective agreements, they now have much more autonomy over people management issues. This means that decisions on staffing levels, staff mixes, recruitment and selection, promotions, redeployments, elements of pay and training and development are devolved to schools, to meet local needs. Since about 70 per cent of a school's budget goes on staffing, this is a highly significant development, providing opportunities and choices in taking people management decisions.

Formula funding, linked to pupil numbers, has introduced market forces into schooling by encouraging schools to compete for pupils like businesses in the market place.

The rationale is that successful schools will attract more pupils and be rewarded with more resources, whilst poor schools will face the threats of diminishing resources and possible closure. Governors and head teachers are concerned to retain or increase their school's share of the pupil market and need to manage their staff efficiently and get good academic results. As heads have been given more responsibility and authority over staff, they have become school managers and many have adopted private-sector management techniques and personnel practices. Those head teachers unwilling or unable to take on this new role have left the profession, whilst some reluctant heads have resisted the imposition of change. The tide has been too strong to stop, and a new people management system in schools is emerging.

LEAs remain the employers of teachers and non-teaching staff. There are still some staffing policies determined nationally but increasingly these set minimum standards and give more scope for local variations and interpretation. Decisions about staffing, grading and payment are taken by school governors and there is more variation than in the past. The role of LEAs is limited, though in some areas they provide consultancy and advisory services to locally-managed and GMS schools.

The new system which is emerging is paradoxically both more centralized and de-centralized than in the past. Teachers have less autonomy and control over their jobs, what they teach and how they teach, such that many claim that they are being de-professionalized. The national curriculum, testing and standard assessment procedures, monitored by the Office of Educational Standards (OFSTED), has led to a massive increase in centralization. On the other hand, decentralizing management to governing bodies has resulted in less bureaucracy and more flexibility in the ways people are managed and rewarded. However, where flexible employment practices have been used to ease budgetary constraints, many staff have experienced work intensification, deterioration in terms and conditions and threats to job security (Sinclair *et al.*, 1993a and b; 1994; Healy, 1994). Decentralization is thus leading to wide variations in people management. What happens increasingly depends on governors and the skills of school managers.

Terms and Conditions in Schools

Until the late 1980s, the pay of teachers and non-teachers was determined by collective bargaining. The teachers' negotiating forum in England and Wales was called the Burnham Committee, in Scotland the Scottish Joint Negotiating Committee (SJNC), with collective bargaining for non-teaching staff conducted in local authority NJCs. In 1987, Burnham was replaced by a pay review body (PRB), known as the Interim Advisory Committee (IAC). The IAC, in turn, was superseded by the School Teachers Review Body (STRB) in 1991. Collective bargaining for teachers in Scotland and all non-teaching staff remains largely unchanged.

Collective bargaining

From 1919 until 1987, the Burnham Committee was responsible for teachers' pay. Burnham was a form of Whitleyism, whose principal purpose was to promote 'joint co-operation' centrally between employers and unions through a consensus approach to industrial relations. Union representatives forming the staff side panel met regularly with the employers (LEAs) or the management side to negotiate matters of common concern. Decisions were taken on the basis of a 'majority decision of each side voting separately' (Farnham and Pimlott, 1995, p. 162) and, in the event of agreement not being obtained, independent arbitration could be used. LEAs and the unions consequently played equally important roles in decision-making.

Burnham Committees for elementary and secondary teachers were established in 1919 and were reconstituted in 1944. The Burnham 'main' Committee was set up by the Remuneration of Teachers Act 1965 (RTA 1965). The composition of the teachers' and management panels of Burnham for primary and secondary teachers was determined by the Secretary of State. Membership of the teachers' panel varied, according to fluctuations in union membership. The panels incorporated representatives of the main teacher associations, local authority associations and DES. The national agreements determined by Burnham were legally binding on LEAs, with little scope for local variations.

During the 1970s and 1980s, Burnham increasingly experienced problems reaching settlements. Deep-seated divisions within the employer and staff panels inhibited the bargaining process. In practice, more time was spent arguing and disagreeing than in negotiating (Seifert, 1989; Seifert and Ironside, 1993). Teachers' pay levels fluctuated in relation to other occupational groups, with prolonged falls followed by catching-up awards. Low pay, reduced funding for education and government's continual attempts to link teachers' pay increases to their performance and duties frequently created the conditions for industrial unrest and arbitration decisions. This contributed to increasing dissatisfaction with the Burnham arrangements, throughout the 1980s (DES, 1987), culminating in the abolition of Burnham in 1987, after prolonged disputes between the employers and teachers in 1984 and 1985–86.

Conditions of service for teachers in England and Wales were negotiated separately from pay. These originally took place in the Working Group on Teacher/Employer Relations and, from 1974, in the Council of Local Education Authorities and School Teachers (CLEA/ST). This included all the unions and LEAs on Burnham but excluded government representation. The agreements, reached in CLEA/ST, were codified in the 'Burgundy Book', covering terms of appointment, dismissal, leave of absence, medical fitness, insurance, travelling and grievance and discipline procedures. They did not cover teachers' duties or working time. LEAs were expected to apply the Burgundy agreements to all permanent teachers, which were used in conjunction with local conditions.

In Scotland, determination of pay and conditions for teachers still follows a Whitley style of bargaining, comprising representatives from the unions – the staff side – and LEAs and the SOED. Bargaining takes place within the statutory SJNC. As with Burnham, pay and conditions negotiated nationally by the SJNC are legally binding, with limited scope for local negotiations. The national agreements on pay and conditions for teaching staff are set out within the Schemes of Salaries and Conditions of Service.

Traditional Whitleyism also remains largely intact amongst non-teaching staff. Manual and non-manual staff continue to have their pay and conditions negotiated nationally through NJCs, supplemented by local agreements. For manual staff, these are determined by the NJC for Local Authorities' Services and for non-manual workers by the NJC for APT&C staff. Conditions for manual workers are contained in the 'White Book' and for non-manuals within the 'Purple Book' (see Chapter 5).

Teachers' pay and conditions in England and Wales since 1987

The IAC, set up to replace Burnham, was a PRB with a statutory, independent panel appointed by government to make recommendations to the Secretary of State on teachers' pay and conditions. Recommendations were made on the basis of evidence submitted by the unions, employers and DES. For the first time, teachers' pay and conditions were determined together and the new statutory conditions of service specified the number of working days and hours of work. The nationally prescribed terms and conditions were set out in the School Teachers Pay and Conditions Documents, which replaced the Burnham reports. The IAC was replaced by the STRB.

The STRB was supported by five of the six teaching unions, on the grounds that PRBs provide benefits to both

workers and government (Saran, 1992). The STRB is intended to reduce industrial unrest and the difficulties
arising from negotiation, whilst enabling government to
control education funding and provide a voice for teacher
unions in the pay determination process (Saran, 1992;
Sinclair *et al.*, 1993b; Seifert and Ironside, 1993). The initial effect of the STRB has been to move towards setting
minimum national rates, to be adjusted locally to meet
variations in local labour markets. The advent of the PRB
has also coincided with changes in the pay structure.

Previously, there was a multi-scale pay structure consisting of four incremental salary scales. Scale one was
the minimum entry scale into the profession and positions on other scales depended on qualifications, responsibility and experience. The salary structure was based on
a unit total system. Each school was given a unit total
and assigned to a school group, which affected the salary scales on which teachers were paid and the number
of promoted posts. The unit total related to size of school
and pupils' age range. Generally, larger secondary schools
received the highest unit totals. Hence secondary teachers
were paid higher salaries and had more opportunities
for promotion than teachers in other schools.

This was replaced in January 1991 with a single 10-
point standard scale for all classroom teachers and spot
salaries for heads and deputies. Appointment of teachers
on the 10-point scale was at the discretion of governing
bodies but was dependent on qualifications, age, experience and the school's recruitment needs (DFE, 1994a).
Almost immediately the new system had been introduced,
spot salaries for heads were replaced by a single 51-point
pay spine which was not incremental but consisted of
salary ranges based on the old school groups. Once again,
boards of governors had discretion on heads' salaries but
were guided by criteria set down by the IAC (Saran, 1992;
STRB, 1993).

In conjunction with the introduction of the standard
scale for classroom teachers, the IAC developed a system of five levels of incentive allowances. These were to
be awarded to at least 55 per cent of classroom teachers

in each school. They were to be given for additional responsibility, teaching children with special needs, recruitment and retention problems and outstanding teaching ability. Further discretionary pay was introduced in 1991, including discretionary points for those on the top of their scale and incremental enhancements. These were to be distributed at the discretion of heads and governing bodies.

Since the 1990 pay settlement, a number of developments can be observed. First, there has been a rise in the size of incentive allowances compared with mainscale increases. Second, there have been relatively higher percentage awards for heads and deputies than for classroom teachers. Third, heads and deputies have received accelerated spinal point increases for additional responsibilities (Seifert and Ironside, 1993; Sinclair *et al.*, 1993a and 1993b; STRB, 1993). These developments appear to offer greater flexibility in the pay structure but also provide additional evidence of a general move towards minimum rate setting, with further opportunities for rewarding individuals differentially at school level.

In reviewing selective pay provisions for teachers, the STRB concluded that head teachers were not making full use of the opportunities for enhancing individual pay (STRB, 1993). Although 57 per cent of standard scale teachers had received incentive allowances, only 44 per cent of teachers in primary schools had. Further, many head teachers avoided using discretionary payments due to insufficient school funds, fear of divisiveness or lack of understanding. The STRB noted the reluctance to reward classroom teaching, with 86 per cent of incentive allowances being awarded for extra responsibilities and only one per cent for classroom performance. On the basis of this information, the STRB proposed further reforms to the pay structure for all teaching staff.

In 1993, a new extended 18-point salary spine was introduced, incorporating 'point scores' allowances. Points are now determined on the basis of: qualifications; experience; responsibilities; special educational needs; recruitment and retention factors; and excellence of classroom performance. The objective of the new system is to improve the motivation and retention of teachers. In addition, the extension of the pay spine is aimed to provide teachers with a further incentive to work to the top. There is potential, however, for more localized conflict in schools over issues of status as a consequence of recent pay and funding reforms (Sinclair *et al.*, 1993b).

The new funding system calculates school budgets for each LEA on the basis of the average teacher's salary rather than covering actual costs of teachers' salaries, which has created financial inequalities for comparable schools. Schools with older, more experienced staff, with higher than average salaries, are facing greater budgetary constraints. In some schools, budgetary pressures have been aggravated by GMS. GMS schools have received extra funding for capital projects, arguably at the expense of LMS. Schools experiencing greater budgetary pressures appear unable to make full use of flexible pay and resort to redundancy, restructuring and redeployment to minimize costs and employ staff more flexibly, with many working longer hours or shorter hours for less pay (Sinclair *et al.*, 1993a and b, 1994; Healy, 1994). However, although budgetary constraints may inhibit use of discretionary payments, they do not appear to be the only factor. Indeed, the Audit Commission (1994) identified schools, with unspent balances of 3.5 to 15 per cent of budgets, which had not made discretionary payments.

Post-Professional Training and Appraisal in Schools

Many reforms introduced into schools over the past decade have grown out of concern to improve the quality of educational provision (Seifert, 1989; Saran, 1992; Sinclair *et al.*, 1993b; Tomlinson, 1993). These concerns have not been the prerogative of any one government and have been on the agenda of both the Conservative and Labour parties since the great 'Education Debate', initiated at Ruskin College in 1976. That debate created a forum in which growing criticisms of the educational system were aired, including demands for higher standards, greater public accountability of schools and a firmer commitment to teaching the skills the country needed. Throughout the 1980s, successive governments have been committed to raising the quality of education, blaming 'industrial decline . . . lawless tendencies amongst the young and the moral crisis of work and authority' (Seifert, 1989, p. 240) on the teaching profession and education system.

Post-professional training and development

Training and staff development in schools have not always been recognized as important by government, LEAs or teachers (Tomlinson, 1993) but they became central to the drive for quality and improved educational standards after 1980. Conservative governments used in-service education and training (INSET) as a vehicle for educational change, to encourage teachers to adopt new objectives and methods in schooling.

Until the 1960s, it was thought that a teacher's initial education and training was sufficient to last an entire teaching career. There was a national training budget, to which all LEAs contributed, but not all LEAs were committed to post-professional training. As a result, training and professional development depended more on the commitment of individual teachers than on the authorities. Following the James report (1972), greater emphasis was placed on post-professional training (DES, 1972). Many of its proposals were taken up in the white paper, *Education: A framework for expansion* (DES, 1972) which stated that expansion of INSET was essential for future quality of the teaching profession. INSET became more school-based and intended training to meet the needs of schools and the educational system, as well as the professional needs of individual teachers (DES, 1977). It was planned to extend INSET from 4500 participants, in 1971, to 18 500 by 1981.

In 1983, the white paper, *Teaching Quality* (DES, 1983), embarked on a centrally directed programme of training.

INSET was expanded and specific grants, known as Education Support Grants (ESGs), were introduced in 1985 to encourage training in specific areas. In 1983, the Technical and Vocational Education Initiative (TVEI) funded by the Department of Employment was introduced. This was primarily targeted at non-academic 14–18 year olds and provided specific grants to LEAs and schools for TVEI in-service training. This became known as TRIST (TVEI-related in-service training). Under TRIST, LEAs and schools had to bid for contracts and monitor results against set criteria. As with ESGs, this specific grant provided government with opportunities to centralize control over IN-SET. It thus found the specific grant a useful model for further INSET programmes.

In 1986, government set up the Local Education Authority Training Grants Scheme (LEATGS). Since then, both the LEATGS and ESG scheme have been run side-by-side. In 1990, a new INSET scheme was introduced – Grants for Educational Support and Training (GEST). GEST is designed to oversee the entire INSET programme and coordinate individual LEATGS funds and ESGs. Under GEST, INSET funds are provided directly to schools from the DFE's national 'school effectiveness' training budget. Schools now have to meet and manage the costs of all INSET activities attended by teachers. They are required to evaluate teachers' training needs annually and produce staff development plans, available for inspection under the quadrennial inspection system. For 1994–95, the total planned expenditure for GEST was £271 million (DFE, 1994b.).

The introduction of teacher in-service days, under the TPCA 1987, allows teachers to undertake more training within schools (Emerson and Goddard, 1993) and, in the last few years, INSET has received a higher profile. However, it can present management problems. Staff on IN-SET are absent from the classroom and, with increasing workloads, there is an opportunity-cost to training. In future, such problems may well hinder in-service training.

Schools have also been urged to recognize the value of non-teaching staff, whose training has traditionally been neglected. Since LMS, schools have been encouraged to make use of LEA training for administrative staff in IT and financial management. However, take-up has been patchy. Although HM's Inspectorate's study, *Non-Teaching Staff in Schools* (1992), identified a need to develop training opportunities for all staff within schools, very few schools to date have considered non-teaching staff in their staff development programmes (Emerson and Goddard, 1993).

Training for management

The decentralization of managerial authority in schools has placed greater emphasis on management skills. In Scotland, the SOED, as well as reviewing its programme of Management Training for Head Teachers and the training needs of School Boards, is urging LEAs to develop management training schemes for schools. Likewise in England and Wales, the STRB has consistently encouraged schools to focus on developing the quality of school management and the School Management Task Force, established by the DES in 1989, has also provided advice on how institutional management may be improved (DES, 1993). Both these bodies have stressed the importance of management training programmes for heads, deputies, teachers and support staff with managerial responsibilities. This is not least because 'the quality of leadership and management' (STRB, 1993, p. 38) has been identified as the 'pre-eminent factor underlying differences in educational outcomes between otherwise similar schools.'

In 1994, the STRB reported that 'there is [still] a need for a comprehensive range of training provision' (1994, p. 35). Although the quality of school management has improved since the ERA 1988, requirements for further improvements have been identified. The DFE has provided specific funding for management training which increased from £4 million in 1987–88 to £10 million in 1990–91 (DES, 1993). The DFE also funded specific training for governors. However, the take-up by heads and deputies has not been high because of the need for matching funds from LEAs. Government hopes the development of the independent inspection service, with the publication of performance measures, will establish benchmarks against which school performance can be evaluated and management developed (STRB, 1994).

Teacher appraisal

In the early 1980s, teacher appraisal was seen as central to the drive for enhanced teaching quality and performance. Sir Keith Joseph, then Secretary of State for Education, saw appraisals as an effective way of weeding out weak, incompetent teachers and, by relating pay to performance, a way of rewarding better teachers (Heywood, 1992).

In the 1983 [white paper] and the 1985 one, *Better Schools*, appraisal was emphasised as an important management tool. It was seen as assisting in more purposeful staff development and training, based on 'systematic assessment of every teacher's performance' (DES, 1983, para. 92). At a time of falling school rolls, appraisal was also seen to be important 'in supplying comprehensive and up-to-date information necessary for the . . . effective provision of professional support [staff]' and the deployment of teachers. Those with 'professional difficulties' could be 'identified for appropriate counselling; guidance and support' and where such assistance does not restore performance to a satisfactory level, 'the teachers concerned being considered for early retirement or dismissal' (DES, 1985b, para. 180).

In the 1985 white paper, a link with PRP was also emphasised but the government backed down. Sir Keith Joseph had come to realize that: 'the value of appraisal is far more in relation to career development, in-service training and promotion and is only indirectly linked with pay' (Heywood, 1992, p. 131). From 1986, LEAs and schools were required to set up staff appraisal systems and, following industrial unrest in 1985–86, the teaching profession was encouraged to sign the Advisory Conciliation and Arbitration Service agreement on appraisal. This sets down the principles upon which teacher appraisal should be developed.

A pilot project was carried out in six LEAs, directed by a National Steering Group consisting of representatives of employers, unions and DES. The findings were published in 1989, along with a parallel report of HM's Inspectorate. Government subsequently published plans to establish a national framework for appraisal in 1991, to be implemented by 1995. To date, the emphasis is on professional development but government is keen to consider establishing links, through performance appraisal, with pay and new PRP schemes. It has instructed the STRB to investigate such possibilities.

The teacher unions have consistently expressed reservations about appraisals and rejected the notion of linking appraisal with rewards. In particular, they have raised concerns about the practicality of evaluating performance in teaching and the problems of developing equitable, objective assessment criteria. Such reservations, however, have not prevented its introduction into schools. So far, however, the school sector has resisted the implementation of PRP. However, the STRB intends to report on the findings of its PRP pilot studies in 1995. The STRB wants a scheme measuring school rather than individual performance. The government, however, would prefer an individually based scheme to reward 'good teachers in poor schools but not poor teachers in good schools' (STRB, 1993, pp. 33–34).

Further and Higher Education

Post-school education is provided in a complex myriad of overlapping and diverse institutions, reflecting their disparate historical origins and growth. In England and Wales, it comprises some 460 FECs – consisting of 180 sixth-form colleges, 220 colleges of further education and 60 other colleges – and 75 universities (FEFC, 1992).

Scotland has no sixth-form colleges, its 46 FE establishments are linked with primary and secondary education and it has 12 universities. Northern Ireland, in turn, has its own FE system and two universities. There is also one 'independent' or private university in the UK, located at Buckingham in England.

Sixth form and tertiary colleges provide academic studies, leading primarily to advanced level (AL) qualifications and university entrance. The CFEs, or their equivalents, offer not only AL but also a wide range of vocational and professional qualifications below degree level, largely to part-time students. In 1994–95, it is estimated that there were 2.6 million students in FE colleges in England and Wales alone.

Until the FHEA 1992, there were 35 polytechnics in England and Wales, which had been created as non-university, HE institutions, after Tony Crosland's binary speech in 1966. On 1 April 1992, the polytechnics were assimilated into the university sector, followed by the six former central institutions in Scotland. This group of institutions is sometimes referred to as the 'new universities', in contrast to the 'traditional' or 'old' universities. Both groups of universities consist of highly differentiated institutions and, in practice, a simple dichotomy between new and traditional establishments is misleading. Amongst the traditional universities, for example, there are 'ancient' universities, 'redbricks', 'plateglass' universities and former 'CATs' or colleges of advanced technology. The former polytechnics are equally diverse in terms of size, academic traditions and status.

In the UK universities, there were over 791 000 full-time and sandwich degree students in 1993–94 and over 337 000 part-time ones. Of these, some 615 000 were doing first degrees, about 97 000 were doing sandwich degrees, with the rest on non-degree courses. There were also over 171 000 part-time first degree students and over 102 000 part-time postgraduates (Committee of Vice-Chancellors and Principals, 1994).

The employers

Until 1993, the employers of teachers and non-teaching staff in the English and Welsh sixth-form colleges and the CFEs were local authorities. Similar arrangements existed in Scotland and Northern Ireland, based on their own systems of local government. Staff working in FE, in the CFEs and sixth-form colleges, were transferred out of the local authority sector on 1 April 1993, as a result of the FHEA 1992. These institutions are now classified as private, non-profit making bodies and are legally constituted as FECs. Each FEC has its own independent governing body and employs its own staff.

The employers in the former English and Welsh polytechnics were, until 1 April 1989, the local authorities. However, the polytechnics and CHEs were removed from LEA control by the ERA 1988 and incorporated as HECs, with their own independent governing bodies dominated by local business people. The 1988 Act made HECs responsible for employing and managing their own staff and constituted the Polytechnics and Colleges Funding Council sector (Farnham, 1988). The university HECs therefore are the employers of staff in the new universities.

Unlike HECs, the UK's 48 traditional universities have always been employers in their own right. They are governed largely by Royal Charters, rather than by Acts of Parliament, and have distinctive systems of governance and ways in which they manage academic staff.

Management styles

When under LEA control, both FE and HE institutions were dominated by bureaucratic rules and procedures, emanating from central government decisions, local government policies and national collective agreements. In essence, FE and HE outside the traditional universities was a national system administered locally, through LEAs. This structure of power and decision-making limited the authority of individual governing bodies and college principals.

Consequently, the style of leadership within institutions was predominantly administrative. Since incorporation, however, both FECs and HECs are becoming increasingly managerialist in the ways that they deal with institutional decision-making and the managing of teaching and non-teaching staffs (Warner and Crosthwaite 1995). With success resting with governing bodies and chief executives, FECs and HECs have had to become more strategic and focused in the ways in which they respond to their education markets. Senior managers now have to 'sell' courses, harbour institutional resources, satisfy student demands and manage staff effectively. This results in different managerial styles being adopted from those during the period of paternalist, bureaucratic, LEA control.

The contrast between management styles pre-incorporation and post-incorporation is most observable within the university sector. Whilst styles of management vary amongst the old universities (Jarrett, 1985), their traditional form of governance is summed up in the concept of 'collegiality'. Loosely defined, collegiality is the process whereby the old universities are managed as self-governing bodies, often through election to office, for fixed-terms, of their senior academic members. Examined objectively, collegiality is an essentially elitist, exclusive and inward-looking form of university governance, based on academic autonomy.

There are different forms of collegiality (Neave, 1991) but Eustace identifies five criteria associated with the collegial governance. These are: equality; democracy; self-validation; absence of non-scholars; and autonomy from society but especially the state. Collins (1994, pp. 3–4) identifies a number of factors likely to promote 'collegiality as [the] dominant approach to governance' within traditional universities. These are their: relatively long history; development on single sites; size and considerable wealth; vice-chancellors who are 'likely to be imbued with a collegial approach'; and committee structures which encourage a democratic and open approach to governance.

The new universities, in contrast, have what Collins

describes (pp. 4–5), as 'a managerialist approach to governance.' The reasons for this are complex but she posits a number of factors determining this. These include their: origins as external qualification-awarding bodies; growth by accretion; lack of financial reserves; governing bodies which are dominated by business people; long relationship with local government, based largely on a bureaucratic and hierarchical structure; and increase in central services supporting the academic function, with the number of support staff often 'considerably larger than the academic and research staff put together.'

There is evidence, however, that collegiality, even in traditional universities, is being challenged by a new managerial elite. This is in response to increased competition for the best students, quality staff and scarce research funding. In searching for vice-chancellors, universities are now likely to seek individuals who not only can command the intellectual respect of academic staff but also have entrepreneurial and managerial talents to lead large, complex organizations. Assessors on selection committees for the appointment of vice-chancellors, therefore, often look for unorthodox qualities in leading academics. According to one commentator, this includes (quoted in Authers, 1994, p. 12):

> The ability to promote and market the university [which] is extremely important, while at the same time having a clear conception as to what happens when managing a complex organisation.

Post-incorporation, concern has been expressed about the apparent weakening of public accountability and openness in the governance of colleges and new universities. With the removal of any obligation from FECs and HECs to have accountable and elected staff and student governors, or independent governors with knowledge of education, there have been tensions between senior managements – or the directorates – and staff in some institutions. In 1993–94, for example, after considerable debate and dissent, the vice-chancellors at Bournemouth University and the University of Portsmouth resigned over matters raised by staff, whilst the retiring vice-chancellor at Huddersfield was involved in controversy about his severance terms.

Rear (1994a; 1994b) writes that it has been claimed that government is seriously eroding academic autonomy and that 'managerialism', as a system of corporate control, is threatening academic freedom. He strongly refutes this, arguing that institutional autonomy is conditional upon fulfilling the purposes for which universities are funded. Any erosion of autonomy, he claims, has been 'largely prompted by the past reluctance of the universities to change and to serve the economy', as well as reluctance to 'give a satisfactory account of their stewardship of huge sums of taxpayers' money.' In his view, 'good management of the universities is essential as a defence against further erosion of their autonomy.' Provided there are safeguards to teach and research freely, he argues, it is the task of senior managers to be the 'defenders of academic faith', by ensuring the economic well-being of their institutions and managing the diverse demands made upon them in conditions of rapid change. Ultimately, Rear concludes, the economic viability of universities 'and the retention of [their] institutional autonomy depend upon effective management' (Rear, 1994a, p. 15).

The Workforce and the unions

The workforce in the FECs and HECs is diverse and segmented. It can be classified into management grades, teaching and research staff and non-teaching staff. Management grades are university directorates, senior managers of institutions or heads of department (HoDs), some of whom are professors. The career grades for teaching staff are lecturer in FE and lecturer and senior lecturer in the new universities, with senior lecturers (SLs) and principal lecturers (PLs) being promoted posts. The workforce in the traditional universities is classified as 'academic and academic related staff', 'clinical academic staff' (doctors and dentists) and 'non-teaching staff'. University teachers are normally recruited as lecturers and those promoted beyond the career grade are designated senior lecturers.

As in school teaching, union membership is high in FE and HE. The main union representing teachers in the English and Welsh FECs, and in Northern Ireland, is the National Association of Teachers in Further and Higher Education (NATFHE). In Scotland, teaching staff are largely represented by the respective College and University Lecturers Associations of the Educational Institute of Scotland (CLA/EIS, ULA/EIS). NATFHE has a long history and its origins can be traced back to its organization of 'technical teachers' in technical schools and technical institutes before the first world war (Farnham, 1974). In 1993, the TUC-affiliated NATFHE had some 76 000 members, about 85 per cent of whom were in FE, with the rest in new universities. A rival FE teachers union, not in TUC, is the ATL. It recruits most members in schools and sixth-form colleges. ATL's membership in FE is not known but it is a minority union.

Support staff in English, Welsh and Scottish FE undertake a wide range of clerical, administrative and technical duties and are recruited largely by the TUC-affiliated UNISON. This is the largest white-collar union in the UK, with members in all the public services and public utilities. Manual staff, such as caretakers, cleaners and kitchen staff, belong to general unions such as the TGWU or GMB.

Unions representing teaching and non-teaching staff in the new universities in England and Wales are identical with those in FE, because these institutions originated in the FE sector, with its 'seamless web' of overlapping FE and HE establishments. The major difference is the absence of ATL in the new universities. There is, however, a minority teachers' union in the new universities, with under 3000 members. This is the Association of University and College Lecturers (AUCL) which is a non-TUC affiliated body. It was formed in 1975 as the Association of Polytechnic Teachers, in competition with NATFHE's predecessor, the Association of Teachers in Technical

Institutions. Its aim was to get separate collective bargaining arrangements for polytechnic teachers (Farnham, 1975).

In the traditional UK universities, both academic and academic related staff, who are mainly senior university administrators, librarians and researchers, are represented by the Association of University Teachers (AUT). The AUT is a TUC-affiliated union with over 30 000 members in 1993. During 1994, the AUT joined with NATFHE to form a higher education 'Confederation' whose primary aim is to provide a common front on HE issues, whilst protecting their own spheres of influence in each of their sectors. It is a significant feature of the AUT that the bulk of its membership is not teachers but researchers and non-teaching staff. This makes it quite a different organization from that of NATFHE, which consists overwhelmingly of teachers (Farnham, 1991b; 1994a). Other features of the AUT are that it recruits in Scotland, has a simpler structure and occupies a centrist position in trade union politics. Remaining non-teaching staff in traditional universities are represented by UNISON, MSF, AEEU, UCATT, TGWU and GMB.

The Personnel Function in Colleges and Universities

The TPM and industrial relations policies of the CFEs and polytechnics were determined centrally by the DES in consultation with the employers and teacher unions, and within the framework of national collective bargaining machinery. These policies were then implemented, interpreted and monitored by LEAs. LEAs had three roles as: filters and executors of national policies; employers of staff; and agents of operational personnel policy for groups of FE and HE institutions.

With 'manpower' policies determined centrally, and operational policy decided within LEAs, the TPM function within polytechnics and colleges was a weak one, even when some institutions grew larger and more complex to manage. The tasks performed by specialist personnel staff, where they existed, were essentially administrative and welfare-centred and focused on keeping personnel records, applying employment procedures and reporting on manpower issues to the LEA. The role was not a dissimilar one in the old universities. Since operational policy was determined by each LEA, policy was implemented, with relatively little variation, across the FE and HE institutions within each local authority, although the polytechnics were generally treated as more mature institutions by the LEAs than were the colleges. But institutions had only limited discretion in implementing policy. What remains of TPM within FECs and HECs is a commitment to the public-service ethic and some vestiges of the local authority ways of doing things.

There are, therefore, significant differences between the personnel function as it was in colleges and polytechnics and what it is now in the incorporated colleges and new universities. Changes have taken place in the old universities too. First, under LEA control, FE and HE institutions had little autonomy on people management issues, although this varied amongst LEAs depending upon the geographical proximity and relationship of the LEA to individual institutions. Second, institutions had to defer to LEA personnel management guidelines, resulting in personnel management structures which were determined at LEA level, duplicated at institutional level and provided standardized practices within individual institutions. Third, personnel decision-making was slow and, with the legal employer being the LEA, most negotiation, consultation and communication between management and unions took place at LEA level.

Since incorporation, the first and probably most fundamental change in people management practices has been the drive by employers to modify contractual relations with their staffs, especially permanent teachers. At the time of writing, this has been successfully achieved within the new universities but not in the FECs, who are in dispute with lecturers over the introduction of a new 'professional' contract (see below). There is, in short, more diversity in contractual relations between employers and staff within FE and HE, compared with when they were under LEA control. There was always, for example, a high proportion of part-timers working in FE and of research staff on fixed-term contracts in universities. But now contractual flexibility for teaching staff is being extended in both colleges and universities. Some universities, for example, or departments within them, are not recruiting teaching staff onto full-time contracts, because of financial constraints and curricula uncertainties. Instead, some staff are being offered fixed-term contracts of under two years' duration, annual part-time contracts and annual hours contracts, not necessarily renewable.

Second, with the devolution of responsibility for people management to institutional level, greater flexibility has also been introduced into employment decision-making and employment resourcing. Although these flexibilities have largely affected the managing of teaching and research staff, support staff are not exempt from these changes (Farnham, 1991a). Personal contracts of employment for senior academic and senior support staff in the new universities are now the norm, which was not the case whilst polytechnics remained under LEA control. Similarly, gradings for support staff are being used fluidly in responding to labour market pressures to recruit and retain staff. With the removal of LEA involvement, managing redundancy has been simplified too. Yet the effectiveness of devolving recruitment and selection decisions within institutions, both post and prior to incorporation, has been questioned (Partridge, 1994).

Third, there have been innovatory responses to equal opportunities by employers but the evidence does not suggest these initiatives have been particularly successful. Some colleges and universities have espoused policies on equal opportunities but there is little evidence that women, ethnic minorities or the disabled are being recruited or promoted to senior appointments in any significant numbers (Giles, 1992). Indeed, representation of these groups amongst college principals, university vice-chancellors, university professors, deans and heads of departments is poor.

Fourth, employers and governing bodies have discovered creative ways of managing pay and conditions within institutions. This has resulted in greater diversity of outcomes than in the past. For example, with senior academic staff now out of national pay agreements, such as college principals, university vice-chancellors and HoDs in the new universities, pay differentials between them and teaching and support staff have widened considerably. It has been shown, for instance, that 'six-figure pay and pensions packages are becoming commonplace for [university] vice chancellors', when the top of the salary scale for a university lecturer was £28 000 (Richards, 1995, p. 1). There has also been pay drift amongst HoDs in the new universities *vis à vis* teaching staff (Farnham and Giles, 1995b).

Fifth, in larger colleges and universities, personnel departments have increased in size and strategic importance and now employ a range of specialists dealing with industrial relations, training and health and safety. In recognizing unions locally, employers have set up institution-wide consultative and communication arrangements for dealing with representatives, sometimes on a single-table basis for involving academic and support staff. This means that decision-making is faster, with employers being able to deal directly with unions and individual staff at institutional level. There has also been an extension of staff development activity within institutions, through staff development officers, staff development units and external consultants. There are indications, too, that the importance of health and safety issues are being recognized by institutions and being addressed by specialists in personnel departments.

Sixth, compared with the past, the industrial relations issues discussed between employers and unions nationally are more limited, giving the employers more flexibility in policy determination and executive action locally (Farnham, 1992). With institutional budgets, controlling employment costs is of prime importance to FECs and HECs. This requires better management information and communication systems at institutional level. Thus incorporation has facilitated the development of institutional personnel information systems, using the latest computer hardware and personnel software. To promote employee involvement, there is also evidence of direct communication channels between institutions and individual staff, such as newsletters, briefing meetings and cascading information downwards.

These developments in the personnel function have been interpreted by those advocating a strategic approach to people management in HE and FE institutions as a necessary condition for responding to the managing of change. According to Crosthwaite and Warner (1995, p. 6), 'the challenge for ... newly independent institution[s] is to develop a human resource strategy which is in line with [their] mission statements and institutional aims.' In helping to shift her employer from a local authority culture to a corporatist one, for example, the Personnel Director of Kingston University claims that there were, and remain, two core objectives within the corporate plan relating to the managing of people: maintaining and developing a flexible, competent and well motivated staff and providing services to support all students and staff. The main human resources areas identified for action within the institution were (Lanchbery, 1995, p. 23f):

- To move away from the local authority culture as quickly as practical ...
- To give local managers as much power as possible within an agreed personnel framework.
- To articulate the role of governors in human resource matters, in particular to ensure that they would not act in the same way as local authority councillors, but would act strategically and allow managers to manage.
- To acknowledge that the trade unions would remain part of the scene, but to stress the importance of the direct relationship between managers and staff and the importance of the individual as well as the collective.
- To gain the ability to change the reward package as appropriate to the needs of the institution.
- To gain the ability to change the organization relatively quickly to be able to respond to the requirements of external influences.

This, Lanchbery argues, requires a 'strong personnel function, not necessarily in numbers, but in expertise and the ability to deliver.'

Pay Determination in the Post-School Sector

Although FE and HE are re-converging, and there is now a unified and commonly-funded university system in the UK, the pay determination processes in the post-school sector are complex, due largely to historical factors. First, there is national pay bargaining for most staff, except university vice-chancellors and HoD grades and above in the new universities. Second, there are a multiplicity of bargaining units covering different staff groups in FE, the new universities and traditional universities. Third, collective bargaining is affected by national geography, with separate negotiating machinery for FE in England and Wales, Scotland and Northern Ireland.

Prior to incorporation on 1 April 1993, negotiating arrangements for FE teachers in England and Wales were conducted in the National Joint Council for Lecturers in Further Education (NJCLFE), established by the TPCA 1987 after the repeal of the RTA 1965. The 1987 Act enabled LEA employers and teacher unions on the former Burnham FE Committee, mainly NATFHE, to set up their own free-standing, national collective bargaining machinery which, unlike Burnham, was outside any statutory provision. The reconstituted NJCLFE – covering at this time the polytechnics and CHEs – had an independent, non-voting chair and the remit to negotiate on all terms and conditions. It also provided binding arbitration, with the consent of both sides, where negotiations broke down (Farnham, 1992). Negotiations on pay and conditions for non-teaching staff in English and Welsh FE took place nationally in separate local government bargaining machinery.

These arrangements have been superseded by new negotiating bodies for teaching and non-teaching staff in FECs and sixth-form colleges. These are the Lecturers National Negotiating Committee, Management Spine Negotiating Committee – for management grade staff – and national negotiating committees for administrative and manual staff. The employers are represented by the Colleges Employers' Forum (CEF), an employers' association speaking on behalf of most of the FECs, and staff by the main teaching and non-teaching unions, NATFHE, ATL and UNISON.

In Scotland, with its different system of local government, FE teachers' pay and conditions were traditionally negotiated collectively, at a national level, through the Scottish FE Joint Negotiating Committee (SFEJNC). However, as of January 1995, the SFEJNC has effectively been abandoned. The pay and conditions of FE teachers are now determined locally by each FE college. Since all non-teaching staff are local authority employees, their pay and conditions are determined by local government collective bargaining machinery. Salaries for FE colleges in Northern Ireland, in turn, are negotiated in the Northern Ireland Further Education Committee. Minor differences exist but scales in Northern Ireland have for many years been the same as those in England and Wales.

In the new universities in England and Wales, collective bargaining machinery is under review because of the need to harmonize arrangements with the traditional universities. But currently, national bargaining for teachers up to HoD grade takes place in the Lecturers National Negotiating Committee (LNNC). There are also an APT&C National Negotiating Committee and a Manual National Negotiating Committee. The LNNC was originally constituted as the Polytechnics and Colleges National Negotiating Committee, in February 1989, comprising three common interest groups. The six unions represented on it were NATFHE, AUCL, NALGO, MSF, TGWU and GMB. At this time, the body representing HECs was the Polytechnics and Colleges Employers' Forum (PCEF), whose role has now been taken over by the Universities National Employers' Committee.

In the new universities, the pay of academic staff above PL grade, such as deans, heads of department and professors – HoD grade staff – is individually based, as it is for senior staff and professors in traditional universities. A study by Farnham and Giles (1995b) confirms that 60 per cent of the 30 new universities surveyed paid 'spot' salaries, within clearly defined bands, to individual HoDs. Salaries at other institutions appeared to be either within incremental scales or, less usually, spot salaries without bands. Some three-quarters of the institutions reported that PRP had been implemented for HoDs over the previous two to three years but that there was no clarity 'about exactly how PRP works' (p. 10). Indeed, despite performance reviews, the criteria used to determine annual pay increases for individual HoDs did not appear to be formally stated at any institution. However, the criteria believed to be used in practice included individual performance, job responsibilities, the nationally negotiated settlement, local agreement and inflation.

Despite the removal of HoD grades from national pay negotiations, Farnham and Giles (1995b) show that in 53 per cent of the institutions surveyed some form of local 'collective machinery' exists for determining the overall pay increases for HoDs. In other institutions, pay increases for HoDs are determined solely by individual negotiation or unilaterally by senior management. Where overall pay increases are collectively determined, this generally involves a discrete HoDs negotiating team or group, sometimes with local union involvement, which meets regularly with institutional management over the academic year. The survey shows that 'there has been a fragmentation and balkanisation of pay, pay determination and the ways in which HoDs are managed within the new universities' (p. 14).

Like the new universities, negotiating arrangements in the traditional universities are under review. Collective bargaining came relatively late for university teachers, during the 1970s. Until 1993, salaries of non-clinical teachers were determined by national two-stage negotiations, first in Academic Salaries Committee A, between the university authorities and the AUT, then in Academic Salaries

Committee B, consisting of representatives from Committee A and government. Similarly, the pay of clinical teachers was determined within the Clinical Staff Salaries Joint Committee, taking account of salaries in the NHS (UCNS, 1988). Now university teachers have a Joint National Council, with representatives from the Universities and Colleges Association and the AUT. This determines the pay of university teachers but conditions of service are determined entirely in each university.

Apart from academic related staff, bargaining machinery for non-teaching staff in traditional universities is organized at three levels. The Central Council for Non-Teaching Staff in Universities acts as an umbrella for four functional JNCs: the Joint Committee for Clerical and Certain Related Administrative Staffs; Joint Committee for Technical Staffs; Joint Committee for Manual and Ancillary Staffs; and Joint Committee for Computer Staff. The terms and conditions determined by the JNCs are implemented in some universities, not all of them.

Conditions of Employment in Colleges and New Universities

Until 1989, there were three sets of conditions of employment for staff: for lecturers, support staff and manual workers. Since then, conditions of employment for staff in FE and the new universities have been disassociated. The changes have been more critical for manual workers and teaching staff than for support staff. Manual work, for example, has been subject to CCT, with the result that either it has been lost to the private sector or terms and conditions of staff have worsened to protect jobs.

Teaching staff

Lecturers in English FE are currently involved in a rancorous, long running dispute with the FECs, who want radical changes made to teachers' contracts of employment. What is at stake is what replaces the conditions of employment embodied in the 'Silver Book'. The Silver Book, negotiated over many years between LEAs and NATFHE, covers length and distribution of the academic year, teaching loads, contact hours, extra payments and other agreements. These include: sick pay, redundancy pay, conditions of tenure, maternity leave, consultation and negotiation, avoidance of disputes and facilities for union officials.

Under the Silver Book, the national scheme for conditions of employment provides for a maximum 38-week working year for lecturers or SLs: no more than 36 weeks of these should be teaching weeks. Teaching staff on the management spine may have to attend more than 38 weeks, subject to not less than 35 working days' annual leave, plus public holidays. A week should not exceed 30 hours, split into 10 morning, afternoon or evening sessions. Furthermore, lecturers cannot be required to teach more than 21 contact hours per week, on average. Teachers on the SL scale, with significant managerial responsibilities, should not exceed 18 hours teaching per week over the teaching year. For staff on the management spine some teaching is required, according to management content of the post.

Since September 1990, additional class contact hours in excess of the 21 hours weekly average can be required by the employers, up to a limit of two hours weekly. These additional hours have to be balanced by reductions in class contact at other times, to keep weekly hours within the average limits. Lecturers should not teach continuously for more than 14 weeks, whilst any continuous teaching between nine and 14 weeks should be followed by a break of at least two weeks. The national agreements provide for at least six weeks' summer leave for lecturers and SLs, plus leave at Christmas and Easter.

What the employers want, ever since the transfer of contracts of employment from the LEAs to FECs on 1 April 1993, is a 'professional' contract and more flexible workforce. When contracts of existing staff were transferred, staff were protected by section 26 of the FHEA 1992, the Acquired Rights Directive of the European Union and TUPE Regulations 1981. Initially, the employers sought to change contracts by national negotiations between the CEF and the unions. But the employers' demands were unacceptable, resulting in a protracted dispute which is unresolved at the time of writing.

In the model contract issued by the employers to new and promoted staff, teaching staff are 'expected to work flexibly and efficiently' and 'comply with any rules and regulations which the Corporation may from time to time issue'. They are also expected to work 'such hours as are reasonably necessary for the proper performance of [their] duties, with a minimum of 37 hours per week', including weekend working and other non-social hours – with 'time off in lieu.' Staff 'will be required to participate in a staff appraisal scheme approved by the Corporation' and, in addition to public holidays, will be entitled to 35 working days holiday per year. Redundancy entitlements are reduced from one year's to three months' notice. There is no specified teaching year and a possible weekly workload of 37 hours (College Employers Forum, 1993).

By mid-1995, the dispute had not been settled. The unions claimed that their members had held their ground, whilst the employers in contrast, though not fully united, claimed that 'most lecturers' in the 'majority of colleges' had signed the CEF's new style, flexible contract (*Times Educational Supplement*, 1995). This includes teaching staff appointed and promoted since incorporation but the proportion of other staff accepting the new contract was difficult to assess. According to the Chief Executive of the CEF, FE employers faced, during 1993–95, a period of intense conflict similar to that faced by HE employers earlier. He reported that DFE had declared its intention of using the 'two per cent holdback mechanism', previously applied in the HE sector in 1989–90 and 1990–91, to push through substantial contractual changes for college lecturers. (Ward, 1995, p. 169). This involved withholding two per cent of the recurrent lecturers' salary bill, until a settlement, satisfactory to both government and employers, had been achieved. In his view:

The challenge for the unions is to repel the encroachment of the 2 per cent conditions. Having failed to do so in higher education, few will give the unions much chance of success. The challenge for the DfE is to determine how far it should go in the application of the 2 per cent holdback mechanism.

There are no nationally defined conditions for teaching staff in traditional universities but the 35 new universities of England and Wales are covered by a national agreement. This was negotiated by the former PCEF and NATFHE, following a dispute between academic staff and the employers in 1990–91. In practice, however, local negotiations took place in most institutions, prior to the transfer of staff to new contracts and the introduction of the associated staff handbook. There are, therefore, variations in conditions of service, applying to academic staff locally. The main provisions of the national agreement include: a maximum 18 hours weekly and 550 hours annually of 'formal scheduled teaching'; a teaching year of 38 weeks including two administration weeks; and 35 days' annual leave, plus statutory days. The remaining time is spent on self-managed research and scholarly activities. There is also a contractual obligation to participate in local appraisal schemes, based on a national model providing for staff development.

Heads and professorial staff

HoD grade staff are no longer covered by nationally negotiated conditions of employment. Even prior to incorporation in 1989, one of the PCEF's central objectives was 'to deny negotiating rights to key senior staff' in the polytechnics and CHEs and the employers were successful in doing this (Farnham, 1992, p. 193). By 1995, although a national minimum for HoDs was still included in the national pay agreement, it had ceased in practice to have any operational effect, since *de facto* pay for these staff is now determined at institutional level.

All HoD grades are now on personal, institutional

contracts, determined locally by employers and senior management, though, in a few cases, NATFHE was involved
in drafting these contracts. Farnham and Giles' survey
(1995b) suggests 90 per cent of new universities surveyed
have institution-wide contracts, applicable to all HoD
grades. However, some respondents, when questioned
about the nature of these contracts, were sceptical about
standard arrangements. It was suspected that, although
it was institutional policy to employ one contract for all
HoDs, individualized contracts, containing new clauses
and improved terms and conditions, were being introduced for some HoDs, especially when new staff were
recruited (p. 9).

Staff Development and Appraisal in FE and HE

There has also been an expansion in training and development in FE, the new universities and traditional universities. According to the OECD (1987), few matters are
of greater importance to the future of colleges and universities than the quality, motivation and productivity of
their academic staff. This requires effective post-professional
training and staff development. Gunn (1987) identifies three
stages in this – prior to appointment, after appointment
and 'further stages' – and 10 components within it. These
are: (1) analysing staffing requirements; (2) meeting these
requirements; (3) recruiting and selecting staff; (4) induction training; (5) appraising performance; (6) counselling
staff: (7) supporting development; (8) providing incentives for good performance; (9) applying sanctions for
unsatisfactory performance; and (10) redeploying staff in
times of change.

The Universities Manpower Review Committee (UMRC,
1988) makes similar claims for non-academic staff. Its main
recommendation was that 'there must be a new major
investment in staff training' and 'as universities expand
their entrepreneurial activities they must look ahead to
identify staffing and skills needs in changing conditions'

(pp. 3 and 18). A key recommendation was that institutions should appoint staff development officers, with responsibility for monitoring and reporting activities. This appears to be happening in both traditional and new universities.

Despite the costs of staff development, facilities in FE and HE appear to be better funded than previously. Staff development officers have been appointed and larger universities have Educational Development Units. Most institutions have in-house career development programmes, ranging from induction to pre-retirement. There are also regional and national centres serving professional training needs. The CVCP's Universities Staff Development Unit organizes courses for university managers and administrators including: introductory, three-day courses for new entrants; one-week courses for middle managers, with five or more years' experience; and specialist courses for those in finance, marketing and estate management (Whitchurch, 1994).

Staff appraisal, linked to staff development, is now widespread within FE colleges and universities, for both academic and support staff. It has been agreed in national negotiations between employers and unions and is a condition of employment for most staff. Where staff appraisal existed previously, it was voluntary, informal, peer-based and poorly resourced. Now it is mandatory, formal and, generally, top-down, with more resources and commitment to it. How staff appraisal is structured, implemented and monitored, in practice, is a matter for local determination, between management and unions. Consequently, there appear to be variations in how appraisal has been agreed and applied within institutions. Yet what actually takes place within appraisal schemes may be less than that expected by government nationally and the employers locally.

In general, staff appraisal has three broad functions: 'those related to personnel management needs; those that are primarily concerned with improving current and future performance; and those which are essentially developmental' (Schofield, 1989, p. 2). The stated purpose of staff appraisal throughout FE and HE is to facilitate staff development. Most schemes state that appraisal does not exist to decide pay or promotion, nor is it linked with grievance or disciplinary procedures. The spirit of the schemes is to identify staff development needs and link them with departmental, faculty and institutional plans and resources. Some academic staff, however, are suspicious that it has covert objectives of monitoring staff performance and allocating rewards. The procedures involved require appraiser and appraisee to review past activities, set future objectives and agree a personal development plan for the appraisee. Appraisers are normally heads or professors.

The philosophy underpinning appraisal is the assumption that staff are entitled to open, objective two-way communications on their job tasks and staff development needs, in line with institutional plans and strategies. It is recognized that their success depends on four main factors. The first is the willingness of participants to make them developmental schemes, not judgmental ones. Second, schemes must promote equal opportunities, by being as objective and fair as possible and removing prejudice in the appraisal process. Third, appraisal interviews involve mutual agreement and commitment between the participants, not compliance by the appraisee alone. Fourth, appraisees must also feel ownership of the process and outcomes and be able to give honest and open feedback to appraisers on their completed tasks and objectives for the future. To what extent these criteria are being met is currently indeterminate.

Conclusion and Evaluation

The legislative and educational reforms of the 1980s and 1990s have presented a major challenge to TPM and industrial relations throughout education. The TPM system, where general staffing policies were negotiated nationally, amongst the DES, LEAs and teaching unions, and then implemented and interpreted locally by LEAs, in consultation with the unions, has been transformed. The introduction of LMS and GMS and the incorporation of FE and HE institutions have simultaneously weakened LEAs and the teaching unions, whilst strengthening the authority of the DFE at the centre and governing bodies locally. As school governing bodies have become directly responsible for a wider range of staffing and training issues, and the extent of budget delegation increases, LEAs are experiencing a continual reduction in authority and assuming an increasingly advisory and facilitating role. In GMS schools and FE and HE institutions, the LEAs have now relinquished their authority to governing bodies.

Governing bodies in schools, FECs and HECs have more flexibility in policy determination locally, resulting in less bureaucracy and faster decision-making than when staffing was under LEA control. As educational institutions are encouraged to operate more autonomously in employment matters, new and more varied people management approaches are emerging locally. These include performance management systems, appraisal systems, institution-based training systems, management development and more flexible payment systems, including PRP. Personnel departments in the FE and HE institutions have grown in size and strategic importance, in response to the range and extent of staffing, industrial relations and training issues now confronting senior management at institutional level.

Decentralization of managerial authority is also leading to variations in people management practices. In schools, FECs and HECs, in particular, manual and teaching staff have been the most affected, experiencing considerable changes in their contracts and wider variations in conditions of service. Manual work in schools, FE and HE has been subject to competition under CCT, with the result that terms and conditions have been changed to protect jobs. Where flexible patterns of employment have been sought to ease budgetary constraints and minimize costs, many employees have experienced work intensification, deterioration in terms and conditions and loss of job security. Some institutions, subject to increased competition for pupils, students and money, are also neglecting their staff development and training responsibilities. As local conditions vary, there are differences in the way people management systems and activities are agreed, implemented and managed.

With decentralization and additional competitive pressures, the effectiveness of institutional decision-making and the managing of staff increasingly depend on the composition of governing bodies and the skills and abilities of senior managers. In HE there is evidence that a new managerialist elite is emerging as independent governing bodies, dominated by local business people, assume greater control over staff and institutional governance. These changes are weakening public accountability and the openness of institutional governance, constraining professionalism and, in the old universities especially, challenging traditional collegiality.

In schools, the teaching unions have experienced a considerable loss of influence at national level with the abolition of national bargaining, the introduction of PRBs after 1987 and increasing balkanization of management authority under LMS and GMS. Although the unions are still recognized within schools and membership remains high, there appears to be a vacuum in union organization at school level.

Unions in FE and HE have also been challenged by recent developments. Changes in the structure, management and organization of FE and HE following, first, incorporation of colleges and polytechnics and, second, assimilation of the polytechnics into the university sector have brought considerable organizational and management problems to the unions. This is not least regarding issues of representation, membership retention and developing a common front on FE and HE issues. In addition, the unions, although still recognized within institutions, have had to adjust to new management initiatives, resulting from changes in management discretion and authority locally. Traditional forms of collective representation, at national and LEA level, have been challenged as institutional-wide consultative arrangements on a single-table basis have been developed within institutions, along with new methods of communication, dealing directly with individual employees. HoD grades in the new universities are no longer represented by nationally negotiated terms and conditions of employment at all.

It is clear that the educational reforms of the 1980s and 1990s are transforming the education sector. There are substantial differences between people management and industrial relations in the past, compared with the new regimes of locally-managed and GMS schools, incorporated colleges and reformed universities. Although there has been considerable change, the reforms continue and their full consequences are not yet entirely understood. Governing bodies, managers, staff and unions will have to go on responding to their changed responsibilities, in an era of continual educational reform.

CHAPTER 7

The Police

Sylvia Horton

The police service is the most recent public service to be subjected to the reforming zeal of Conservative governments. Between 1979 and 1984, there were major increases in police expenditure (Jones and Silverman, 1984), as government honoured its pledges to implement the Edmund-Davies report on pay and raised police establishments. These were part of a broader strategy to strengthen the police and win them over to government's law and order and industrial relations policies (Scraton, 1985; Nash and Savage, 1994).

Police reforms have taken a similar path to those in other public services. FMI came first, aimed at curbing waste and getting value for money. This was linked with all police forces adopting rational approaches to policy making through 'policing by objectives'. Home Office Circular 114/83 required all 'Chief Officers . . . to identify problems, set realistic objectives and clear priorities, keep those priorities and objectives under review, deploy staff and other resources in accordance with them, and provide themselves with the practical means of assessing the extent to which Chief Officers are achieving their objectives' (para. 15). Her Majesty's Inspectorate of Constabulary (HMIC), monitored and assessed performance and required all police forces to develop relevant performance measurements, PIs and financial and management information systems.

One strategy to reduce costs was civilianization and contracting out of services. A second was to improve performance through training and development, especially management training, linked to performance management. There was some resistance to these changes because policing and management 'are not terms which sit easily together'. More than any other public service, 'the policing function presents specific dilemmas as far as attempts to introduce coherent managerial approaches is concerned' (Leishman and Savage, 1993a, p. 211). This is due to the wide discretions exercised by police constables, the reactive nature of policing and traditional police culture.

By the end of the 1980s, police management was exhibiting greater efficiency and had taken on some of the practices found in the private sector and the USA (Butler, 1983; Lubans and Edgar, 1979). Some forces had been more proactive than others, as reports of HMIC reveal, but the combined effects of Home Office Circulars and HMIC were leading towards greater standardization. Important changes had also occurred in recruitment, training and staff development, with personnel high on the agenda. There was less evidence of improvements in value for money, with overtime payments and pay awards well above inflation.

The 1992 Election, and the appointment of Kenneth Clarke to the Home Office (HO), brought the long anticipated moves to restructuring, marketization and quality culture which had been systematically imposed on other public services. The HO launched two major reviews in 1992: one into the relationship between the police and local and central government; the other into police management, pay and conditions. The white paper and report that followed (Cm. 2281, 1993: Sheehy, 1993) led to the Police and Magistrates' Courts Act (PMCA) 1994, heralding fundamantal changes in the organization and management of the police.

Organization, Functions and Structure

Organization

There are 43 Police forces in England and Wales, eight in Scotland and one, the Royal Ulster Constabulary, in Northern Ireland. The Police Act 1964 established a tripartite structure to administer policing, consisting of the Home Secretary and Secretaries of State for Scotland and Northern Ireland, local police authorities (LPAs) and chief constables (CCs). It gave the Home Secretary powers to promote the efficiency of the service, make regulations governing pay and conditions, approve the appointment of CCs and provide support services to all police forces.

LPAs were responsible for maintaining adequate and efficient police forces, setting police budgets, supplying resources and manpower and appointing CCs. They did not determine policy, which was the responsibility of the Home Secretary, nor could they direct or control the local police force. In fact, their powers were limited and to some extent neutralized, during the 1980s, by the close relationships between CCs and the HO.

Each CC was responsible for the direction and control of the police in his area. He recruited, trained, disciplined and deployed staff and controlled all police operations. He could not be given instructions, either by the LPA or the Home Secretary, on police operations, although he had to account to both for his actions. This operational independence of the police was the keystone to political relationships within the tripartite structure.

LPAs formed part of local government, except in Northern Ireland (Oliver, 1987). They coincided with regions in Scotland. In England and Wales there were 27 county forces, eight covered two or three counties and six metropolitan forces covered the former English metropolitan counties. The latter were controlled by joint LPAs. London had two police forces, the City and the Metropolitan Police Service (MPS). The LPA for the former was the City of London Corporation and for the latter, the Home

Secretary. This structure reflected the traditional view that policing should be a local rather than a national service and should be close to the community it serves rather than an arm of the state.

Policing is jointly funded by central and local government, although the former now contributes over 90 per cent of the total. All provincial LPAs receive a specific grant of 51 per cent of expenditure which, until 1995, was not cash limited. Local authorities contribute the remaining 49 per cent, although most comes from the Department of the Environment's revenue support grant and non-domestic rates. The MPS receives a specific grant of 52 per cent with local authorities contributing 48 per cent through a precept.

The 1964 structure created confusion over policing responsibilities and impeded many of the management changes that government sought to introduce. Although the tripartite structure remains, the PMCA 1994 changes the respective roles and powers of each institution, including LPAs. The Home Secretary now has a more strategic role and sets down national objectives, providing a framework within which LPAs and CCs operate. He also sets down performance targets, issues national guidelines and codes of practice and supplies central services. Central funding is provided in the same proportions as before but police spending is now cash limited. The major change is that the Home Office no longer controls establishment numbers, or issues regulations on terms and conditions of service. The Home Secretary remains responsible for overall police efficiency and effectiveness and retains powers to alter the numbers of police areas, after consultation.

The new LPAs are now independent corporate bodies separate from local authorities. They exercise statutory powers and duties in their own right. Their size is limited to 17 to 19 members, consisting normally of nine nominated local councillors, three magistrates and five independents representative of the community. The method of appointing independents proved highly controversial and government was forced to limit its own role in their selection. They are now appointed by LPA members from short-lists prepared by the Home Secretary, advised by a selection panel. Initial evidence suggests that most are local business and professional people (Vize, 1995).

The principal function of LPAs is now 'to secure the maintenance of an efficient and effective police force in its area'. It is responsible for: establishing police priorities in consultation with the CC; setting its own budget; approving a costed plan related to key national and local objectives; monitoring the financial and other performance of the force; and publishing annual performance results. It appoints the CC, soon to be on a fixed term contract, subject to approval of the Secretary of State. The reforms are intended to give LPAs substantially greater powers and responsibility for levels and standards of policing. However, as Loveday points out, 'the new "freedoms and powers" given to the Police Authority would continue to be exercised by working within a national framework of police objectives set by the centre' (Loveday, 1994, p. 8). This makes it likely that there will be less autonomy and local control than the legislation implies.

CCs are now 'the professional managers and leaders of the police service' with more power than in the past. They draft the local police plan and budget, and have responsibility for staffing, buildings, supplies and equipment. The CC is the *de facto* employer of all police staff and responsible for their deployment, direction and control. CCs are accountable for the efficiency and effectiveness of their forces and are subject to performance review and annual inspection by HMIC. CCs are now the providers of police services and LPAs the purchasers.

Functions

The role of the police is to uphold law and order, enforce the law, prevent crime and apprehend criminals. These functions are often seen as difficult to reconcile and prioritize. Effective policing requires the consent of the public, as police powers inevitably infringe the freedoms of individuals. Without public cooperation, the police are unable to function. Crime has to be reported, and the public willing to give evidence, if criminals are to be convicted. The cooperation and support of the public, however, depends on their perception of the police in satisfying public needs.

Policing priorities are set down by the HO, which is currently reviewing core and ancillary functions. All non-core functions will be considered for privatization, contracting out or 'specials' and 'volunteers'. A core policing function requires the exercise of police powers and cannot be performed by civilians. Large areas of traditional policing, such as information gathering, scene of crime investigations, dealing with emergencies, traffic control and beat patrolling, have already been identified as non-core activities. There is concern, however, that if the police are restricted to crime fighting and maintaining public order, they will become associated with state power and control.

Structure

The police is a uniformed, disciplined service based upon the military model, with a hierarchical, rank command structure. There have traditionally been nine ranks, 11 in the MPS. The rank structure, as shown in Figure 7.1, has dictated police management. The top three ranks (five in the MPS) known as Association of Chief Police Officer (ACPO) ranks, constitute top management. They take key policy decisions, with functional responsibility for the central tasks of operations, administration and staffing and training. Operations covers uniform general policing, criminal investigations (CID) and traffic. Administration covers all support services, and staffing and training cover all aspects of personnel. The middle ranks, from chief superintendent to inspector, have responsibility for either territorial or functional divisions, whilst sergeants the lowest level of management, supervise constables.

Provincial Forces	Metropolitan Police
ACPO ranks	
	Commissioner of Police
	Deputy Commissioner
Chief Constable	Assistant Commissioner
Deputy Chief Constable	Deputy Assistant
Assistant Chief Constable	Commander
Federation ranks	
Chief Superintendent	Chief Superintendant
Superintendent	Superintendent
Chief Inspector	Chief Inspector
Inspector	Inspector
Sergeant	Sergeant
Constable	Constable

FIGURE 7.1   Traditional rank structure in the police

The functional command structure is overlaid by specialized units such as drug squads, firearms, public order, CID and training. Most police officers work within territorial divisions, responsible for geographical units. The average police force has between three to six divisions, although there are more in larger forces like Greater Manchester, which has 13, and the MPS, which has 75, grouped into eight areas. Divisions, headed normally by chief superintendents, contain sub-divisions, headed by superintendents. Sub-divisions or Basic Command Units (BCU), in turn, are organized into sections, which provide 24-hour policing, headed by inspectors. The whole service 'is held together by an immense apparatus of procedure. In accordance with the quasi-military style of the organisation these are codified as "standing orders" in a huge reference book known as "General Orders"' (Bradley *et al.*, 1986, p. 120).

Traditionally, force structures were highly bureaucratic, with top-down authoritarian management styles. The rank structure was criticized by the Sheehy report (1993), which made radical proposals for its reform. These included the removal of three ranks – Deputy CC, Chief Superintendent and Chief Inspector – and general delayering. Sheehy argued that the basis of the new command structure should be role rather than rank. Under the PMCA 1994, the ranks of Deputy CC and Chief Superintendent have been abolished and police forces now have more scope to determine their own rank structures.

The Audit Commission (1991) recommended that forces adopt an organizational structure based on BCUs, with responsibility for all policing and financial matters. By 1992, 28 forces had moved to a BCU structure and some others are doing so. One of the first to restructure was Kent, which replaced its divisional structure in 1992 and now has only two levels, headquarters and 13 BCUs. Headquarters determines strategy, targets, standards and value for money. Area superintendents ensure that policies are implemented and key PIs are achieved in the BCUs. Each BCU is managed by an Operations Manager (chief inspector), a Crime Manager (chief inspector) and a civilian Support Manager, responsible for budgetary and other support functions.

New police management structures are becoming increasingly similar, as HMIC and the Audit Commission put pressure on for restructuring. Forces have senior policy/management teams of ACPO ranks that draw up mission statements and corporate plans and undertake structural reviews. Most have de-layered, eliminating divisional or sub-divisional units. The impending capping of police budgets, after 1995, will add a further incentive to de-layer and concentrate management responsibility at operational level where the new national and local objectives have to be delivered. Getting force structure right is essential to implementing the new management regimes required after April 1995 (House of Commons, 1994).

Restructuring is a precondition of devolved budgeting and responsibility for resources management. The Audit Commission (1994) recommended that all forces delegate operational, financial and personnel control to BCUs or sub-divisional units. Progress is slow, because training has not kept pace with structural reform and information systems are not in place. The major constraint, however, may prove to be the reluctance of HQs to let go of control over spending decisions. LPAs may appeal to local authorities for supplementary payments but, if this is not forthcoming, they may go into deficit.

A further feature of restructuring is the introduction of internal markets, requiring units or cost centres to compete for 'business' and develop service-level agreements. Cost centres already exist in areas such as training. Contracting out is also used, where services can be provided more cheaply by outside organizations. After reorganization, market testing of all non-core activities is likely.

The Workforce

The police service consists of two groups of personnel, uniformed officers and civilian staff. Apart from wearing a uniform, police officers are subject to a discipline code and have distinct terms and conditions of employment. Civilians have normal contracts of employment and are employed by LPAs under separate rules and procedures.

All police establishments, before 1995, were set down by the Secretary of State. Not all forces recruited up to their establishment level but they could not exceed it. The numbers of officers have increased throughout the postwar period, particularly since 1961. As Table 7.1 shows, there was a 25 per cent increase between 1961 and 1978 and a further 20 per cent between 1978 and 1992. Law and order policy, during the 1980s, with its attempt to reduce crime, led to a major expansion of police numbers. Since 1992, however, numbers have fallen slightly. They are likely to fall further with increased civilianization, de-layering and efficiency savings.

All police officers are recruited to the basic rank and most remain constables. In 1994, over 76 per cent were constables, 15 per cent sergeants, seven per cent inspectors and 1.5 per cent senior ranks. These ratios may change

TABLE 7.1 Police and civilian staff by headcount 1961–94

Year	Police	Traffic Wardens	Cadets	Civilians	Total
1961	75 600	300	Not Known	37 700	133 600
1978	109 075	4678	3229	39 821	156 803
1979	113 309	4275	3597	39 801	160 982
1980	117 423	4296	3098	41 872	166 689
1981	119 575	4455	1973	41 783	167 786
1982	120 951	4597	1292	41 883	168 723
1983	121 003	4914	960	42 106	168 983
1984	120 573	4860	583	42 563	168 579
1985	120 702	4769	356	42 251	168 078
1986	121 550	4793	428	43 383	170 154
1987	124 102	4754	419	44 692	173 967
1988	124 759	4650	356	45 500	175 265
1989	126 110	4604	388	47 241	178 343
1990	127 090	4808	385	49 226	181 509
1991	127 127	5006	352	50 236	182 721
1992	128 045	5074	Not Applicable	52 342	185 461
1993	127 658	4997	Not Applicable	53 618	186 273
1994	127 534	4681	Not Applicable	54 093	186 308

Source: derived from Home Office, Annual Reports 1961–94.

as the Sheehy reforms are introduced. The majority of police officers are men, although female and ethnic minority officers are increasing.

Civilianization

Table 7.1 shows a small increase of 2000 civilians between 1961 and 1978 but a significant growth since then. Civilian personnel increased by over 25 per cent between 1978 and 1992. Including traffic wardens, this rise is 32 per cent.

There is no central control over civilian appointments and their numbers are determined by individual forces. They are employed in manual, mechanical, clerical, administrative and professional tasks and recruited at any level. In the MPS, there have been senior civilian administrators since its creation in 1829. Also, until after the second world war, many top police jobs were filled by ex-military men. However, as Loveday points out 'if senior management of the police was civilian controlled, this was not reflected in civilian employment lower down the organizational structure' (Loveday, 1993 p. 118).

The reasons for increased civilianization are economic and linked to demands for professional management and police presence in the community. In the past, uniformed police were cheap to employ and the epitome of mixed skilling. After 1961, police became more expensive but there was strong opposition to civilianization from uniformed ranks who were possessive of their jobs and unwilling to accept control by civilians. The Edmund-Davies pay award in 1978 altered the cost equation significantly and the drive to employ cheaper civilian staff accelerated. Home Office Circular 114/83 required all forces to look at civilianization, whilst Circular 105/88 identified specific posts to civilianize.

HMIC issued guidance in 1993 on the categories of work suitable for civilianization. All posts are now classified into A posts, which only police officers can perform, B posts with mixes of staff, and C posts employing only civilians. By 1994, 44 per cent of total staff were civilians and 80 per cent of C posts were civilianized. Areas with scope for further civilianization include IT, finance, personnel, scenes of crime work and administrative support (House of Commons, 1994).

Civilianization is increasingly seen as bringing in expertise to operate the new public management. There may be a counter-trend, however, as police work is market tested and there is an increase in contracting out. Some of the issues arising from increased civilianization and contracting out are raised below.

Special Constabulary

An increasingly important part of the workforce is the Special Constabulary. The number of specials, a part-time volunteer group, has increased throughout the 1980s. Between 1988 and 1993, they rose from just over 15 000 to over 20 000. Government has set a national figure of 30 000 to be reached by 1996 which would be about 25 per cent of the regular establishment (House of Commons, 1994). They have a high drop-out rate but offer a cheap supply of labour and fit in with the government's move to more foot patrols.

The Personnel Function

People management has traditionally been different for uniformed and civilian staff. Civilians, mainly local authority employees, had their terms and conditions determined separately (see Chapter 5). This anomalous position resulted in underdeveloped personnel policies. There was usually a civilian, within the personnel division, responsible for civilian staff but this was a routine task. There was little training, no career structure or career development, no appraisal and little in the way of welfare support for civilians (Parrett, 1992).

Uniformed personnel worked within a clearly defined, hierarchical structure, with pay and conditions determined centrally and incorporated into regulations, made by the Home Secretary. All terms, conditions and rules relating to discipline were statutory. Responsibility for police management rested with the CC but people management was the responsibility of an ACC Personnel in charge of recruitment, training, personnel administration and welfare.

Establishments were determined by the HO, which also set down regulations for recruitment, probationer training and promotion. This centralized, bureaucratic system ensured uniformity and conformity throughout the country. The personnel department's role was largely administrative, with low status. Uniformed officers had no training in personnel work and rarely held the post for more than three years. Training was the responsibility of a separate training division, under the ACC. Individual forces had considerable discretion over what training they supported and who provided it.

During the 1980s, major changes in personnel work took place. Departments grew in size, extended their functions and took on a more strategic role. The personnel department in Sussex Police, for example, now comprises five units: Career Development; Personnel Planning; Employee Relations; Welfare and Occupational Health; and an Administration Unit. Additionally, a Training Department has its own command structure.

Personnel work has been extensively civilianized and some forces have appointed civilian personnel managers. Hampshire has a woman Personnel Director in charge, with a department of 34 staff, 31 of whom are civilians. She is a member of the ACPO Policy committee and advises on all personnel matters. Increasingly, civilian appointees have to obtain professional qualifications and some police officers are also seeking professional status.

The latest development is devolving responsibility for personnel management from headquarters to the BCUs, reflecting patterns evident in other public services which are ahead in the introduction of public management. Over the next few years the personnel function is likely to become fully civilianized, professionalized and more diverse as each police force develops its own devolved responsibilities and flexibilities. Headquarters will exercise control by setting down strategic frameworks and monitoring and evaluating outputs. Central personnel departments are also likely to provide advice, although they will be faced increasingly with competition as contracting out is extended to this area.

Recruitment, Selection and Promotion

The police experienced recruitment problems from 1945 till 1980. Low pay, anti-social hours and the dangers inherent in police work made it an unattractive job during a period of full employment. Standards set for recruitment were not high and most recruits were working class with low educational qualifications. Rigid height and fitness criteria also limited the supply of recruits.

To raise the quality of entrants, a Graduate Entry Scheme was introduced in 1968, later called the Accelerated Promotion Scheme for Graduates (APSG). Between 1968 and 1992 over 550 graduates were recruited to the scheme, although far more entered by the normal method. By 1994, approximately 15 per cent of entrants were graduates. The drop-out rate of APSG graduates was 26 per cent between 1968 and 1992 (Parker-Jones, 1993) but numbers of applicants continue to rise, with 2700 in 1994 compared to 915 in 1989.

Since 1980, there has been no difficulty in recruiting. Applicants exceed places by a ratio of 10:1. Each police force decides on its recruitment strategy. A difficulty remains in attracting women and ethnic minority recruits although there were rises of 26 per cent and 74 per cent respectively between 1988 and 1992. Equal opportunities is currently high on the police agenda.

The traditional entrant to the police was between 19 and 24, but today 24 is effectively the minimum and some recruits are up to 40. Candidates do not require formal educational qualifications but more emphasis is being placed upon them. Education is only one criterion as: 'there appears to be a tradition in the force that too much education, while useful for those who seek promotion, will not make for a satisfied constable' (GLC, 1986, p. 32). Preference is now given to those with relevant experience such as service in the armed forces or work within the community.

Sifting and screening is a lengthy process. Nearly 80 per cent of applicants are screened out before the interview stage. The remainder attend interviews or assessment centres for further screening. In most forces, the final selection decision still rests with the CC.

Recruitment to the uniformed service is at constable rank. All senior positions are filled by promotion, with no lateral entry to middle or top management except civilian posts. This practice developed in the 1950s (Leishman and Savage, 1993a). The case for direct entry and creation of an officer class have both been considered in the context of how to increase the professional status of the police and improve their general managerial performance (Leishman and Savage, 1993b). Ironically, although proposals to open up recruitment have met with objections from the police federations (Reiner, 1992), there has been little opposition to the steady flow of entrants *via* civilianization.

The strongest case for direct entry rests on the arguments that direct entry could further equal opportunities; facilitate recruitment of people with competences needed to operate the new public management; and force a reform of the career management of the operational police constables who are the 'backbone of the service' (Leishman and Savage, 1993b).

Promotion to sergeant and inspector is based on passing examinations and selection at the promotion board or assessment centre. Promotion above inspector is based solely on a promotion board or assessment centre. In future, it will also require completion of relevant development courses. All officers seeking promotion have to be supported by their line managers in a promotion appraisal. Appointment to ACPO rank officers involves open advertisements and successful applicants are interviewed by a panel of the LPA.

Over 50 per cent of forces still use panel interviews as the main method of selection. Around 20 per cent use assessment centres, with the remainder using both methods. Larger forces use assessment centres and so over 50 per cent of all police personnel are now subject to them, with all forces being encouraged to adopt them (Bright, 1994).

The insular nature of police work and the difficulty of police transferring to other organizations means that promotion is the only means of career advancement and reward. Failure to get promotion is often perceived as professional failure and a cause of low morale, although not all constables want it. Promotion is also the only means of filling managerial positions. The emphasis in the 1990s has been to refine promotion procedures, ensuring that selection is based upon competences and skills and conforms with equal opportunity requirements.

De-layering, abolition of intermediate ranks and increased civilianization will greatly reduce promotion opportunities and increase competition over the next few years. What effect this will have on recruitment and retention has yet to be seen but it may make the police less attractive as a career, unless attention is given to career development and rewards for constables.

Equal Opportunities

Women

The police has traditionally been dominated by white males. There were only 260 women officers in Britain in 1939 and numbers remained small until the 1980s, and concentrated in a limited range of policing activities. The police failed to recognize the social and political importance of women in policing, until required to do so as a condition of Britain's entry into Europe in the 1970s (Taylor and McKenzie, 1994). The ratio of men to women was 31:1 in 1960 and 10:1 by 1983. However, the police moved slowly on equal opportunities and in the 1980s some forces maintained unofficial recruitment quotas, which were arguably unlawful. Between 1983 and 1993, the percentage of women increased from 9.2 per cent to 13.2 per cent of force strength.

Most women are concentrated at constable rank as Table 7.2 shows. There were only five women serving at ACPO level in early 1995, including two DCCs and three ACCs. In the MPS, there were no women in the 48 ACPO posts. ACC Alison Halford brought a case of discrimination against Merseyside CC, the Home Secretary and the North West Regional Inspector of Constabulary in 1990, after failing to gain promotion to DCC on four occasions. This

TABLE 7.2 Police in post by rank and gender, 1978–94

Year	Association of Chief Police Officers Males	Super Grades Males	Super Grades Females	Inspector/C 1 Grades Males	Inspector/C 1 Grades Females	Sergeant Males	Sergeant Females	Constable Males	Constable Females	Totals Males	Totals Females	Aggregate
1978	257	2075	–	8280	44	17 897	188	72 011	407	100 520	7 916	109 075
1979	259	2092	–	8420	43	18 213	186	74 852	411	103 837	8 832	113 309
1980	260	2128	–	8526	39	18 351	178	77 728	425	106 993	9 788	117 423
1981	261	2147	–	8588	39	18 406	169	79 401	456	108 803	10 108	119 575
1982	263	2181	–	8750	32	18 484	178	80 258	482	109 936	10 323	120 951
1983	255	2160	–	8780	37	18 541	173	80 166	520	109 927	10 346	121 003
1984	257	2138	–	8780	33	18 665	182	79 650	572	109 490	10 296	120 573
1985	238	2147	2	8841	36	18 856	181	79 317	626	109 399	10 458	120 702
1986	242	2114	3	8918	33	18 975	182	79 593	704	109 842	10 786	121 550
1987	238	2141	3	8982	35	18 936	193	81 192	724	111 489	11 658	124 102
1988	241	2131	3	9004	36	18 868	204	81 390	768	111 630	12 118	124 759
1989	239	2132	2	9034	35	19 075	211	81 801	794	112 281	12 787	126 110
1990	232	2108	1	9102	40	19 229	239	81 906	857	112 577	13 376	127 090
1991	238	2086	4	9031	41	19 324	256	81 387	932	112 066	13 828	127 127
1992	235	1985	5	8983	41	19 319	292	81 515	999	112 037	14 671	128 045
1993	214	1760	5	8730	40	18 971	307	81 230	1072	110 905	15 329	127 658
1994	210	1599	4	8465	44	18 643	303	81 226	1141	110 143	15 899	127 534

Source: derived from Home Office personnel returns for the police service, 1978–94.

did much to raise equal opportunities to the top of the police agenda.

Women were clearly facing barriers to promotion and discrimination was widespread in the 1980s. The MPS was the first to introduce an equal opportunities policy and grievance procedure. The adverse publicity, arising from women successfully taking cases to industrial tribunals, led the HO to issue Circular 87/1989. This instructed CCs to take steps to identify and eliminate discriminatory practices and guard against discriminating unwittingly (Home Office, 1989).

Every force now has an equal opportunities policy and many have appointed EOOs to head EOUs. Traditional areas such as CID, traffic and firearms have been opened to women. Equal opportunity awareness training is a requirement for all ranks and flexible working patterns have been introduced, along with paternity leave, career breaks and job-sharing. All officers are referred to now as police constables.

Sexual discrimination continues to be widespread (Young, 1991; Anderson, Brown and Campbell, 1993) and there are still barriers to career advancement, deployment in specialist areas and benefits such as overtime, whilst sexual harrassment is widespread. There is also evidence of blatant disregard of equal opportunity principles and procedures (Coffey, Brown and Savage, 1992). However, the first woman CC, Pauline Clare, was appointed to lead Lancashine police in June 1995.

Ethnic minorities

Recruiting ethnic minorities before 1980 was insignificant. The Scarman report (1982) recommended recruitment from ethnic minorities and there has been a small increase as shown in Figure 7.3. This is mainly the result of concerted efforts by LPAs with large ethnic populations. The MPS has undertaken a major advertising campaign in both the national and the ethnic press and has introduced access courses to assist those failing the entrance examinations,

FIGURE 7.2   Percentage of minority ethnic officers in England and Wales, 1988–93
   Source: derived from Home Office, *Annual Report 1993*.

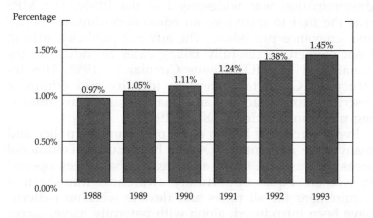

first time, to retake them. Monitoring was introduced in 1982 along with a special procedure for complaints. Although there has been an increase in the number of ethnic recruits the success rates are still much lower than for either women or white males. In 1993, 12.8 per cent of 7572 formal applications to the MPS were from ethnic minorities, 5.2 per cent of those selected for the assessment stage and 7.8 per cent of the final 937 probationers. This compares favourably with the national figure of 2.9 per cent for England and Wales (House of Commons, 1994). The overall strength of minority representation is still, at 1.45 per cent, well below their five per cent representation in the overall population. Within the police, ethnic minorities continue to face discrimination (Campbell, 1990).

In 1992, HMIC reviewed progress on equal opportunities (Home Office, 1993a). They found all forces had comprehensive equal opportunites policies and grievance procedures, supported by training, but there were wide variations in practice. Follow-ups have revealed continuing inadequacies. Areas still underdeveloped and impeding progress include: absence of tenure policies and standardized procedures or criteria for selection; absence of job descriptions and person specifications; and failure to advertise internal posts (Home Office, 1994; Holdaway, 1991).

Pay and Conditions of Service

As with civil servants, who the employer of the police is remains a grey area. Common law states that the police constable is an officer of the Crown, exercising original authority derived from the office. Constables are answerable to the law and are not servants of either the LPA or the CC, although they are paid by the LPA and work under the direction and control of the CC (Fredman and Morris, 1989). However, since 1964, CCs have had vicarious liability for torts committed by officers in carrying out their duties and on that basis it is normal to recognize the CC as the *de facto* employer. The CC exercises the traditional powers of appointment, promotion, reward and discipline. On appointment, officers receive a statement of their terms and conditions of service, including regulations made by the Home Secretary.

At one time it was thought the police were outside employment law but they have exercised rights of appeal to industrial tribunals in cases of discrimination. However, the right of appeal for breach of contract on other employment matters remains unclear, because of the statutory 'code of discipline'. Under this, it is a statutory offence for any officer to refuse to obey a 'lawful order'. This effectively gives the CC virtually unlimited discretion. Although the police have standard terms and conditions, they may be ordered to work overtime, relinquish holiday time, act up or transfer to another unit. In the absence of job descriptions, and with the discipline code, they have little basis for appealing against breach of contract.

Police contracts are traditionally permanent and it has been difficult to dismiss officers on grounds of incompetence. The Sheehy report was critical of conditions of employment which, it argued, were more favourable than those in the private sector and other public services. It rejected the 'job for life' and 'security of tenure' tradition in favour of fixed-term appointments, recommending that all police officers should have normal employment contracts under employment law. Initial appointments should be for 10 years, including probation, to make sure that the force recoups the cost of training but all subsequent appointments, including those on promotion or transfer, within the 10 year period, should be for five years. No officer should have an automatic right of renewal of appointment. Refusal could be on grounds of misconduct, inadequate performance, structural reorganization or ill-health. Sheehy recommended the introduction of compulsory redundancy, as well as giving power to managers to get rid of incompetent staff.

Most of the proposals were referred to the Police Negotiating Machinery and many are being adopted, albeit gradually. The Police (Discipline) Regulations are being replaced by a national non-statutory code of standards. This will set down minimum national standards and form part of the terms and conditions of police officers. All matters not laid down in the code will be subject to the discretion of CCs or negotiated locally with police representatives. The National Code of Standards will cover only those areas where it is considered that a common approach is required. These are likely to include basic pay scales, normal hours of work, annual leave, maternity and paternity leave and sick leave, rank structure, pension rights, staff association rights and discipline and grievance procedures. All other matters, previously covered by regulations, will be left to individual forces to determine. In future, only a limited number of matters will be covered by police regulations, including restrictions on civil and political activities and the duty to carry out lawful orders.

Discipline

Because of the statutory basis of police regulations, any case where police officers fail to meet required standards of behaviour or performance constitutes a disciplinary offence. The discipline procedures require a full formal investigation, which is heavily legalistic in approach. The regulations call for proof beyond 'reasonable doubt' and are conducted along criminal court lines. The system is ineffective in dealing with minor misconduct or poor work and more serious offences. The system being proposed is based on the ACAS Code of Practice. There will be four stages and remedies available to police managers including an informal warning, written warning, suspension or dismissal. Ultimately police managers will be able to dismiss and appeals will go to industrial tribunals.

Restrictions on civil and political activities

The police have traditionally accepted that their role requires restrictions on their social and political freedoms. Like civil servants, police are disqualified from membership of the House of Commons and the European Parliament and, under the LGA 1972, from taking a seat on any local authority which is an LPA. In addition, police regulations state that police officers shall not take part actively in politics (Home Office, 1987). It is currently a disciplinary offence for police officers to communicate with LPAs. Furthermore, it is a disciplinary offence to disclose any police information without proper authority. Under the Police Act 1919, police are denied the right to belong to a trade union or to take industrial action.

Pay and related conditions

Police pay has always been a controversial issue. During the 1970s, morale was low and there was grave discontent about pay, extending to talk of strike action. The

TABLE 7.3   Police pay settlements, 1983–89

	1983/4	1984/5	1985/6	1986/7	1987/8	*Per cent rises* 1988/9	1989/90
Inflation	4.0	5.2	6.9	3.0	4.2	3.9	8.0
Average earnings	7.5	7.7	7.5	7.5	7.75	8.5	9.25
Police (indexed)	8.4	5.4	7.5	7.5	7.75	8.5	9.25
Civil Service	4.9	4.55	4.9	6.0	4.25	4.5	4.0

Source: derived from Beaumont, 1992.

Labour government set up the Edmund-Davies Inquiry in 1977 to review police negotiating machinery and report on police pay. Its recommendations led to pay increases of almost one-third. The Committee recommended that pay should be up-rated annually, linked to the monthly index of annual earnings. Edmund-Davies argued that police were a special case and needed to be compensated for the fact that they could not take industrial action. Throughout the 1980s, the police did well compared with other public services, whose pay was not indexed. From 1983 to 1990, they received increases almost twice the level of inflation and well above increases in the Civil Service, as shown in Table 7.3.

In 1988, government sought to change the Edmund-Davies formula on the grounds that there were no longer staff shortages. The Police Federation (PF) reacted strongly, threatened to reconsider their position on industrial action and withdrew from the Police Council. A compromise was reached and the pay of new recruits was frozen for a year.

In addition to generous pay, the police have received other unusual, pay-related conditions of service. They have had unlimited sick leave on full pay and a range of payments and allowances attached to particular posts. All police officers outside ACPO ranks have been paid overtime. Given the nature of police work, this has often represented a substantial part of police pay. Other payments have included housing allowances and private medical insurance.

Sheehy recommended radical changes, proposing that the benchmark for police pay should be the median of private-sector white-collar agreements, not the Edmund-Davies formula. It proposed an immediate reduction in the pay of recruits, with other scales to be adjusted over time. Pay was to be related to responsibilities and performance, thus ending the standardized system of payment for rank and length of service. PRP should be introduced, with top officers having the opportunity to receive performance bonuses of up to 30 per cent, but poor performance would not be rewarded. Pay flexibilities should be introduced, enabling regional and local variations to reflect local market conditions. Sick pay should be limited; pay allowances should be incorporated into the pay structure; overtime for all ranks, except constables and sergeants, should be abolished; and housing allowances should be phased out.

The Home Secretary, under pressure from the PFs, referred Sheehy's proposals to negotiation, with an instruction that the starting point was to be long-term savings in pay, overtime and allowances. A new pay structure was agreed with overlapping scales, enabling higher salaries to be paid to those of lower rank based upon responsibilities, tasks and performance. Annual increments remain but are no longer based on length of service. PRP is to be introduced in 1996, with pay increments subject to satisfactory performance based on annual appraisals. There will be an opportunity for officers at the top of the scale to earn additional, non-pensionable, performance payments with outstanding performance. Housing allowances have been abolished for all new recruits and frozen for all existing staff.

Overtime and other payments are being adjusted. Overtime has been bought out for inspectors for £3500. They are now salaried and no longer qualify for overtime or special payments for rest days or bank holidays. Lower ranks continue to qualify for overtime at present. The introduction of fixed contracts for ACPO ranks has been accepted and range from four to seven years. It will be up to LPAs to decide the length and content of the new fixed contract.

Before 1995, civilan pay was fixed by local authority NJCs (see Chapter 5). When civilians became employees of the new LPAs, they took their existing terms and conditions with them, under TUPE regulations. This protected them for a year, whilst new arrangements for negotiating salaries and conditions were being worked out.

Pensions

Pensions have been an important element in the reward package of police officers. They are eligible to retire on half pension after 20 years and on two-thirds pension after 30. They are required to retire at 55, although extensions are sometimes permitted on a yearly basis. Contributions, fixed at 11 per cent, are high compared with other public officials.

Sheehy made radical proposals for changes in pensions, which would have brought the police more in line with other public services. It recommended the abolition of the fast accruals of benefits, with normal half-pay pension paid after 40 years. The pension contribution was to be reduced to 7.5 per cent, with provision for transfer and commutation of pension for those on non-renewed, fixed contracts. The Sheehy proposals were rejected but it is likely they will be revisited once the changes underway are consolidated.

Industrial Relations

There are two systems of industrial relations in the police service, one for police officers, the other for civilians. The outcomes in both cases have been national agreements uniformly enforced locally.

The police federations

Police officers, though denied the right to belong to unions, belong to police federations not having union aims and objectives. The original PF emerged out of the last industrial dispute in the police in 1919. The Desborough Committee proposed, in addition to a substantial pay rise, that a PF, for constables, sergeants and inspectors, should be formed to represent police in matters of welfare and efficiency (Desborough, 1920). These recommendations were incorporated in the Police Act 1919, which outlawed the police union, making it a criminal offence to cause disaffection within police ranks (Judge, 1994).

In the inter-war period, the PF played a limited role in representing police interests but after 1945 its status and position changed. First, a soft form of collective bargaining was introduced and the PF was represented on the new negotiating machinery. Second, it was given the status of a free association. Third, in 1964, membership of the PF became compulsory for all ranks below superintendent, thus making the PF, in effect, a statutory closed shop. Fourth, from 1953, the PF was permitted to raise subscriptions on a voluntary basis. Within weeks, it had 99 per cent of members paying the fee.

The PF represents all ranks up to and including chief inspector. Its constitution is laid down in detailed regulations, issued by the Home Secretary. At national level, there are three boards, representing constables, sergeants and inspectors, which, in turn, are represented on a Joint Central Committee. This speaks for the whole Federation on matters of common interest. The tripartite structure is reproduced at regional and local levels. Locally, each board reflects the different sections within the force.

Superintendents and chief superintendents have their own federation, formed in 1952. Membership of the Superintendents Federation (SF) is compulsory, though it is not a statutory body, and it raises a voluntary subscription from its members. It falls outside the legal definition of a trade union and therefore outside the trade union legislation.

ACPO was formed in 1948 from the County Chief Constables Club and the Chief Constables Association of England and Wales, which had existed since the nineteenth century. ACPO represents all senior officers above the Chief Superintendent rank. There are currently 270 ACPO members, 50 of them in the MPS. The role of ACPO is to act as a staff association for chief officers and an advisory body, seeking to influence police policy and represent the police position. It has a large number of committees and working parties covering all aspects of policing.

The legal restrictions imposed upon the PFs have not prevented them from acting as pressure groups and seeking to influence government and public opinion. The PF has been very active in this role and has a parliamentary adviser, public relations staff and conducts political campaigns. ACPO has influenced policy more covertly. Indeed, all three bodies openly opposed Sheehy. This has led to questions of whether the political pressure-group role of the police is compatible with the legal requirement that the police should be politically independent. There are moves to separate the professional and policy advisory roles from the staff representation role in collective bargaining, by creating an independent Institute of Policing.

Collective bargaining

There was no collective bargaining until 1953 and from 1919 until post-1945 industrial relations were dominated by central government. The system was highly centralized, standardized and proceduralized. All pay, allowances, pensions and other conditions of service were uniform and determined by the Home Secretary. A Police Council, set up by the Police Act 1919, consisting of representatives of local authorities, the PF and other senior police officers, advised government. Each police interest could approach the Home Secretary independently, although it was encouraged to work through the 'round table' of the

Council. There was no collective bargaining or joint regulation, only a limited system of consultation (Judge, 1994).

In 1949, the Oaksey report recommended that a system akin to Whitley councils should be introduced into the police. A new Police Council, consisting of an 'official' side, representing the HO and local police authorities, and a 'staff' side, representing the federated ranks of England, Wales and Scotland, was set up to negotiate pay, hours, leave and allowances. Where agreement could not be reached, provision was made for conciliation or arbitration. The old Police Councils for England, Wales and Scotland were renamed Advisory Boards and continued to advise on non-negotiable matters, including training, discipline and recruitment.

New negotiating machinery was introduced in 1953 and the Police Act 1964 finally established the Police Council on a statutory basis as a negotiating body. It also appointed a Police Advisory Body to allow the Home Secretary to consult the police associations and the local authorities on non-negotiable matters. Further changes occurred between 1977 and 1979, after the PF withdrew from the Police Council. Based upon the Edmund-Davies Committee's recommendations, a Police Negotiating Board (PNB) replaced the Police Council and its jurisdiction was set out in the Police Negotiating Board Act 1980.

The PNB currently considers pay, hours, leave, allowances, pensions, clothing and related matters. It operates through five autonomous standing committees for: chief officers; superintendents; inspectors, sergeants, constables and cadets; pensions; and issues common to all ranks. These boards advise government, making recommendations which must be considered by the Secretary of State before he issues regulations. He cannot by-pass the Board and usually accepts its recommendations, meaning that bargaining outcomes are incorporated in law.

Civilian administrative, clerical, technical and manual staff have their terms and conditions determined nationally, through local authority NJCs. National salary scales are applied but there are also locally agreed terms (see Chapter 5). As LPA employees, civilian staff are free to join or not to join a union of their choice. About 40 per cent belong to UNISON, TGWU, AEEU or UCATT.

Joint consultation

Non-negotiable matters include training, promotion and discipline, where the Secretary of State is only required to have regard to representations from police interests. Statutory Police Advisory Boards are consulted on these issues at national level. Locally, there are joint negotiating and consultative committees which consider the local application of national agreements and grievances. Practices on local consultation vary, depending on the willingness of CCs to consult and the degree of organization and leadership of the federations.

There is no formal consultative machinery for civilians within individual forces, although this may change. Since 1980, HMIC has monitored relations between management and civilian staff representatives and the evidence confirms a general lack of local consultation and representation, although this varies.

The Sheehy report

The Sheehy report pressaged a period of strained industrial relations. The inquiry was set up by government without any consultation over its terms of reference or membership. The Committee, chaired by Sir Patrick Sheehy, head of British-American Tobacco Industries, consisted entirely of people without direct knowledge of the police, from top management positions.

All the PFs gave evidence to the inquiry, although it was not coordinated and often conflicted. ACPO, along with the HO, and HMIC, took a managerialist position on many issues. The PF, in contrast, represented the interests of rank and file officers. There was confidence of a positive outcome in all associations.

The Sheehy proposals were, however, universally

criticized. These ranged from outright condemnation by the PF, which described it as a 'blueprint for disaster', to ACPO's more measured response that implementation would need to be carefully considered. In the main, ACPO welcomed those changes which would increase the power of CCs to manage but was sceptical about the proposal for short-term contracts. The PF, which rejected the report in its entirety, saw it as a management cost-efficiency exercise, designed to reduce the size of the force, subject it to more control and increase productivity.

Training and Development

The HO has overall responsibility for police training in England and Wales and individual forces are responsible for ensuring that officers are trained. Each force has a training department and training centre. Before 1979, there was a lot of discretion left to individual forces but throughout the 1980s there was an attempt to standardize training and set down national guidelines. In 1985, the Police Training Council (PTC) set out a 'Police Training Strategy', prescribing areas of training and setting down national standards. A review in 1993 showed that the strategy was not being translated into practice, because there was inadequate coordination of training needs and provision. As a result, the HO centralized training and appointed a National Director responsible for all training and training staff (Home Office, 1993b).

The National Director has a line management responsibility for all staff engaged in the provision of national and regional training courses, national curriculum design and promotion examinations. He is also responsible for central services staff delivering national and regional training programmes (Ryan, 1994). Additionally, he is responsible for all national and regional training and for all training courses developed nationally for use locally. The Police College and the seven district training centres (DTCs), where probationer training takes place, are under his control (Cm. 2281, 1993). The National Directorate is seen as a provider of training and the PTC as the purchaser. This centralization of training has met with resistance but has been justified by the need to rationalize training resources and focus training to meet service needs.

Major changes in operational training have been to make some training mandatory, limit the location of training, make it conditional for promotion or advancement and impose service delivery standards on all courses. These changes are intended to raise the general standards of training, increase its cost-effectiveness and enhance police professionalism.

The National Directorate performs a strategic role. It identifies the core business and values underpinning training; sets the volume and quality of training against targets; and monitors implementation of training policies. Regional coordinators, responsible for quality control and providing support services, act as links between the centre and training establishments. Training takes place at the Police College at Bramshill, the DTCs and local training centres. Over 70 per cent of police training is now set down nationally and only 30 per cent is determined locally.

Changes in training provision

Traditionally, police training was done by police officers trained at the Central Planning Unit (CPU), Harrogate. Few officers attended universities or colleges to obtain degrees or management qualifications. There was an anti-intellectualism pervading the police service, which influenced attitudes towards recruitment and training as well as police practice. Criticisms of training, voiced in the Scarman report (1982) and the PSI Report (1983), combined with the changes imposed by government after 1983, have led to fundamental reforms in the content of training.

Probationer training

Probationer training was criticized in the 1980s for its content and style of delivery. Changes to the curriculum were introduced and the period of training was lengthened but there were still wide variations between forces. In 1989, a new national system was adopted. It consists of a Foundation Phase of 31 weeks and a Post-Foundation Phase of 73 weeks. The programme is modular with two modules, totalling 15 weeks, conducted at the DTCs, with the remainder at provincial training centres. All modules must be delivered by officers trained at the CPU where the course was designed. The MPS continues to operate an independent scheme and has developed a distance-learning programme with the University of Portsmouth, which leads to a Certificate in Higher Education. Officers can then go on to study for a degree in Police Studies.

Probationer training now emphasises personal and interpersonal skills, has a social science content and involves more active learning. A centrally designed appraisal system has been introduced, with identified competences and strict guidelines on assessment levels required to graduate from probation. Regional quality control groups monitor the scheme.

OSPRE

Before 1990, constables and sergeants took examinations to qualify for promotion and further training and development. Both examinations consisted of written papers across a range of police law and procedures. Constables could take both examinations and be eligible for promotion to both ranks, although few were successful at the first attempt. Once qualified it then took four or five attempts to pass a promotion board. Both examinations encouraged rote learning and placed no emphasis on skills or management competences.

In 1989, a new system, based on competences, was

introduced involving objective structured performance-related exercises (OSPRE). Part one consists of a written examination, based on knowledge and ability to apply the law; part two, held at an assessment centre, has nine exercises assessed by independent assessors. The pass rate in the OSPRE examinations is very low. Only 31 per cent passed part one and 46 per cent part two in 1993, giving an overall pass rate of 17.8 per cent in the sergeants' examination.

A significant innovation since 1990 is that the inspector's examination can only be taken by substantive sergeants. Partly because of this and very high failure rates, there is concern about the number of officers qualified for promotion and management development. The numbers of officers putting themselves forward for the examinations is also falling. Research suggests this is due to uncertainty about the availability of promotion and the limited financial awards attached to it (Collins, 1994).

Accelerated promotion scheme

In an attempt to attract able young people into the service, the Accelerated Promotion Scheme was started in 1962. It was designed to improve career prospects by providing training for young officers, selected by their CC, for showing leadership skills. Since 1985, a new scheme provides for a sandwich course and promotion to sergeant for all those selected to attend it (Mead, 1990). Those passing OSPRE first time are automatically considered for recruitment to the scheme, although they have to pass a further interview (Parker-Jones, 1993). Starred sergeants are expected to move quickly on to inspector rank. The numbers attending the Bramshill's Special Course (SC) increased after OSPRE and, since 1991, an index of high-lighted officers is kept and monitored by regional HMIC. Like OSPRE, the SC is competency-based and linked to NVQs and MCI competency profiles.

Management training

Management training was not developed before the 1980s. This was partly because management was seen as alien to policing and because controlling staff was according to the book and the discipline code. The style of management was one of command and control, in which rigid application of rules was the practice. Promotees might receive some job training but not in management theory or in management skills. The approach is summed up as follows:

> the managerial requirements of command at the various levels were very much left to nature; that is, a promoted officer would have to rely upon his own experience 'on the job', his rank, his knowledge of force policy and general orders and whatever help or advice he could informally pick up in order to learn how to do the job of police management (Bradley *et al.*, 1986, p. 36).

Leishman and Savage (1993b, p. 228) refer to the 'recurring concerns of politicians, academics and, indeed, the police themselves about how best to train and retain the managers they need'. The merits and demerits of fast tracking, developing an officer corp, recruiting directly into management grades, particularly at highest levels and of internal development and promotion from the ranks have been continually debated (Reiner, 1992; Wall, 1993; Leishman and Savage, 1993c).

Management training is now provided by individual forces, regional centres and Bramshill. A carousel of courses for supervisors, mainly sergeants, middle managers and top managers has been developed and all sergeants and inspectors attend management development courses provided regionally. In 1992, the ACPO Personnel and Training Committee clarified the philosophy of the training, arguing for regional training as a way of obtaining cross-fertilization of ideas and diversity of policing experience (ACPO, 1992).

There are three key in-service management courses run

at Bramshill including the Junior Command Course (JCC), designed for chief inspectors, the Intermediate Command Course (ICC) for superintendents and the Senior Command Course (SCC), for chief superintendents and above. These are designed to train police leaders and provide a professional development programme. Each course develops appropriate skills and competences and enables members to focus on the central issues in policing at the time.

Following a HO Circular 12/87, the JCC became compulsory for all chief inspectors. Now known as the Leadership Development Programme, it involves an assessment appraisal by the Police College Career Development Centre to identify the training needs of individual officers and plan a training programme.

In 1988, major amendments were made to the SCC and ICC. The role of the ICC, now the Advanced Leadership Development Programme, was enhanced to act as a conduit for those to be admitted to the SCC. Reports from the ICC are now used in the selection for SCC. Officers who have not attended ICC and wish to be considered for SCC, now the Strategic Leadership Development Programme, must attend an extended interview. Officers on the SCC increased significantly after 1989, because of concerns about possible shortages of officers qualified for ACPO ranks. In 1994, 200 officers were eligible for promotion. Restructuring and delayering, larger spans of control in operational policing, increased civilianization of senior posts and likely amalgamation of police forces over the next five years will, however, squeeze promotion opportunities.

The content of Command Courses is focused on management skills and leadership. At first, instruction was in rational approaches to management, underpinning policing by objectives after circular 114/83. Since then, the emphasis has moved to performance management and new approaches to managing people, including TQM. The latest trend is 'structural reengineering'. With the reduction in the number of ranks post-Sheehy, and civilianization, it is likely that the Police College will provide training for mixed groups of officers, civilians and LPA members in the future.

Career development

Promotion has traditionally been the only route for police officers to obtain financial advancement and more responsibility, although nearly 80 per cent of police officers are constables and the majority remain so throughout their careers. The emphasis is now on developing and rewarding officers who remain in the same rank, as well as those that are promoted (Home Office, 1991). This is based on regular staff appraisals, identification of training needs, formulation of individual development plans and the opportunities under the post-Sheehey pay structure to award responsibility and excellence with additional payments. Most police forces have appointed Career Development Officers, usually located in personnel departments. They liaise with training departments, line managers and individual officers to identify needs and advise and assist in constructing plans.

Innovations have included secondments to other public and private organizations and encouragement to obtain degrees and professional qualifications (Reiner, 1991; *Police Review*, 1994). The latter has been seen as a way of breaking down the negative aspects of the police occupational culture (Bradley *et al.*, 1986; Burke, 1993; Wright, 1994). This emphasis on raising the educational qualifications of police officers has to contend with the pervasive anti-intellectualism of the 'cop culture'. In 1968, only 0.2 per cent of police officers were graduates; in 1992 it had reached 6.4 per cent (Smithers, Hill and Silvester, 1990; Morgan, 1994). The increase in the numbers of graduates, whilst an essential element in moving towards a professional police force, poses problems if the expectations of graduates about career progression and greater responsibility are frustrated.

The New National Director appears to favour NVQs over academic qualifications, as the former focuses on behaviour and competences in the workplace, whereas the latter emphasises cognitive and diagnostic skills. Involvement of external institutions also has its drawbacks, as there is loss of control over the syllabus and methods of assessment. There appears to be a move towards introducing more control over the educational development of police officers and a preference for training, rather than educating police managers.

Staff appraisal

Staff appraisal is not new, although its form and function has varied. It developed in the 1960s, using narrative reports on officer performance during the previous year to identify those suitable for promotion. During the 1980s there was a move towards more objective and participative appraisal systems, designed to enable the performance of officers to be reviewed in the context of objectives, thus reinforcing moves towards management by objectives and performance management. The new appraisals are designed to inform officers of how they are rated in terms of efficiency and prospects for promotion, and to guide senior officers in making decisions about promotion, transfers and career development. Appraisals tend to combine performance, development and promotion functions, although these are not always spelt out clearly. The new appraisals are open and joint systems, with appraisees involved in setting the interview agenda and counter-signing the final report.

In the mid 1980s, performance criteria were often based upon the Beatcraft Manual PIs, with narrative assessments. Rating systems were restricted to officers thought suitable for promotion. These schemes were introduced, however, without training interviewers or the interviewees and there was widespread dissatisfaction.

Appraisal interviewing skills are now part of management training. Assessment is based upon performance criteria and targets, objectives and standards agreed in the previous review. More emphasis is placed on counselling and mentoring to encourage individuals to identify their own weaknesses and agree training needs.

Appraisal is now central to performance management and career development. Sheehy spelt out that appraisal should cover planning performance, managing performance, appraising performance, and monitoring. It should involve officers and line managers in agreeing specific objectives and outputs related to a time period and the skills and competences required to achieve those results. The appraisal should result in a single performance rating, from one to five, which can then inform pay. The assessment system now has a central role as part of the appraisal-related pay system being introduced in 1996.

Conclusion and Evaluation

Since the mid-1980s, all aspects of people management have been subjected to investigation and reform and the service is being managerialized. In many ways, however, the management problems of the police are unique. This is because most decisions are taken at the bottom of the hierarchy and long hierarchies have been developed to control police staff. It is also because the militaristic style and culture of the police is not receptive to the new ideas of flexible, consumer oriented and quality focused management or to the people centred management approaches.

Along with other public services, governments have sought to make the police more efficient, less bureaucratic and more responsive to the public. The special status of the police and its role in maintaining law and order has constrained the speed with which the changes have taken place, so has the resistance of the police themselves. Of all public services, the police was probably the least affected by the Thatcher revolution. Although the FMI and more rational approaches to management, introduced after 1983, established a new climate, and a more questioning ethos, new working practices and methods were slow to take root, because of the inherent conservatism of the structure.

Since 1990, the pace of change has quickened. This is due partly to actions taken by ACPO and the PFs in improving service delivery and quality and setting standards in policing (ACPO, 1990). But it is also because of the actions of the government, Audit Commission and HMIC to force through change. Kenneth Clarke's appointment as Home Secretary signalled the government's intention to take on the police.

In many ways the change process in the police is not distinctive. The direction of change has followed patterns throughout the public services. The initial thrust was towards more rational management and a search for value for money. Policing by objectives, initially challenged by many CCs, is now universally practised. A system based upon management by objectives requires procedures for evaluating performance, thus the police have been steered towards performance management. Managers, using PIs, can identify organizational achievements and can also assess the efficiency of individuals. Further, it increases police accountability and enables the HO to compare the efficiency of police forces and monitor the achievement of national and local police objectives. League tables are likely to become more important after 1995, as all LPAs will have to set down their objectives and HMIC will examine how forces perform against their local policing plans. The PMCA 1994 also ensures that the government's national objectives are followed by all LPAs, as well as cash-limiting LPA funding.

There has been considerable centralization, especially in training, and in the setting of national objectives under PMCA 1994. But decentralization, now a dominant feature of other public services, may well follow the restructuring programme which is under way. There is some evidence to suggest that financial and personnel will be devolved over the next few years, when the emphasis will be turning to the 'social market' and developments in community policing.

Although there are still many vestiges of the traditional

culture of people management, there are also many new people management practices. The police remain a uniformed service but are losing much of their military character, as command and control functions of senior ranks are becoming management roles. Strict discipline is giving way to more instrumental and pragmatic approaches to people management. In particular, training and staff development are fostering a more professional ethos in the service. The traditional authoritarian style of police management has been replaced, in part, by a more participative and performance-oriented approach, although deference to rank still persists.

Performance management has both required and enabled new approaches to people management. Staff appraisal now provides the basis for monitoring performance and identifying training and development needs. From 1996, pay increments, except for ACPO ranks, will be based upon appraisal ratings. Line managers are using performance as the basis for control and development. Individuals are expected to take the opportunity, in performance reviews, to participate equally in the setting of their own objectives. The ownership of agreed objectives, it is assumed, will motivate officers to perform.

Performance management is far away from the discipline forms of control characterizing TPM. Managers are required to have skills in appraising, motivating, counselling and mentoring, as well as competences in establishing development strategies and identifying training needs. New systems of management training are equipping officers for these new roles. Younger staff are adapting to the new performance culture more readily than the older ones, who see the changes as increasing line management control. In particular the impending changes to the discipline code will give managers more power to dismiss officers on grounds of incompetence, whilst PRP will give them control over rewards.

At first, it appeared that the marketizing strategies of the government would not be applied to the police, although civilianization was encouraged during the 1980s to reduce costs. In the 1990s, however, a more radical agenda has been imposed. Many non-core policing activities have been civilianized or contracted out, and internal markets are generating a business culture in which contracts and service agreements are being introduced. Market testing has not yet been imposed but once structural de-layering and the introduction of BCUs is complete, and budgets devolved, it will be possible. There is now a much wider acceptance of private policing and the present Home Secretary has expressed a preference for marketized services (Howard, 1994).

There is likely to be a further reduction of police forces, after local government reorganization. Civilianization will continue, as management and support services are separated from core policing. More specialists and general managers will probably be recruited. Support and administrative activities will be done increasingly by civilians or contracted out. All of this has implications for civilian and police staff. The rationalization of police forces will also lead to reductions in ACPO posts. Policing will no longer offer job security, whilst competition with private security companies may lead to the creation of operational policing business units. The areas already identified for contracting out or privatization include: policing public areas, private estates and public events; motorway patrol and traffic policing; and scene of crime reporting. Government's commitment to expanding neighbourhood watch and the Special Constabulary is indicative of its preference for volunteer policing.

The police have always had a distinctive, bifurcated system of industrial relations, with a centralized, soft form of collective bargaining for uniformed staff but normal collective bargaining for civilians. Neither have enjoyed full consultative rights at local level, although the PFs have had a more institutionalized system. The police has never been very pluralistic, because it is a highly unitary organization. There are challenging implications for industrial relations in the changes taking place. It is possible to see the police moving to decentralized bargaining, which is emerging in the other public services. As terms and conditions of uniformed police are being removed from a statutory to non-statutory basis, LPAs are likely to assume responsibility for local collective bargaining across a range of issues. Civilian staff, whose terms and conditions are still linked to Whitley negotiating procedures, will have to establish their own bargaining arrangements with the LPAs. Four LPAs have already negotiated local bargaining for civilians and more are likely to follow. If local bargaining is developed it is likely that some single-table bargaining will emerge.

Another scenario is that the PFs will be permitted to extend membership to civilian staff of comparable status who agree to sign away their trade union rights. ACPO is balloting its membership over whether to allow civilians holding ACPO ranks to be members. The outcome is likely to lead to other federations doing the same. That would require a change in the law, as PFs cannot have non-officer members. Opinion seems at the moment to rule out the possibility of Police being given trade union rights. A third scenario, and a most probable one, is that the police will close ranks, maintain their special status and exclude civilians. They will focus on core policing activities, supported by a highly professionalized cohort of civilians.

Parallel systems of industrial relations are developing, with individualized communications increasing. Collectivist structures have always been weak and the new direct approach by management is not perceived as undermining the staff associations but rather as an improved system of management. Paradoxically, although there was initially a rejection of public management as alien to policing, the unitary structure of the police and its legacy of rank, command and discipline makes it more receptive to managerialism than some other public services.

In summary, people management changes have seen a move away from a highly centralized, bureaucratized, autocratic system of control towards a more flexible, responsive managerial system, but not excessively so. Police are still steeped in a traditional culture, with its emphasis on rank, superordination and subordination. It is still male-dominated and inherently sexist, although beginning to change. It is still task and action oriented with an under-developed approach to people management. It continues to represent a career for most officers, although there may be less job security in the future. What is clear is that the police will no longer be so favoured in terms and conditions as in the past and there will be greater lateral movement in and out of the force. Civilians may well benefit from the changes and see their terms and conditions improve. But this will be offset by greater uncertainty as market testing and contracting out take hold.

PART III

Assessment

CHAPTER 8

Towards a new people management?

David Farnham and Sylvia Horton

Earlier chapters have identified and discuss significant shifts in people management policies, activities and systems in the UK public services, during the 1980s and 1990s. The changes originated in political ideology and have been driven by government policy and environmental turbulence. The aims of government have been to reduce the size and costs of the public services, make them more responsive to the needs of 'customers' and 'clients' and fashion them into lean and efficient organizations, modelled on private-sector lines. A major thrust of governmental change has been legislative, including privatization, restructuring, CCT and market testing. Another thrust has been the injection of private-sector management methods and techniques into the public services, including devolved budgetary and financial accounting systems, TQM and HRM policies and practices. Although these new management systems have been initiated by ministers, advised by businessmen and management consultants, responsibility for implementing them has rested with senior managers within each service. The net impact of these fundamental political, organizational and managerial changes has been the 'quiet revolution', outlined in previous chapters.

There is no longer a broadly uniform pattern of people management across the public services. During the heyday of TPM, the principles underpinning it – an administrative personnel function, a paternalist style of management, standardized employment practices, collectivist patterns of industrial relations and the state's role as a model, good practice employer – were incorporated, to varying degrees, within each service discussed in this book. TPM, in other words, was a broadly universalistic and homogeneous set of policies and activities across the public services. TPM in the public services also contrasted with people management in the private sector, where there were wider variations in policy and practice. This was accounted for by the differing patterns of ownership, size, accountabilities, product markets, organizational structures and managerial ideologies of private businesses. Historically, too, the UK private sector placed great emphasis on financial short-termism, enterprise autonomy and the right to manage (Hutton, 1995). Its personnel and employment policies, in turn, were subordinated to these ends.

The remaining question to be examined is to what extent do the new developments in people management represent a shift towards a 'new people management' (NPM) in the public services? NPM is defined as those recent developments in the people management process, taken largely from the private sector, to make the public services more efficient as the political and economic demands placed on the state change and are redefined. This central question incorporates four subsidiary issues. What, if any, are the essential features of NPM? How does NPM differ from TPM? Are elements of TPM incorporated into NPM? And is NPM a homogeneous or heterogeneous set of policies, activities and systems? It is these conceptual and theoretical issues which we attempt to address in this final Chapter.

Pressures for People Management Change

Since the late 1970s, there have been a number of pressures leading to people management change in the public services. These were both endogenous and exogenous to the services, but collectively they have significantly affected the contexts of people management and the ways in which it is organized and structured within public organizations. These are summarized below.

The political contingency

The ultimate source of change has been government policy. This is the political contingency (Ferner, 1985 and 1988). As outlined in Chapter 1, since 1979 successive Conservative governments have adopted New Right economic and social policies, in reaction to Keynesianism, the Welfare State and Postwar Settlement, although there is little evidence that the Conservatives had a detailed blueprint for change when they assumed office. Up till 1987, they reacted incrementally and pragmatically in implementing their neo-liberal socio-economic reforms but since then their approach appears more strategic and coherent, a situation unquestionably helped by their winning four consecutive general elections (Savage, Atkinson and Robins, 1994).

The macro-goals of governments included reversing the UK's relative economic decline, improving the efficiency of the economy, destroying 'socialism' and reasserting Britain's role in world politics. At meso-level, government sought to revitalize private enterprise, improve the competitiveness of British business and strengthen the right to manage. The micro-goals of government included optimizing consumer choice and consumer sovereignty in the market place and freeing individuals from the 'culture of dependency' on the state. Government also wanted to motivate individuals to take personal responsibility for themselves and their families and encourage the enterprise culture (Farnham and Horton, 1993).

These principles of market individualism and the enterprise culture were spelt out by the incoming Thatcher government in its first budget statement. The government's espoused aims were (Hansard, 1979):

> First the strengthening of incentives, particularly through tax cuts, allowing people to keep more of their earnings . . . so that hard work, ability and success are rewarded; second, greater freedom of choice by reducing the state's role and enlarging that of the individual; third, the reduction of the borrowing requirement of the public sector which leaves the rest of the economy to prosper; and fourth, through firm monetary and fiscal discipline bringing inflation under control and ensuring that those taking part in collective bargaining are obliged to live with the consequences of their actions.

Similar themes were repeated 13 years later in the Conservative's Election Manifesto in 1992. This claimed that government's main task was to provide 'an economic environment which encourages enterprise'. Accordingly, the Conservative party's stated aims were to achieve price stability, control public spending, reduce taxes, 'make sure that market mechanisms and incentives are allowed to do their job' and 'reduce the share of national income taken up by the public sector' (Conservative Party Manifesto, 1992, pp. 5–7).

Government used three main policy instruments to implement their political objectives: deregulating the economy, creating a strong centralized state and promoting 'popular capitalism'. By deregulating the UK's financial, product and labour markets, government aimed to increase market competition, foster business enterprise and develop a business culture – in both the private sector and public services. This was done through legislation, creating private and public-service regulators and abandoning the postwar commitment to full employment. Further, government's search for value for money in the public services made public managers more cost-conscious and resourceful in the ways that they deployed and utilized their people or human resources. This was compounded by the strict financial contraints put on the public services during this period.

Governments also attempted to reduce the size of the public sector within the economy by privatization, hiving off organizations into bodies such as Next Steps agencies, and contracting out public-service functions into the private sector through CCT, which has affected all public services. One writer described CCT 'as one of the most fundamental changes to affect the management of local authority services' (Fowler, 1988b, p. 9). Similar pressures on people management derived from the creation of internal markets in the NHS.

The creation of a strong centralized state was aimed at weakening other public bodies, especially local government. This was done through legislation, administrative directives and financial controls. GMS schools were allowed to opt out of local authority control, over 400 FE colleges were taken out of LEA control and the 30 former polytechnics became higher education corporations. Over 100 Next Steps agencies were created in the Civil Service, whilst over 400 trusts were set up in the NHS. All these measures have implications for the ways in which public workers are managed.

The promotion of popular capitalism sought to empower individuals and weaken their attachment to the Welfare State. Measures included: enforced sale of council housing; de-nationalizing the public utilities; and encouraging share ownership. Promoting popular capitalism was aimed at fostering possessive individualism and the view that people are personal consumers in the market place, rather than collective groups in the workplace, thus strengthening individualism inside and outside work.

The managerial contingency

There are four dimensions to the managerial contingency and its impact on people management policies and practices. First, throughout the 1980s and 1990s, ministers were convinced that cost-efficient and effective public services were dependent upon 'good management' and 'sound business practice'. As Michael Heseltine (1980), then-Secretary of State for the Environment, wrote shortly after coming to office: 'Efficient management is a key to the [national] revival. . . . And the management ethos must run right through our national life – private and public companies, civil service, nationalized industries, local government, the National Health Service.' Underlying this assumption was the belief that private-sector management methods, based on 'bottom-line' accountancy concepts, were superior to those of public administration and, if public services were to be successful enterprises and provide value for money to taxpayers, then management techniques, most closely associated with the 'efficient' private sector, should be introduced into the public services too. Accordingly, it became the task of government to promulgate these views, propagandize them and inject them into the 'new' public services (Farnham and Horton, 1993; Pollitt, 1993).

Second, one way in which ministers encouraged the adoption of private management ideas and practices was by calling on notable 'captains of industry' to conduct investigations, write reports and advise them (Griffiths, 1983 and 1988; Efficiency Unit (Ibbs), 1988; Sheehy, 1993). It was largely through the advocacy and authority of business leaders that private-sector management practices were initially justified and subsequently introduced into the Civil Service, NHS, local government, education and the police. Another strategy was to appoint senior businessmen, often on secondment, to senior posts within the public services.

Third, a further way of facilitating change, and introducing managerialist values and techniques into the public services, was by recruiting outsiders committed to the new managerialism into key managerial positions. This was particularly the case for general, financial and personnel management posts. One example was Len Peach, sometime director of personnel and corporate affairs at IBM. He became director of personnel in the reformed NHS and was later appointed to the NHS Executive Board.

His influence was instrumental in introducing individual performance reviews and PRP into the health service, policies which were central to IBM practice at the time. By ensuring that such appointments were advertised and recruited by open competition, employing authorities had the opportunity of selecting managers with private-sector backgrounds and experience, especially in the Civil Service, NHS and local government and most recently the police.

Fourth, the public services have also been affected by trends in management, and in some cases by passing fads and fashions, copied from the private sector. These include HRM, TQM, customer-care programmes, HRD and business process re-engineering, some of which have been introduced into public services by multi-national management consultants such as Peat Marwick, Hay-MSL and Andersons. The attraction of these private-sector innovations to public managers has arisen from the financial and competitive pressures facing them. The ideas underpinning these practices originated from north American management researchers (Moss Kanter, 1985 and 1989; Juran, 1989; Deming, 1986), management gurus and management consultants (Peters and Waterman, 1982; Peters, 1987; Peters and Austin, 1985) and the cross-fertilization of ideas between public and private managers, largely through attending conferences, seminars and management development programmes together. It was partly through these processes of transferral and diffusion that the new managerialist ideas have become common currency and practice within the public services. They are now the staple diet provided by internal and external management training courses.

Socio-technical contingencies

The 1980s and 1990s have been a turbulent period of intense and radical socio-technical change. The rate of change has been accelerating, with innovations in ideas, social attitudes, products, services, markets and technology. These have challenged traditional institutions such as the family, religion, Fordist production methods and largely national communication systems (Horton, 1993).

There have been fundamental changes in the social, economic and technological spheres which, in turn, have affected the people management process. The changing roles of women, for example, have been bolstered by equal opportunities legislation, and, in particular, the decisions of the European Court of Justice and UK industrial tribunals. This has necessitated employers, including public ones, reviewing their people management policies and employment practices, as the proportion of women in the labour market increases.

Demographic changes, especially the ageing profile of the population, have forced employers to reconsider those available for work by recruiting and training older workers to fill jobs normally taken by school leavers. The steady increase in the proportion of the elderly has also made impacts on housing, social services and health care, whilst some employers are reviewing their pensions policies as people live longer. On the other hand, there have been increases in the numbers of students in higher education, with the implications this has for labour supply and the labour market.

Another major contingency has been technology. Microelectronics has transformed the means available to collect, store and transfer information. The convergence of computers, telecommunications and automation has had profound effects on employment patterns and work processes in the public services, as they have in the private sector. Public services, like all large organizations, depend on information which is their most strategic resource. New technology has made it possible to restructure information systems and decision networks. Without IT, most if not all the management changes introduced since 1979 would not have been possible.

The FMI, MINIS, PIs, de-layering, de-concentration, centralization and decentralization have all been facilitated by IT. The Civil Service has rationalized IT through the Central Computing and Telecommunication Agency and,

FIGURE 8.1 TPM and NPM compared

	TPM	NPM
Personnel Function	administrative	strategic
Management Style	paternalist	rationalist
Employment Practices	standardized	flexible
Industrial Relations	collectivist	dualist
Role of the Employer	model	new mode

by 1991, over 90 per cent of local authorities had or were developing IT strategies. The NHS and police have introduced computer networks throughout their organizations. IT has been a major factor in public-service change. It has enabled changes to be made in organizational structures, work processes and the ways in which people are managed. And it has provided means for information transmission upwards, downwards and outwards to facilitate more control, decentralization and responsiveness to public-service clients and consumers (Bellamy and Taylor, 1994; Isaac-Henry, 1993).

People management in transition

We are now able to summarize the impact of the pressures for change on the people management process in the public services. These are set out in Figure 8.1. This compares TPM with NPM and provides ideal typologies of TPM and NPM respectively. TPM is those elements of the people management process which evolved in the public services, over many years, as the political and economic demands placed on the state grew and expanded, reaching their zenith in the period 1945–79. NPM, in contrast, encompasses those recent developments in the people management process, taken from the private sector to make the public services more efficient, as the political and economic demands placed on the state change and are redefined. Evidence suggests that the people management process in the public services is changing and that it is shifting from a TPM approach to a NPM one, although to differing extents within each service and their operational units. In practice, elements of both TPM and NPM can co-exist in the same organization, or in part of it, but, as ideal types, TPM and NPM are likely to have the distinctive features shown in Figure 8.1. In the move away from TPM to NPM, five key features of people management stand out:

- the personnel function becomes more strategic than administrative
- management style shifts to being more rationalist than paternalist
- employment practices are more flexible and less standardized
- industrial relations are dualist rather than collectivist, containing both pluralist and individualist elements
- the role of state employers shifts from being that of a model employer to that of a 'new mode' employer, meaning that public services lean heavily on private-sector people management ideas and practices, rather than acting as exemplars to the private sector

It is these aspects of NPM which we explore in the sections below.

The Personnel Function

A major feature of NPM in the new public services is the attempt to create a strategic role for the personnel function and move it away from its traditional administrative role. By a strategic role, we mean the adoption by senior managers of a forward looking and proactive approach to people management policies and activities, which can incorporate personnel specialists in business planning. From being largely reactive, and applying standardized rules and procedures, as with TPM, those leading the personnel function are actively seeking to influence the direction in which people management policy and practice are focused. A key feature of personnel strategy is that it becomes central to the business planning cycle. This is largely in response to the forces of competition facing the public services, their increasing customer focus and managerial concerns with quality outputs and performance targets. As Lanchbery (1995, p. 31) argues: 'a human resources strategy only makes sense in the context of an overall organizational strategy' and 'must be continually reviewed and updated.'

The locus of power for this strategic role varies. In the Civil Service, for example, it is located in the OPS and in the health service in the NHS Policy Board. It is less easy to generalize about its location in local government, education and the police. In these cases, the location of the strategic role varies but, in principle, it operates at top policy-making levels within the appropriate public or corporate authority. In some local authorities, for example, there are policy and resources committees, with personnel sub-committees. Some universities have human resources committees, established as sub-committees of their governing bodies. And in the police, the strategic role can be found in the ACPO teams of the police forces.

Two crucial factors are driving the development of a strategic role for the personnel function: government policy and the changing goals, cultures and structures of the public services. The overriding aim of recent public-service reforms is to slim down their size and make what remains of them more efficient, customer-centred and quality-driven. One way of doing this is by utilizing people as productively and cost-effectively as possible, so requiring appropriate people management strategies.

The goals of the public services are increasingly business-oriented, underwritten by the culture of value for money, consumerism and continuous improvement. Similarly, as shown earlier, structural reform within them has been endemic over the last decade. The Civil Service, for example, is now organized into central departments, functional departments and agencies. The concept of a unified and uniform Civil Service is breaking down and it now consists of a quasi-federal structure, with core and satellite units. The NHS, too, has effectively been de-layered, consisting of a centre, the DoH, and hundreds of de-centralized, semi-autonomous units of purchasers and providers. Local government has lost some of its functions and powers, is moving towards an enabling role and it too is about to be restructured. GMS schools are funded directly from the DFE, whilst schools remaining in LEAs now manage their own budgets. HECs and FECs are also directly-funded units and are responsible for their financial and staff resources. The police are also likely to be reorganized, with fewer forces after local government reform. There have already been changes to its tripartite system of control and internal structures. This would complete a cycle of public-service structural change, beginning with Next Steps agencies in 1988.

The changing nature of the public services necessitates a strategic rather than administrative approach to people management. This is compounded by the labour-intensive nature of public organizations and their large numbers of professional staff but is constrained by the relative strength of their unions and professional associations. These forces for people management change are being reinforced by other organizational developments including: the breakup of monolithic public authorities; the heterogeneity of de-centralized public-service units; and delegation of managerial authority within them. The result is that centralized people management systems are no longer appropriate to emerging public-service organizations.

All these developments are prompting a changing role for the personnel function. First, a distinction is being drawn between strategy formulation and strategy implementation (Johnson and Scholes, 1993). It is central personnel units, in cooperation with senior management teams, which are determining the strategic direction of people management, with operational units implementing strategy through devolved authority. This leads to local managerial discretion in implementing people management policy, much more so than in TPM. Second, the personnel function is increasingly concerned with human resources utilization and is becoming human resource-centred, rather than 'people-centred'. The ideas underpinning this approach to people or human resources management (HRM) originated in the private sector (Storey, 1989). It implies 'recruiting, developing and retaining people with the right combination of specialist know-how and the broader skills and attitudes needed to match the changing demands of the business' (Personnel Standards Lead Body, 1993, p. 14). From management's point-of-view, individual workers need to be integrated into the organization, motivated and trained to meet its changing requirements. People, in short, are seen as both sources of knowledge and skills for organizations and investments in their future.

Third, personnel departments are helping to manage change, rather than deal with stability. Indeed, managing organizational change has a central place within the NPM paradigm. As two members of the University of Brighton's directorate put it (House and Watson, 1995, p. 19): 'managing change successfully, ultimately depends upon understood and shared values and objectives, for the managers and managed.' Public-service change has taken a variety of forms and has not simply been structural. It has involved technological change, policy change, procedural change, changes in personnel systems and practices and, above all, culture change. Since organizational culture incorporates the dominant values and beliefs driving the behaviour of people within organizations, changing it facilitates behavioural change (Parry, 1990). The task facing those seeking culture change has been to shift public organizations from producer-driven bureaucracies, led by professionals, to customer-driven public businesses, led by managers. As a unit personnel manager in the NHS reported in research conducted by Storey (1992, p. 165):

> In the 1970s, relationships were managed as if the whole thing was about 'contract-negotiating'. That's not my view what we are [now] here for. We are here to deliver a service to patients – our clients. The role of personnel in this is to

promote the conditions which will allow this to happen. Quality of service is the key and our immediate customers who set the appropriate service level are the unit general manager and the rest of his management team.

Fourth, personnel departments are likely to perceive all the people they serve as their 'customers', not just managers. Personnel's customers can include governing bodies or boards of management, chief executives, senior managers or chief officers, heads of units or departmental heads, individual managers, employees, union officials and members of the public. The services provided include: policy formulation; information; advice; policy monitoring; administration; and controlling staff costs.

Fifth, in developing a strategic role, the personnel function develops a business-orientation and becomes more closely integrated into corporate management. Some would identify this with an HRM approach rather than a TPM one. Yet the term HRM is inherently problematic. It has a variety of meanings and has been subject to considerable academic debate over the last decade, much of it speculative and focused on private-sector evidence rather than what has happened in the public services (Storey, 1989; Storey, 1992; Tyson, 1995; Hendry, 1995). Beardwell and Holden (1994) summarize the debate, arguing that HRM is characterized by four predominant approaches: as a renaming of the basic personnel management function; as a fusion of personnel management and industrial relations but with a managerialist agenda; as a wider conception of the employment relationship, stressing the potential of individual employees as investments rather than as costs; and as part of the strategic managerial function, making a contribution to corporate strategy. The emerging personnel function in the public services appears to incorporate each of these approaches, to varying degrees, but underpinning it is 'the question of control and the manner in which it is exercised and mitigated' (p. 687).

Sixth, with changing public-service orientations and change in the personnel function, some personnel tasks are being devolved to line managers. The relationship between line managers and the specialist personnel function is often a sensitive one. As early research by Legge (1978, p. 52) shows:

(1) Line management tend to have a confused, hazy and/or stereo-typed perception of the potential nature and scope of a personnel department's activities.
(2) Middle and junior line management in particular tend to consider that personnel departments are 'out of touch' with the problems and constraints which face them.

There is always some degree of ambiguity about which aspects of people management should be left to line managers and which to personnel specialists. However, as Storey (1992, p. 214) indicates, recent organizational responses to environmental change are inducing changes in the human resources roles of senior and middle line managers. Structural and culture changes are giving new emphases to 'customer orientation, innovation and competitiveness', with implications for the ways in which people are being deployed and managed. And 'steerage with regard to these matters has increasingly been taken up by operational managers rather than personnel specialists.'

As earlier Chapters have shown, the sorts of people management tasks being devolved to line managers include: recruitment and selection decisions, performance management, staff appraisal, staff development, PRP, career advice, staff counselling and welfare. Line managers are also making decisions about pay allowances, extensions of leave and compassionate leave. Tasks remaining the prime responsibility of personnel specialists include dealing with the unions, human resources planning and payment administration.

A major strategic concern for the personnel function is the requirements for market testing and CCT for personnel services. In November 1992, government announced that it would be extending CCT to six professional and corporate support services in local government, including personnel services. The Department of the Environment's (DoE) draft definition of personnel services included: corporate and advisory work; organizational development; human resource management; training and development; pay and non-pay benefits; equal opportunities; health, safety and welfare; industrial and employee relations; and 'client-side activity.' The expectation was that initially up to 25 per cent of personnel work would be subject to CCT.

In a study commissioned by the DoE, Peat Marwick management consultants (1994) were asked to review: the base quantum for the defined activities within local authority personnel services; factors affecting its determination; and factors to be taken into account in determining the competition requirement. The consultants' main findings from their data collection exercise amongst 22 local authorities were that: the quantum of services was dominated by training and development and human resource management; the case-study authorities experienced difficulties in allocating activities amongst the constituent definitions; training included large elements which were externally funded; a large number of authorities provided both centralized and de-centralized services, with some activities devolved to line managers; and an average of 20 per cent of activities were already subject to competition or externalization, especially training.

Turning to the competition requirement, the report came to three conclusions. First, local authorities stressed the need for in-house personnel capabilities supporting the core organization, performing an effective client role and maximizing the value of external providers. Second, 30–40 per cent of personnel services could be subject to externalization. Third, there was genuine concern that a requirement for further market testing of internal providers could lead to 'a large number of small value packages with associated extra client cost' or 'packaging of services that may constrain an authority's freedom to organise itself in ... the most effective fashion' (Peat Marwick, 1994, p. 55).

In responding to Peat Marwick's study, SOCPO's Core Group on CCT (1994) made three points. First, it accepted that the report showed a good understanding of the role and structure of the personnel function in local government. Second, it considered that an extension of CCT to personnel services could force authorities to re-centralize the function. Third, it added (p. 4):

> Requiring more than 25% of personnel activities to be subject to a statutory competitive regime ... could lead to areas generally accepted as unsuitable for competition being exposed to CCT, in particular the core and corporate role undertaken by personnel in supporting the work of authorities.

Management Style

The dominant management style emerging in the public services, which is largely replacing paternalism, may be described as a rationalist one. Essentially, a rationalist style of management is goal oriented. It is one where those in authority scan the environment facing them, set themselves and the organization explicit goals, objectives and targets and plan the ways most likely to achieve these goals, objectives and targets, using all their resources, including human resources, to this end.

A rationalist management style differs substantially from public-service paternalism in at least three ways. First, it is not driven by concepts of fairness, the welfare needs of employees and the need to maintain good relations with the unions. It is driven by the demands of those leading public organizations for effective job performance, high quality of output, service to customers and value for money. Second, as a management style, a rationalist approach to management is not just concerned with the effective managing of people. Rather, it adopts a comprehensive approach to management by seeking to integrate the needs of the 'business' with the effective managing of people and to integrate the needs of the organization with the aspirations of those working in it. Third, a rationalist style of management does not rely upon the techniques of classical public administration but leans heavily on private-sector concepts, nostra and experiences, drawn largely from north American and Japanese case studies and literature (Pascale and Athos, 1980; White and Trevor, 1983; Moss Kanter, 1985; Peters, 1987 and 1992; Thurley and Wirdenius, 1989; Kotter, 1990; Moss Kanter, Skein and Todd, 1992). Fourth, and above all, rationalist management is not concerned with managing stability but managing continual change.

A rationalist style of management derives from the economistic view that public services are public businesses, requiring mission statements, business plans and corporate strategies together with accompanying objectives, goals and targets to be achieved and evaluated, using techniques adapted from private-sector practice (Johnson and Scholes, 1993). Those adopting a rationalist style of management argue that the best way in which managers can achieve effective and efficient organizations, which meet performance targets and satisfy customer needs, is by utilizing the knowledge, skills and competences of staff and gaining their commitment to corporate values, goals and objectives (PSLB, 1993; IPD, 1995). It thus becomes incumbent upon managers: 'to articulate clearly the objectives and core values of the organisation within which local managers will be required to operate.' As one chief personnel officer in local government writes (Parvin, 1995, p. 19):

> This demands a high profile for people management within the organisation and I use the term 'people management' advisedly. I do not subscribe to the term 'Human Resources'. Employees are not 'human resources' to be passively exploited like an inanimate piece of machinery or seam of coal. They are people with minds and motivations of their own. If they are to make the maximum possible contribution to the organisation in which they work they need to feel an identity with the objectives and culture of that organisation, and to feel that their contribution is valued.

A number of British managers in leading-edge organizations, including some in public services, have written about their experiences in the proactive managing of change and the problems associated with this. And there is considerable overlap between vocabularies used in the public and private sectors by those dealing with organizational change. Connock (1993, pp. 143 and 159), for example, based on his experiences in insurance, electronics and a public utility, emphasises 'the power of vision': 'know what you want to achieve; know your underlying values; reinforce the business mission' and 'be proactive!'. This theme is taken up by the Director of Personnel and Management Development in a rural district council. She argues (Holmes, 1995, p. 4) that the role of her organization's central personnel department is now focused on 'vision and direction'. This involves 'monitoring the external environment and anticipating the need for cultural or organisational change' and 'supporting managers, proactively and reactively, with high level knowledge and expertise.'

The Personnel Officer for Nottinghamshire County Council describes how the appointment of a new chief executive heralded the 'beginning of a new approach to the management of the Council' (Gorman, 1995, p. 8). He outlines how the authority moved from being a departmentally-focused, bureaucratic and reactive organization 'to one with corporate objectives, that was customer and quality oriented with a broader vision, mission and values'. In defining its 'vision' for the human resources function, he writes, the Council sought (pp. 9–11) to:

— develop latent skills in the workforce
— improve employee ability to participate in developing and improving services
— recognise personal effort and achievement and improve job satisfaction and career development
— enable the Council to be more self sufficient by developing the potential of its employees
— advance the commitment to equality of opportunity
— retain staff with particular specialist knowledge and experience

To achieve this vision, seven 'human resource objectives' were agreed within the Council. These were to:

— Foster a corporate identity to enhance the fact that the County Council is one organisation
— Improve human resource planning to facilitate achievement of the Council's aims and objectives
— Promote and facilitate the appointment of staff of the highest calibre who are appropriate in terms of disability, race and gender
— Provide appropriate training and development of staff to facilitate the highest standards of work throughout the Council for the best interests of all our customers
— Promote and facilitate the highest possible level of staff performance, motivation, job satisfaction and commitment and with the Occupational Health Unit, care for the health, safety and welfare of all County employees
— Work positively towards and influence the direction and implementation of organisational development in line with the Council's aims and objectives
— Support the Council in its wider community role in relation to providing employment opportunities throughout the county

In Gorman's view (p. 12), his role has moved away from being a maintenance one to one focused 'much more on supporting the Chief Executive in . . . culture change' and 'in being a member of his team in driving forward the concepts of customer care, quality services, line management empowerment and organisational development'.

These themes are repeated throughout the plethora of documentation, position papers and consultancy reports circulating within and emanating from the public services since the early 1980s. A recent example is the police reform white paper (Cm. 2281, 1993). This argues that the police service faces many of the problems of other large organizations and that it 'should use the best techniques of modern management commonplace in the private sector' and 'increasingly in other parts of the public sector.'

These include: clear statements of aims and objectives, resources related to these objectives, delegation of responsibility to the lowest possible level and 'freedom for managers to marshal the available resources to achieve their objectives in the most effective way' (p. 9).

What then are some of the common themes emerging in what Armstrong, a manager with senior experience in banking and manufacturing, (1993, p. 1) calls 'the shift from "resolution of inevitable conflict" to "active management of change"'? For him, the key issue for contemporary managers is to learn from past mistakes and accept responsibility (p. 9) 'that what we are about is creating the capacity within the organisation through people to design, develop and deliver the future we are looking for.' Whilst conceding that there is no single effective style of the 'new' management, he encapsulates the common features of what he calls 'winning organisations' which 'have changed dramatically in recent years'. These include (p. 11):

— their structures are now flatter and less hierarchical;
— power is devolved to smaller, customer-based units;
— aims and purposes are absolutely clear;
— headquarters offices are reduced in size, so that they provide strategic direction but do not attempt to take or vet (far less implement) most operational decisions;
— distinctions between line and staff functions have become blurred in management teams made up of people with complementary talents;
— management specialization has been discouraged, with individuals acquiring a portfolio of 'generalised' skills;
— boards have accepted clear responsibility for creating the vision, allocating resources, developing managerial talent and rigorously monitoring performance against targets and external competitors.

Armstrong then summarizes what he considers to be 10 'radically altered approaches to people management' tending to accompany these organizational changes (pp. 12–13). These organizations:

- create clear senses of purpose and values
- set targets for the organization and individual employees
- emphasise the primacy of customers
- recruit for potential to raise the overall competence of the workforce
- treat employees as respected contributors to success
- adapt working patterns to fit the needs of the organization
- develop flexible systems of reward, linked to contribution and performance
- invest heavily in training and encourage self-development
- take employee involvement seriously
- take an optimistic view of human nature

For Armstrong (p. 19), the search for improved organizational performance and people contribution to success does not rest on 'exhortation and academic analysis' but on management experience.

Performance management, quality management and customer care need again to be briefly addressed here, because they are dominant themes in the new public management, whilst the values underlying them are at the core of the rationalist approach to management. There are five basic elements in a comprehensive PMS. First, top management defines the organization's mission, values and goals. Second, departments and sub-units use these corporate benchmarks to determine their objectives, plans and activities. Third, specific objectives and targets are determined for individual staff, which are later reviewed in the staff appraisal scheme. Fourth, decisions are made about performance payments to staff. Fifth, action plans are produced for the next performance management cycle. Initially introduced into the private sector, PMSs, based on these principles, have been introduced on a wide scale into the public services since the mid-1980s.

Further, according to Storey (1989), it is the search for improved performance in organizations which has provided the impetus for developments in HRM techniques.

These include more sophisticated selection methods, performance-review appraisal schemes, contribution-based (PRP) reward systems and increased interest in management development and staff training. Indeed, research reveals 'a considerable degree of revitalized attention in many of Britain's major companies to each of these four constituents of selection, appraisal, rewards and development' (1989, p. 6; 1992).

There are a variety of approaches to quality management (ACAS, 1991), including 'hard' statistical approaches, 'soft' behavioural ones and combinations of the hard and soft versions. A model which has taken root in many parts of the public services is Total Quality Management (TQM), based again on private-sector experience. An operational definition of TQM is provided by Russell and Dale (1989, p. 2):

> The aim is that everyone in the organisation should be dedicated to the never-ending improvement of their activities with the objective of satisfying their customers. Teamwork is an essential aspect of the improvement process, and the organisation is committed to improving the quality of working life of their people and to their development through participation at all levels. External customers and suppliers are also integrated into the quality improvement process.

According to Mortiboys and Oakland, in a Department of Trade and Industry publication (1991, pp. 8 and 37), TQM 'is a way of managing an organisation so that every job, every process, is carried out right, first time and every time. It affects everyone.' They identify the key facets of TQM as:

- Recognising customers and discovering their needs and expectations
- Setting standards which are consistent with customer requirements
- Controlling processes and improving their capability
- Establishing systems of quality
- Management's responsibility for setting quality policy,

> providing motivation through leadership and equipping
> people to achieve quality
> ■ Empowerment of people at all levels . . . to act for quality
> improvement.

Quality initiatives, along these lines, are now common-place across the public services.

Employment Practices

A central feature of emerging employment practices amongst public employers is their focus on flexibility. In this respect, the public services are again going along the pathway of private-sector employers, where the concept of the flexible firm has long been accepted and debated (Atkinson and Meager, 1986). This contrasts with the old public services, with their record of job stability, planned career pathways and employment security. The institutional 'push' factors driving public services towards greater flexibility include: de-centralization and de-layering; pressures on labour and employment costs; and the opportunity provided for managers to control their staff and the work process. The social 'pull' factors include: demands by some groups, such as parents and carers, for non-standard working arrangements; individuals wanting the flexibilities available from freelance employment; and pressures on employers arising from equal opportunities legislation.

The shift towards flexible employment practices starts with recruitment, which now tends to be open, continual and speedy, and is more market-driven than in the past. As Fowler (1988b) reports, public employers have questioned and redefined selection specifications to increase volume of candidates and achieve a more flexible workforce, representative of the community-at-large. They have tried to eliminate unjustified age limits and unnecessarily high standards of educational qualifications, although conditions of service can place restrictions on recruitment, particularly those defining salaries and working time. As a technical officer in local government commented, 'personnel can assist by monitoring the market, ensuring that remuneration packages are appropriate to the market in which we are recruiting' (quoted in Fowler, 1988b, p. 55).

There are also tendencies for public employers to identify new sources of recruitment, use a wider range of recruitment methods and target particular populations or locations for their staffing requirements. These can counteract shortages of particular types of staff, facilitate equal opportunities and are cost-effective.

Public-service employers are also using a wide range of working patterns. The Mueller report (1987), which has since been implemented, identified, for example, the main influences on working patterns in the Civil Service. These were: pressures to reduce costs; demand for services outside working hours; technological change; levels of unemployment; the number of married women seeking employment; skills shortages; and constraints of the CSMC. It examined the case for change, arising from the needs to reduce costs, improve productivity and compete with employers to employ premium staff. The MPO recommended the extension of part-time employment, period contracts and homeworking. It also recommended introducing three new working patterns: recurring temporary contracts, nil-hours contracts and annual hours contracts.

These working patterns are duplicated across the public services. Staff with full-time, tenured contracts are declining in relative importance. Whilst there have always been non-standard contracts in public employment, such as supply teachers, part-time nurses and support staff in central and local government, the proportion on part-time and fixed-term contracts is increasing, especially amongst female staff. Fowler (1993) lists the variety of part-time contracts found in the public services today. These include contracts for: fixed five-day schedules; full daily hours for some days each week; variable weekly hours; unspecified hours to complete specific tasks; term-time only; performance, with employment ceasing on job completion; standby employment; weekend or evening shifts; and job sharing. There are, in addition, fixed-term contracts, which are increasingly being used for senior managerial jobs, where completion of the job and termination of employment are known in advance.

There is greater flexibility in pay and benefits too. Historically, public-service units paid little attention to rewards management, because of standard, national pay agreements. This has changed, largely because of skills shortages, rigidity of national agreements, government pressure to abandon national pay bargaining and the impacts of CCT and market testing. One of the biggest changes has been the introduction of PRP, strongly supported by government. Fowler (1993) identifies the main variants of PRP used in the public services: salary progression within defined pay scales; salary progression above scale maxima for high performers; lump sums; and combinations of salary progression and lump sums. In some cases, spot salaries are paid, with pay increases based solely on performance.

Flexibilities have also been introduced in non-pay benefits, such as relocation and fringe benefits. In some public services, repayment of fees for estate agents and solicitors, temporary housing accommodation and mortgage subsidies are available. Other benefits include: leased cars for certain grades of staff; nominal private mileage charges; life insurance; private health insurance; and pension options, such as additional voluntary contributions. There are also benefits covering: childcare assistance; career breaks; welfare and stress counselling; health promotion facilities; and grants for personal study.

There have always been opportunities for promotion in the public services, especially for white-collar and professional staff, normally based on merit and seniority. Merit continues to be a main criterion for promotion but seniority, or time-serving, is much less important. This is because applications for some senior posts, such as in the Civil Service, NHS and local government, are no longer limited to internal candidates. In fact, appropriately qualified external candidates are sometimes actively sought. This is supported by the belief that the opening-up of posts to individuals in the private sector, or private professional practice, is likely to raise the quality of applicants. It is also expected to enrich the public services, and transfer private-sector know-how into them, where high quality external applicants are appointed.

Promotion was also linked with training and career progression and those applying for promotion were usually amongst the best qualified in their occupations. But, again, circumstances are changing. In the Civil Service, for example, the Oughton report (Efficiency Unit, 1993, p. 6) made proposals for providing a better basis 'for identifying, training and developing individuals to ensure a pool of supply for senior posts.' It also made recommendations about selection and appointment procedures for filling senior posts, 'where, as in the private sector, developing staff from within is right in most cases but there is likely to be a greater use of open advertisement and competition.'

The standing of public services in training provision has always been high. But now training and HRD are taking a central role in facilitating change and flexibility. Continuous change results in old skills becoming redundant and new ones being required. Further, change itself is facilitated by effective training, staff development and management development. Despite the relatively good record of public services in providing training for staff at all levels, there are three areas where public organizations are showing increasing interest. First, there is management training to develop new skills and competences, such as managing people, finance and information. Second, public organizations are also developing awareness of the 'learning organization', rooted in the belief that organizations have to learn from their own experiences, adapt and develop accordingly. Third, with the emergence of national training strategies, such as NVQs and the MCI, public services are relating training to national developments.

Industrial Relations

Under TPM, industrial relations in the public services were strongly pluralist. Even very senior managers were union members and their pay and conditions were negotiated with representative organizations in national pay forums, such as Whitley bodies in the Civil Service, NHS and local government and the Police Negotiating Board (ACAS, 1980). In NPM, industrial relations tend to become dichotomized. This means that there is a move away from the collectivist tradition to a dualist one. This new system contains elements of both collectivism and individualism, in which some groups are treated pluralistically by their employers, with elements of individualism, and others wholly individualistically. A basic fission is often between the ways that employers deal with managerial staff and non-managers.

The preferred method for managing employment relationships with managerial staff is on an individual basis, through introducing personal contracts of employment. This has happened, especially at senior levels. Top managers in Next Steps agencies, the NHS, new universities and the police are employed on fixed-term contracts. Other senior staff on personal contracts, which may or may not be for fixed terms, also negotiate individually with their employer. It is the governing bodies of organizations, such as NHS trusts and new university corporations, which set the parameters of individual negotiation. Employers establish pay and benefits packages for these staff, in line with what they believe 'the market will bear' and what is necessary to attract and retain the right quality of individual postholders. It is a pattern of employment relations imported from the private sector, where individual salaries are negotiable, within set ranges, and normally contain a performance-related element.

Such arrangements effectively de-recognize trade unions who previously negotiated pay and conditions for these staff (Claydon, 1989). There is little or no evidence about union membership and membership density amongst such staff except in the new universities, which may be a special case. Here it appears that average density of union membership for managerial grades in 1994 was 52 per cent. This appears to be relatively high but at some institutions there is partial collective bargaining for this group locally (Farnham and Giles, 1995a). Other occupations where senior staff appear to have retained or even increased union or professional association membership is amongst doctors, nurses and other professional groups (Farnham and Giles, 1995b). All chief constables are members of ACPO, even where they are on fixed-term contracts.

More realistically, managerial staff are effectively denied representation at their places of work, where their unions and staff associations have been de-recognized nationally, except where individuals retain membership for purposes other than collective bargaining. Where this is not the case, it makes some individuals vulnerable when in conflict with their employers. There are instances, privately known to the authors, where senior managers have been in dispute with their employers but were unable to remedy their complaints. As a result, they resigned and lost their jobs.

A major feature of the non-collectivist approach to managing staff on personal contracts is individual performance reviews and performance management systems (PMSs). As discussed earlier, PMSs have become commonplace in the public services. Indeed, according to Fowler (1993, pp. 48–9):

> It has . . . been evident that in some [public sector] organisations, a failure to define corporate aims and standards has left individual managers to decide for themselves which aspects of performance and quality to pursue. The result has sometimes been conflict or inconsistency between different parts of the same organisation.

Attempts have been made, therefore, to introduce coordinated PMSs in the public services, to facilitate managerial efficiency and motivate the whole workforce.

Performance management begins at the very top and

senior managers have to agree, normally annually, their own managerial goals or targets with those to whom they report. It is a rebirth of 'Management-by-Objectives' (Humble, 1961). Such targets are specific to the purposes and tasks of each manager's job and are intended to support corporate aims and values. At top levels, personal targets derive out of the organization's corporate mission statement, its core values and long-term and short-term priorities and include plans to operationalize the postholder's objectives. The same process is cascaded downwards to departmental and unit heads and, through them, to subordinate staff. There are periodic reviews of achievements against targets, with new targets and action plans set for the next review.

This approach to managing people management has been described as a 'neo-unitary' one (Farnham and Pimlott, 1995). It builds on the classical unitary ideas of team work and common purpose at work but is more sophisticated in the ways that it is articulated and applied. Its underlying aim is to integrate all staff into the organization, including those in non-managerial or professional positions. The public services, like their private-sector counterparts, share a number of ways in which they seek to achieve this integration (p. 46):

> ... they try to create a sense of common purpose and shared corporate culture; they emphasise ... the primacy of customer service; they set explicit work targets for employees; they invest heavily in training and development; and they sometimes provide employment security for their workers.

In managing the employment relationship between non-managerial staff and their employers, on the other hand, the collectivist tradition continues to predominate and remains strongly rooted. Collective bargaining procedures cover most professional and non-professional grades, despite structural reorganizations, changes in corporate culture and the introduction of new, private-sector management techniques. National collective bargaining persists in the Civil Service, parts of the NHS, local government and further and higher education but not for school teachers, nurses and midwives and the professions allied to medicine in the NHS.

It is arguable that the employers' emphasis in managing non-managerial staff is now a 'neo-collectivist' one. First, reforms of collective bargaining structures are taking place. In the Civil Service, for example, collective bargaining and personnel management flexibilities are being devolved to departments and Next Steps agencies (Treasury and Cabinet Office, 1991). Local pay bargaining is being encouraged in NHS trusts (Huddart, 1994a). Some local authorities are opting out of national bargaining for certain groups of staff (Bryson *et al.*, 1993) and, in the new universities and further education colleges, new style bargaining arrangements, modelled on private-sector procedures, have been established, replacing a more bureaucratic and slower-reacting NJC system (Farnham, 1992).

Second, trade unions and staff associations, whilst not being actively discouraged by public employers, do not appear to be actively encouraged either. This differs from past practice, when union membership was positively promoted by most public authorities, to maintain the representativeness of staff organizations and their legitimacy. Now some public employers appear to be non-committal towards union organization and the role that unions play in managing the employment relationship.

Third, the frame of reference held by public-service employers appears to be moving towards a 'soft' pluralist one, away from traditional pluralism (Clegg, 1975). Whilst accepting collective bargaining as an authoritative system for managing industrial relations, some employers seem to be encouraging joint problem-solving and non-adversarial approaches to the employer-union relationship. They are also attempting to harmonize and rationalize staff representation on negotiating and consultative committees, especially locally. In some cases, such as in the NHS and FE colleges, employers and staff organizations are involved in single-table bargaining, incorporating union, professional association and non-union staff representatives, from TUC and non-TUC organizations. Another indicator of a softer style of industrial relations management is attempts by some employers to communicate directly with their staff through briefing groups, newsletters and house journals.

Role of the Employer

It is doubtful whether the state as an employer is any longer the traditional model employer, which it previously purported to be, even if, in practice, it sometimes fell below the best standards it set for itself (Beaumont, 1981). In the past, in conditions of expansion and full employment, an assumed symbiosis existed between the role of the public services as providers of public goods and their role as good employers. The underpinning assumption was that the state had a triple responsibility: to its citizens, as taxpayers and beneficiaries of public services; to its employees, as agents of provision; and to employees outside the public services, working for employers where labour standards were low. The state was expected to be a good employer, not only to meet its moral duty as an employer, but also to provide examples of good practice for private employers to follow.

The extent to which the traditional good employer role can any longer be upheld is, on the evidence available, questionable. In some areas, state employers continue to be models of good practice; in others, less so. In the Civil Service, for example, an internal review of the respective responsibilities of the Civil Service Commissioners and departments in the recruitment process, commissioned by the Head of the Civil Service, made a 'number of recommendations designed to reinforce the principles of openness, fairness and merit in recruitment', which is very much in line with the traditional position. The review team also clarified 'responsibilities for ensuring that these principles are properly and effectively applied', whilst acknowledging that, in future, 'recruitment is likely to be limited in scale' (Cm. 2627, 1994, pp. 9 and 30). Further, in order 'to make

use of its most important resource – the staff of departments and agencies', the Civil Service stated its intention
of providing 'the prospect of a career with a good employer', developing staff 'skills to meet ... managerial,
technical and competitive challenges' and ensuring 'equality
of opportunity for all members of staff, irrespective of
background, gender, race and disability' (p. 31).

In other areas, the Civil Service has diverged from traditional good employer practices, driven by the 'need to
manage reductions in the size of its workforce as a result
of competition and in the interests of efficiency' (p. 46).
The principle underlying pay, for instance, is now guided
by government's belief that it 'should be set on a fair
basis which reflects the need to recruit, retain and motivate
staff of the right quality' but 'recognises good performance', taking into account 'that pay increases have to be
covered from efficiency savings and other economies'.
Indeed, this is a policy which appears to be increasingly
applied within other public services. Additionally, government has disaggregated its centralized pay arrangements
for civil servants, on the assumption that 'pay and grading systems, like other management arrangements, should
be attuned to individual circumstances and relevant labour
markets' (pp. 26–27). Again, this policy-emphasis is apparent in the NHS, local government and other public
services.

Government has also said that job security will continue to be weakened in the Civil Service, adding that
'there is a belief in some quarters that civil servants have
jobs for life. That is not the case'. Whilst staff reductions
are to be achieved as far as possible without redundancies, and on a voluntary basis, with every effort being
'made to ensure that civil servants will be treated in a
way which is fair and reasonable', government's underlying aim is to continue 'reductions in the size of the Civil
Service'. In the future, too, there may well be fewer distinctions in 'job security between employment in the senior
levels in the Civil Service and that at comparable levels
in the public sector or ... private sector'. Accordingly, to
the extent that this is the case, 'there will be less justification

for the present discount in Senior Civil Service salaries'
(pp. 30, 43 and 44).

Similar statements have been made in local government.
A senior manager in a leading local authority, for example,
has questioned the continuing validity of the model employer role. In his view (Griffiths, 1993, p. 45):

> The imminent extension of compulsory competitive tender-
> ing to 'white collar' professional services emphasises the fact
> that the model 'good employer' public sector tradition, with
> its implied security and continuity of employment and cen-
> trally negotiated pay and conditions, is at odds with 'free
> market' principles.

The head of employment policy in a large urban, local
authority also identifies the central importance of CCT
in producing a range of managerial problems in local
government. He argues that (Manning, 1995, p. 29):

> [CCT] has ... forced both managers and elected members
> to challenge their existing value systems concerning what it
> means to be 'a good employer', and what the costs to
> employees might need to be in retaining jobs in-house. A
> clear tension has developed between what the good em-
> ployer would like to do and what might be necessary to win
> contracts.

The traditional philosophy of the model employer, then,
is being eroded and is being replaced by a new notion:
that the public services are increasingly public businesses,
aimed primarily at satisfying individual client needs in
the market place, in conditions of resource constraint, with
the role of the state as an employer becoming subordinated to this political priority. One consequence is that
the employment function of the state becomes secondary
in importance to its business functions, which are associated with customer care, quality service and organizational efficiency. A second consequence is that the
management function increases in importance, becoming
the prime agency of change, control and cost-effectiveness. A third consequence is that the state treats its

employees like private-sector employers treat theirs, rather than as old-style public servants. State employers, in short, are no longer the model for private-sector employers to follow: private-sector employers become the model for state employers to follow. From being leaders of people management policy and practice, the public services become followers of what is perceived to be best practice in the private sector. This is the 'new mode' public-service employer.

Examined in this way, the emerging role of the new mode employer (NME) becomes easier to understand and put into context. It explains the shifts towards a number of people management developments: personal contracts of employment; PRP; PMS; staff appraisal; external recruitment; flexible patterns of work; increases in part-time workers; cafeteria benefits; union de-recognition; prime union deals; local pay bargaining; the weakening of Whitleyism; challenges to pluralism; emphases on training and HRD; and less job security. Most of these practices, and the ideas and policies underpinning them, have their origins in the private sector.

The NME, however, also incorporates legacies of the past. Whilst most public employees are subject to staff appraisal and performance management, and some have enhanced training opportunities, not all elements of the new employment practices apply universally or evenly across the public services. Only selected groups of staff, for example, are on personal contracts; PRP is not used throughout the public services; and external recruitment is more firmly rooted in some services, such as the Civil Service, than it is, say, in education or the uniformed police. Even flexible patterns of work and increases in part-time employment vary across different services. Indeed, in the NHS, education and local government, employers have always relied on relatively large numbers of part-timers to maintain services. Cafeteria benefits are not widespread and are mainly limited to selected managerial and professional staff groups. To date, union de-recognition has been limited to senior managers, teachers, nurses, midwives and PAMs, and staff at GCHQ.

Prime union deals seem to be limited to the NHS, whilst the shift to local pay bargaining remains limited to the NHS and local government. Further, whilst the principles of Whitleyism and industrial relations pluralism have been weakened in the Civil Service, parts of the NHS – such as amongst PAMs – and schools, they are still strongly rooted in other parts of the NHS, in local government and in post-school education. And even if jobs in the public services are less secure than in the past, they are still safer than in most parts of the corporate sector.

The NME in the public services, then, incorporates elements of tradition and change in the ways that staff are treated. The employment function becomes subordinate to the needs to control employment costs, change working methods and improve productivity. As a former member of the NHS Executive starkly summed up (Caines, 1993, p. 34): 'personnel officers [in the NHS] must learn to talk the language of productivity and must know how productivity gains can be achieved.' If there is an emerging pattern, good employment practices in the public services are primarily to facilitate organizational efficiency and customer satisfaction, in conditions of resource constraint. As such, public employers aim to reflect best standards in the private sector, such as pay policy, equal opportunities and training and development, rather than to influence private-sector practice. At the same time, certain traditional model employer practices, such as employment security, universal support for collective bargaining and full incorporation of unions into the consultative process, are being weakened.

Conclusion

There is little doubt that the ways in which people are being managed in the reformed public services are qualitatively different from people management during the heydays of TPM, during the 1960s and 1970s. In this, the public services are no different from what has been happening in the private sector, where people management policies, activities and systems are also changing.

Sisson (1994) argues that the significant developments taking place in private-sector personnel management may even be described as a 'transformation'. This transformation is what Guest (1990) calls the 'new orthodoxy' of personnel management. He identifies this with the HRM model associated with the central goals of commitment, flexibility, quality and strategic integration. According to Sisson (pp. 41–2), however, 'this transformation in the direction of the "HRM" organization' is only happening in a small number of cases. What appears to be more widespread is 'the substitution of individualism for collectivism, a reduction in standards and an assertion of management freedom from constraints.' For Sisson, the reality of HRM is very different from its rhetoric. Most large British companies, he argues, faced with competition and resource constraints, 'will seek what they perceive to be the benefits of the [HRM] model . . . yet will be unable to incur the costs involved in implementing it in full.' As a result, 'they are likely to exhibit an odd "hybrid" of HRM practices, further moves away from collectivism, and bouts of macho management', with personnel management in many organizations being 'locked into a vicious circle of low pay, low skill, and low productivity.'

In terms of the HRM paradigm, NPM can be viewed in a number of ways: as another 'failed' or partial model of HRM; as a relatively successful 'implant' of HRM, taken from the private sector and injected into the public services; or as a public-service mode of HRM, drawing on some of its classical features but omitting others. Rather than enter into a complex and sterile debate, since cases could be made out for each of the above models, we prefer to restate our analysis so far. First, the developments in people management outlined in this book represent a significant shift towards a NPM paradigm in the public services. Second, as pure typologies, TPM and NPM incorporate contrasting personnel functions, management styles, sets of employment practices, patterns of industrial relations and roles for public employers. Third, elements of TPM are inevitably incorporated into NPM in the public services, largely because of the legacy of history on them, their continuous evolution for over a hundred years and their high levels of union membership. Fourth, NPM is not a homogeneous set of policies, activities and systems. As public services fragment, diversify and devolve, NPM develops in different ways, with various emphases, at variable speeds, in each service and within their constituent parts. NPM, in short, represents successive waves of change, with ebbs and flows of activity, not a tidal torrent.

What has changed are the contexts of the public services. Since the late 1970s, the British polity has been shifting from a Welfare State to a Contract State. In the former, the emphasis was on the provision of universal public and social services by largely expanding public bureaucracies, dominated by producers, especially professionals, their unions and staff associations. In the latter, the emphasis is on more diverse provision of 'public goods' by a 'mixed economy' of public, private and voluntary organizations, driven by managers, client needs and constraints on public spending. There is a dialectic between these two political philosophies, the definitive outcomes of which have yet to be determined. But this political and ideological dimension to the public services, and its implications for containing employment costs, controlling work activities and managing people, cannot be ignored. In successive general elections, since 1979, the Conservative party has continually claimed to be the party of 'low taxation'. Limiting public spending, including cutting income taxes prior to elections, has been central to defending this position and has impacted on public-service and people management change.

Another changing context is the labour market. During the heydays of TPM, the UK labour market was dominated by Keynesian economic policies and the tradition of collective *laissez-faire* or voluntary collectivism (Wedderburn, 1986; 1991). Government took responsibility for maintaining full employment; autonomous employers and independent unions participated in free collective bargaining; and the state provided a minimum floor of employment protection rights for workers (Farnham, 1993a). Since the late 1970s, however, full employment and collective voluntarism have been abandoned to a deregulated labour market and voluntary individualism. Employment is expected to find its 'natural' level through the operation of free market forces, industrial relations are more individualized and government policy no longer supports collective bargaining. As government stated in its 1992 white paper (Employment Department, 1992, pp. 1–2):

> There is new recognition of the role and importance of the individual employee. Traditional patterns of industrial relations, based on collective bargaining and collective agreements, seem increasingly inappropriate and are in decline ... Many employers are replacing outdated personnel practice with new policies for human resource management ... [and] There is a growing trend to individually negotiated reward packages which reflect the individual's personal skills, experience, efforts and performance.

The public services have not been exempt from the emergence of de-regulated labour markets and individualized employment relationships. Indeed, CCT and market testing have contributed to the de-regulating process, whilst senior public officials and top public managers, supporting ministerial policies, have helped implement new individualized modes of people management.

A third contextual change is that public services are no longer stable bureaucracies. The introduction of contractorization, for example, de-stabilizes those parts of public organizations affected by it. This arises from the intense demands and uncertainties placed upon managers and staff to coordinate and deliver contracts, which have to be continually drafted, applied and reviewed. As two local government officers have put it (quoted in Pratchett and Wingfield, 1994, p. 25):

> ...[the] emphasis is changing to be more cost conscious. Beyond broad cost comparisons this often becomes esoteric nonsense. Services often suffer and priorities are sacrificed for academic fiscal exercises.
>
> ...[also the] introduction of market philosophies leads to a selfish, self-seeking mentality which is difficult to integrate with social need; but value for money and being held responsible for performance is good.

The creation of internal markets also results in organizational disequilibrium, with much time and effort being spent in balancing the expectations and responsibilities of purchasing and providing units. The new culture associated with markets, competition, value for money and managing uncertainty is alien to traditional public servants. As a senior manager in local government has commented: 'for many managers there is a requirement to metamorphose from career local government officers to entrepreneurial team-based or individual operators' (Griffiths 1993, p. 45).

The effects of these contextual changes on those working in public organizations are far-reaching: senior public servants become public managers, responsible for managing resources rather than applying rules; public servants become public workers, some as part-timers, subcontractors or with non-tenured contracts, employed to meet defined job standards; professional staff become deprofessionalized, driven by managerialist agendas rather than by their own professional standards and codes of conduct; employment security is weakened for some, replaced by uncertainty about their futures; and quality of working life declines.

Additionally, there are increases in the proportions of support staff working in public services, often at the expense of professionals or 'service deliverers'. They are there to organize, manage and administer the implementation and monitoring of CCT, market testing, internal markets, financial management systems, IT and people management policies. In consequence, the traditional public-service ethos associated with reliability, service to the community and loyalty, is weakened. It is displaced by new values associated with efficiency, quality, innovation and informatization. A study of the changing public-service ethos in local government by Pratchett and Wingfield (1994, p. 33), for example, concludes that: interpretations of accountability are shifting from political accountability to contract and market accountability; acceptance of bureaucratic rules are diminishing; fragmentation into discrete business units is weakening collegiality; and loyalty is moving away from a 'Council-wide focus' towards 'more personally located loyalties.' Above all, the key feature of the emerging ethos:

... emphasises a competitive, contractual, insular and adversarial culture. This new ethos will not provide cohesion in the face of fragmentation, but will gradually compound the divisive elements of the new local government, leading to a disaggregated and disunited range of local services.

Another consequence is that the fair pay principle is undermined, if not replaced, by the market pay principle. This takes place at two levels. Public organizations want more flexibility in the ways in which they attract, recruit and retain staff, and the ways they reward them, whilst staff, especially professional ones, have expectations and aspirations about their individual worth to the organizations employing them. Employers seek entrepreneurial employees, rather than time-serving bureaucrats, using market and performance criteria in designing reward systems. Employees or potential employees, in turn, expect their personal contributions and efforts to be recognized by employers, although this can result in collaboration amongst colleagues being superseded by competition amongst intrapreneurs, for limited positional goods and rewards (Hirsch, 1976).

What, briefly, are some of the potential benefits of NPM? Within public-service organizations, people management becomes more proactive, rational and focused. For managers, there is potential for becoming more skilled in people management tasks, whilst management development opportunities enable managers to update and train in current best practice and 'state of the art' techniques in people management. NPM also provides more jobs and rewards for managers. It reinforces their right to manage, providing more scope for controlling and coordinating human resources. Where unions are de-recognized, or with local bargaining, trade unions and staff associations are weakened and opportunities for taking industrial action are limited. It is also easier for managers to get rid of incompetent or underperforming staff.

For some staff, NPM provides more open management systems, potential for better rewards, enhanced promotion opportunities and better chances for staff development. Staff are also likely to have more open appraisal systems, with the best managers providing feedback on performance, opportunities for training and openings for career potential. There are also possibilities for direct employee involvement, through team briefings, quality initiatives and more information provided by top management. Staff can also be treated more individualistically by managers, taking account of their personal expectations, as well as enhancing equal opportunities. For other staff, flexible working enables them to work in ways best suiting their personal needs and family responsibilities.

The potential disadvantages of NPM to managers and staff include intensification of workloads, less employment security and fewer promotion prospects, as organizations are de-layered, restructured and downsized. The de-professionalization of public-service professionals, and the corresponding rise of the salariat, weakens professional power and influence in organizational decision-making, whilst strengthening the position of support staff. The weakening of joint negotiating machinery and JCCs makes staff more vulnerable to unilateral managerial changes in pay, working methods and conditions of work, as well as the potential for 'dividing and ruling'. Whilst there may be increased equality of opportunities for individual staff, parity of participation in decision-making, by staff representatives, is reduced. NPM also creates 'winners' and 'losers', with the latter being particularly drawn from older staff, non-tenured workers, the less skilled and disadvantaged groups.

So how, finally, can the drift towards NPM be interpreted? We conclude with three perspectives: a 'managerialist' one; a 'labour process' one; and a 'politico-economic' one. The managerialist interpretation of NPM is an 'optimistic' one, starting from the assumption that the introduction of professional managers into state agencies is the best way to ensure the delivery of efficient, effective and quality public services to their customers, in conditions of economic constraint and continuous change. NPM becomes the means of achieving the ends of management, and of government, by attempting to integrate the needs of public-service organizations, as producers of public goods, with those of their workforces as human resources in the production process. The people working in them, at all levels, are seen as the key resource for achieving organizational and public-service success. The prime function of NPM is to ensure the recruitment and retention of the best staff, committed to the core values and beliefs of the organizations employing them. Staff are paid according to their market value and contributions they make and are continuously trained, developed and enculturated, so they can adapt to the demanding changes facing the public services.

The labour process perspective derives from the work of Braverman (1974), Friedman (1977) and Littler (1982). It is a 'structuralist' analysis, rooted in the assumption that management's central concern in organizations is maintaining control of the labour process and that production systems are geared towards this end. At its simplest, managerial control of work ultimately necessitates labour becoming de-graded, de-skilled and de-humanized. Friedman's contribution to the debate is important because he identifies a continuum of job design and control structures. These range from directly controlled, low trust, de-skilled jobs to high discretion, high trust, skilled ones. Managements can vary their work control strategies, using direct methods for the first, peripheral, group of workers but indirect ones for the second, core, group.

Those supporting the labour process interpretation of NPM would posit that it is directed at controlling the work process in the public services. This results, for some of the workforce at least, in: de-skilled job tasks; intensified work activity; reduced individual discretion; weakened employment security; limited trade union power; diluted collective bargaining; a smaller workforce; workers segmented into core and peripheral groups; and compliant workers, whose real wages are forced down.

The politico-economic interpretation of NPM is a 'pragmatic' one, based on the objective study of the employment relationship. It perceives NPM to be rooted in the nature of the employer–employee relationship in a market economy. Those proposing this perspective view the relationship between public-service organizations and their workforces as little different from any other employer–employee relationship: it rests on a mutually agreed wage–work bargain, albeit within a political contingency. This bargain involves organizations hiring the workers whose knowledge, skills and experience they need and providing them, in exchange, with wages and other employment benefits. It is essentially a reciprocal and instrumental relationship, based on the existing balance of power between the parties in the labour market and workplace. Employers seek to minimize their total wages costs, commensurate with achieving their organizational objectives, whilst employees seek to maximize their rewards for labour services, commensurate with their personal needs and aspirations.

Seen in this light, NPM reflects recent political changes within the UK and changes in the balance of power in the labour market between public-service employers and their workforces. Political change has been associated with free market economic policies, the strengthening of the powers of central government and globalization of markets (Gamble, 1988; Hutton, 1995). This is the context of NPM. The balance of power in the labour market, in turn, has shifted to employers, both public and private, because of high levels of unemployment, weaker trade unions and more assertive and sophisticated styles of management. The politico-economic interpretation of NPM perceives it as a product of political and managerial responses to the managing of people, where public workers have a weak position in the labour market and workplace, confronted by a strong state.

Bibliography

Ackroyd, S. and Helliwell, C. (1991) 'What happened to objectives?'. *Policing*, 7(2).

Advisory Conciliation and Arbitration Service (1980) *Industrial Relations Handbook* (London: ACAS).

Advisory Conciliation and Arbitration Service (1991) *Total Quality Management* (London: ACAS).

Anderson Report (1923) *Report of the Committee on Pay etc. of State Servants* (London: HM Treasury).

Anderson, R., Brown, J. and Campbell, E. (1993) *Aspects of Sex Discrimination within the Police Service in England and Wales*. Hampshire Constabulary/Police Research Group.

Anstey, E., Fletcher, and Walker (1977) *Staff Appraisal and Development* (London: Allen and Unwin).

Armitage Report (1978) *Report of the Committee on the Political Activities of Civil Servants*, Cmnd. 7057 (London: HMSO).

Armstrong, G. (1993) (ed.) *View from the Bridge* (London: IPM).

Armstrong, W. (1969) 'Whitleyism in the Civil Service', *Whitley Bulletin* x/ix.

Armstrong, M. (1993) *Human Resource Management: Strategy and Action* (London: Kegan Page).

Assheton Report (1944) *Report of the Committee on the Training of Civil Servants*, Cmd. 6525 (London: HMSO).

Association of Chief Police Officers (1992) *Towards a Future Training Strategy*, report of the Personnel and Training Committee (ACPO).

Atkinson J. and Meager N. (1986) *Changing Working Patterns: how companies achieve flexibility to meet new needs* (London, NEDO).

360

Audit Commission (1989) Police Paper 4 *The Management of Police Training* (London: HMSO).

Audit Commission (1990) Police Paper 8 *Effective Policing: Performance Review in Police Forces* (London: HMSO).

Audit Commission (1991) Police Paper 9 *Reviewing the Organization of Provincial Police Forces* (London: HMSO).

Audit Commission (1992) *The Management of Police Training* (London: HMSO).

Audit Commission (1994) *Adding up the Sums: school's management of their finances* (London: HMSO).

Audit Commission (1995) *Paying the Piper. People and Pay Management in Local Government* (London: HMSO).

Authers. J (1994) 'Management academe plc'. *Financial Times*, 14 December.

Bach, S. (1995) 'Restructuring the personnel function: the case of NHS trusts'. *Human Resource Management Journal*, Vol. 5, No. 2.

Bach, S. and Winchester, D. (1994). 'Opting out of pay devolution? The prospects for local bargaining in UK public services'. *British Journal of Industrial Relations*, Vol. 32, No. 2.

Bacon, R. and Eltis, W. (1976) *Britain's Economic Problems: Too Few Producers* (London: Macmillan).

Bains Report (1972) *The New Local Authorities, Management and Structure* (London: HMSO).

Beardwell, I. and Holden, L. (1994) *Human Resource Management* (London: Pitman).

Beatson, M. and Butcher, S. (1993) 'Union density across the employed workforce'. *Employment Gazette*, January.

Beaumont, P. (1981) *Government as Employer – Setting an Example* (London: RIPA).

Beaumont, P. (1992) *Public Sector Industrial Relations* (London: Routledge).

Behrens, R. (1989) 'Equality of opportunity in the Civil Service'. *Public Money and Management*, Winter.

Bell, D. (1973) *The Coming of Post-Industrial Society* (London: Heinemann).

Bell, L. (1995) *Spinning the Wheel. Joint Initiative for Community Care*. February (London: LGMB).

Bellamy, C. and Taylor, J. (eds) (1994) 'Towards the information polity? Public administration in the information age'. *Public Administration*. Vol. 72, No. 1.

Benn, T. (1979) *Arguments for Socialism* (London: Jonathan Cape).

Bevan, S. and Thompson, M. (1992) *An Overview of Policy and*

Practice in Performance Management in the UK (Wimbledon: IPM).

Beveridge, Sir W. (1942) *Social Insurance and Allied Services*, Cmnd. 6404 (London: HMSO).

Bird, D. and Corcoran, L. (1994) 'Trade union membership and density 1992–3'. *Employment Gazette*, June.

Blunkett, D. and Jackson, K. (1987) *Democracy in Crisis: The Town Halls Respond* (London: Hogarth).

Bolger, A. (1995) 'Threat of BMA sanctions averted'. *Financial Times*, 10 February. P 11.

Bradley, D., Walker, N. and Wilkie, R. (1986) *Managing the Police* (Brighton: Harvester Wheatsheaf).

Braverman, H. (1974) *Labor and Monopoly Capital* (New York: Monthly Review Press).

Bridges, Lord (1966) *The Treasury* (London: George Allen and Unwin).

Bright, P. (1994) 'Police promotion assessment centres'. Unpublished BA Dissertation. University of Portsmouth.

Brindle, D. (1993) 'NHS trust plunged into crisis after NHS contract withdrawn'. *The Guardian*, 17 September.

Brindle, D. (1994a) 'NHS to cut back managers by renaming'. *The Guardian*, 22 October.

Brindle, D. (1994b) 'NHS bosses boom as nurses work harder'. *The Guardian*, 19 August, 6.

Brindle, D. (1995) 'Spending up £1 billion on NHS bureaucrats'. *The Guardian*, 6th February, p. 3.

British Medical Association (1994) Letter to junior doctors from Dr Edwin Borman and Dr Paul Miller, 27 July.

Brittan, S. (1973) *Capitalism and the Permissive Society* (London: Macmillan).

Brooke, R. (1989) *Managing the Enabling Authority* (Harlow: Longman/LGTB).

Bryson, C., Gallagher, J., Jackson, M., Leopold, J. and Tuck, K. (1993) 'Decentralisation of collective bargaining: local authority opt outs'. *Local Government Studies*, Vol. 19, No. 4, Winter.

Buchanan, M. (1975) *The Limits of Liberty: Between Anarchy and Leviathan*. (Chicago: University of Chicago Press).

Bunyan, N. (1994) 'Bullied doctors says NHS chief must go'. *Daily Telegraph*, 2 November, p. 9.

Burden, D. (1976) 'New model office project in the Department of Health and Social Security'. *Management Services in Government*, February, Vol. 31, No. 1.

Burke, M. (1993) *Coming out of the Blues* (London: Cassell).

Butler, A. (1983) *Police Management* (Farnborough: Gower).

Butler, A. (1994) 'Pruning the rank structure'. *Policing*, Vol. 10, No. 1, Spring.

Butler, R. (1993) 'The evolution of the Civil service – a progress report', *Public Administration*. Vol. 71.

Cabinet Office (1984) *Programme of Action on Equal Opportunities for Women in the Civil service* (London: HMSO).

Cabinet Office/OMCS (1988) *Equal Opportunities for Women in the Civil Service. Progress Report 1984–87* (London: HMSO).

Cabinet Office (1991) *Pay and Management Flexibilities* (London: Treasury/OMCS).

Cabinet Office (1993) *Encouraging and Supporting the Delegation of Human Resource Development Responsibilities to Line Managers* (London: HMSO).

Cabinet Office (1994) *Next Steps Agencies, Third Report* (London: HMSO).

Cabinet Office (1995) *Next Steps Briefing Note* (London: Cabinet Office).

Caines, E. (1993) 'Personnel procedure', in Armstrong, G. *View from the Bridge* (London: IPM).

Callaghan, J. (1953) *Whitleyism* (London: Fabian Publications).

Campbell, D. (1990) 'The forces of prejudice'. *The Guardian*, October 31.

Cassels, J. (1983) *Review of Personnel Work in the Civil Service. Report to the Prime Minister* (London: HMSO).

Central Statistical Office (1994) *Economic Trends*, No 471, January.

Certification Office (1989) *Annual Report* (London: HMSO).

Certification Office (1993) *Annual Report* (London: HMSO).

Certification Office (1994) *Annual Report* (London: HMSO).

Chapman, L. (1978) *Your Disobedient Servant* (London: Chatto and Windus).

Chapman, R. and Hunt, M. (eds) (1987) *Open Government* (London: Croom Helm).

Charles, R. (1973) *The Development of Industrial Relations in Britain* (London: Hutchinson).

Civil Service Commission, *Annual Reports* (1986 to 94) (London: HMSO).

Civil Service Department (1970) *CSD Report 1969* (London: HMSO).

Civil Service Department (1975) *Civil Servants and Change* (London: HMSO).

Civil Service Department (1979) *Application of Race Relations Policy in the Civil Service* (London: HMSO).

Clarke, J. and Langan, M. (1993) 'The British welfare state: foundation and modernization', in Cochrane, A. and Clarke, J. *Comparing Welfare States* (London: Sage in Association with The Open University).

Claydon, T. (1989) 'Union derecognition in Britain in the 1980s. *British Journal of Industrial Relations*, 27(2), July.

Clegg, H. (1964) *General Union in a Changing Society* (Oxford: Blackwell).

Clegg, H. (1975) 'Pluralism in industrial relations'. *British Journal of Industrial Relations*, November.

Clegg, H., Fox, A. and Thompson, A. (1964) *A History Of British Trade Unions since 1889. Vol 1 1889–1910* (Oxford: Oxford University Press).

Coates, R. (1972) *Teachers Unions and Interest Group Politics* (Cambridge: Cambridge University Press).

Cmd. 3909 (1931) *Report of the Royal Commission on the Civil Service* (Chairman Lord Tomlin) (London: HMSO).

Cmnd. 9508 (1983) *Financial Management in Government Departments* (London: HMSO).

Cmd. 1730 (1991) *Competing for Quality* (London: HMSO).

Cm. 2281 (1993) *Police Reform: A Police Service for the Twenty-First Century* (London: HMSO).

Cm. 2464 (1994a) *Review Body on Senior Salaries Report No 34 Sixteenth Report on Senior Salaries* (London: HMSO).

Cm. 2464 (1994b) *Review Body on Senior Salaries Report No. 34 Annex to the Sixteenth Report on Senior Salaries* (London: HMSO).

Cm. 2519 (1994) *Public Expenditure: statistical supplement* (London: HMSO).

Cm. 2627 (1994) *The Civil Service Continuity and Change* (London: HMSO).

Cm. 2729 (1994) *Ending Discrimination against Disabled People* (London: HMSO).

Cm. 2748 (1995) *The Civil Service: Taking Forward Continuity and Change* (London: HMSO).

Cm 2764 (1995) *Review Body on Senior Salaries Report No 35 Seventeenth Report on Senior Salaries* (London: HMSO).

Coffey, S., Brown, J. and Savage, S. (1992) 'Policewomen's career aspirations: some reflections on the role and capabilities of women in policing in Britain'. *Police Studies*.

Cohen, E. (1941) *The Growth of the British Civil Service 1780–1939* (London: Frank Cass).

Cole, G. D. H. (1923) *Workshop Organisation* (London: Hutchinson Educational).

Colleges Employers Forum (1993) *Model Contract of Employment* (London: CEF).

Colling, T. (1993) 'Contracting public services: the management of compulsory competitive tendering in two county councils'. *Human Resources Management Journal*, Vol. 3, No. 4, Summer.

Collings, D. (1994) 'An examination of incentives and disincentives for constables and sergeants to take the sergeants and inspectors promotion examination'. Unpublished BA Dissertation. University of Portsmouth.

Collins, J. (1994) 'Collegialism and managerialism: a new model of university governance?'. Unpublished MA Dissertation. University of Portsmouth.

Commission for Racial Equality (1988) *Ethnic Minority School Teachers: a survey in eight local education authorities* (London: CRE).

Committee of Vice-Chancellors and Principals (1994) *Index of UK Universities, 1994/95* (London: CVCP).

Connock, S. (1993) 'The power of vision', in Armstrong, G. (ed). *View from the Bridge* (London: IPM).

Conservative Party (1992) *Manifesto: The Best Future for Britain* (London: Central Conservative Office).

Corby, S. (1992) 'Industrial relations developments in NHS trusts'. *Employee Relations*, Vol. 14, No. 6.

Corby, S. (1994a) 'How big a step is "next steps"? Industrial relations developments in civil service executive agencies'. *Human Resources Management Journal*, Vol. 4, No. 2.

Corby, S. (1994b) 'Hurdles to equality'. *The Times*, 8 December.

Corby, S. (1995) 'Opportunity 2000 in the NHS: a missed opportunity for women'. *Employee Relations*, Vol. 17, No. 2.

Corby, S and Higham (1995) 'Decentralization of pay in the NHS: diagnosis and prognosis'. (unpublished).

Crosby, P. (1984) *Quality Without Tears*. (New York: McGraw-Hill).

Crosthwaite, E. And Warner, D. (1995) 'Setting the Scene' in Warner, D. and Crosthwaite, E. (eds) *Human Resource Management in Higher and Further Education* (Buckingham: Open University Press).

Cuming, M. (1978) *Personnel Management in the National Health Service* (London: Heinemann).

Deming, W. (1986) *Out of Crisis: Quality, Productivity and Competitive Position* (Cambridge: Cambridge University Press).

Department of Education and Science (1972) *Teacher Education and Training*, (the James Report) (London: HMSO).

Department of Education and Science (1972a) *Education: a framework for expansion*. Cmnd 5174 (London: HMSO).

Department of Education and Science (1977) *Education in Schools: a consultative document*. Cmnd 6869. (London: HMSO).

Department of Education and Science (1983) *Teaching Quality*. Cmnd 8836. (London: HMSO).

Department of Education and Science (1985a) *Better Schools*. Cmnd 9469. (London: HMSO).

Department of Education and Science (1985b) *Better Schools evaluation and appraisal conference*. (London: HMSO).

Department of Education and Science (1987) *School Teacher's Pay and Conditions Document* (London: HMSO).

Department of Education and Science (1989) *School Teacher's Appraisal: a national framework* Report of the national steering group on the school teacher appraisal pilot study (London: HMSO).

Department of Education and Science (1993) *Effective Management in schools* (London: HMSO).

Department for Education (1992) *Choice and Diversity: a framework for schools* (London: Department for Education).

Department for Education (1994a) *School Teachers' Pay and Conditions Document* (London: HMSO).

Department for Education (1994b) *Departmental Report: the Government's Expenditure Plans 1994–95 to 1996–97* (Cmnd 7510). (London: HMSO).

Department of Employment and Productivity (1971) *British Labour Statistics: Historical Abstracts* (London: HMSO).

Department of Health (1994a) 'Extending the benefits of fundholding is the key priority of the health reforms says Virginia Bottomley'. *Press release*, 24 March.

Department of Health (1994b) 'Virginia Bottomley outlines way ahead for NHS'. *Press release*, 29 March.

Department of Health and Social Security (1972) *Development of the Personnel Function*. HM(72) 65 (London: HMSO).

Department of Health and Social Security (1973) *Organization for Personnel*. HRC (73) 37 (London: HMSO).

Department of Health and Social Security (1975) *Management Education and Training in the NHS: Review of Guidelines*. HS Circular 189 (London: HMSO).

Desborough, Baron (1920) *Committee on Police Service of England, Wales and Scotland*. Report Part 1 1919 Cmd. 253; Part 2 1920 Cmd. 574 (London: HMSO).

Dines and others v. (1) Initial Health Care Services and (2) Pall

Mall Services Group Ltd (1994) *Industrial Relations Law Reports*, 336.

Donovan, Lord (1968) *Royal Commission on Trade Unions and Employers Associations: Report* (London: HMSO).

Dr Sophie Redmond Stichting v. Bartol and others (1992) *Industrial Relations Law Report*, 366.

Drewry, G. (ed.) (1989) *The New Select Committees* (Oxford: Clarendon Press).

Drewry, G. and Butcher, T. (1992) *The Civil Service Today*. 2nd Edition (Oxford: Blackwell).

Duncan, S. and Goodwin, M. (1988) 'Removing local government autonomy: political centralisation and financial control'. *Local Government Studies*. November/December.

Dunleavy, P. (1989) 'The architecture of the British central state', *Public Administration*, Vol. 67, Nos. 3 and 4.

Dunsire, A. and Hood, C. (1989) *Cutback Management in Public Bureaucracies* (Cambridge: Cambridge University Press).

Dyson, R. (1991) *Changing Labour Utilization in NHS Trusts: the reprofiling paper* (Keele: University of Keele).

Edmund-Davies, Lord (1979) *Committee of Inquiry on the Police, Reports 1 and 2*. Cmnd 7283 and 7633 (London: HMSO).

Efficiency Unit (Ibbs Report) (1988) *Improving Management in Government: The Next Steps* (London: HMSO).

Efficiency Unit (Fraser Report) (1991) *Making The Most of Next Steps: The Management of Ministers' Departments and their Executive Agencies* (London: HMSO).

Efficiency Unit (Oughton Report) (1993) *Career Management and Succession Planning Study* (London: HMSO).

Elcock, H. (1991) *Change and Decay* (London: Longman).

Elcock, H. (1993) 'Strategic management' in Farnham, D. and Horton, S. *Managing the New Public Services* (London: Macmillan).

Eliasson, K. and Kooiman, J. (1993) *Managing Public Organizations* (London: Sage).

Emerson, C. and Goddard, I. (1993) *Managing Staff in Schools* (Oxford: Heinemann).

Equal Opportunities Commission (1991) *Equality Management: Women's Employment in the NHS* (Manchester: Equal Opportunities Commission).

Equal Opportunities Review (1989) 'Equal opportunities in the civil service' (London: Industrial Relations Services).

Equal Opportunities Review (1994) 'Equal opportunities in the health service: a survey of NHS trusts' 53, January/February.

Employment Department (1992) *People, Jobs and Opportunity* (London: HMSO).

Eustace, R. (1987) 'The English ideal of university governance: a missing rationale and some implications'. *Society for Research into Higher Education.*, 12 (1).

Farnham, D. (1974) 'The Association of Teachers in Technical Institutions 1904–1914: a case study of a white-collar organization'. *International Review of Social History*, XIX (3).

Farnham, D. (1975) 'How apt is APT?'. *Higher Education Review.* 7 (3).

Farnham, D. (1978) 'Sixty years of whitleyism', *Personnel Management.* Vol 10, No 7.

Farnham, D. (1988) 'Employee relations in the PCFC sector: what happens after vesting day? *Higher Education Review.* 21 (1).

Farnham, D. (1991a) 'From model employer to private sector model: the PCFC sector. *Higher Education Review.* 23 (1), Autumn.

Farnham, D. (1991b) 'Post-binarism and academic staff unions in the UK'. *Higher Education Review*, 24 (1).

Farnham, D. (1992) 'Union recognition in polytechnics and colleges'. in Winstanley, D. and Woodall, J. (eds) *Case Studies in Personnel* (London: IPM).

Farnham, D. (1993a) *Employee Relations* (London: IPM).

Farnham, D. (1993b) 'Human resources management and employee relations', in Farnham, D. and Horton, S. (eds) *Managing the New Public Services* (Basingstoke: Macmillan).

Farnham, D. (1994a) 'From confederation to federation or where? Recent developments in AUT and NATFHE relations'. *Higher Education Review*, Vol. 26 No. 3.

Farnham, D. (1994b) *Employment Relations and the Rebirth of History.* Inaugural Lecture, University of Portsmouth.

Farnham, D. and Giles, L. (1995a) *Pay, Contracts and Collective Organization of Departmental Heads in New Universities: A National Report 1993–94* (London: National Association of Teachers in Further and Higher Education).

Farnham, D. and Giles, L. (1995b) 'Trade unions in Britain: trends and counter trends since 1979'. *Employee Relations*, Vol. 17, No. 2, May.

Farnham, D. and Horton, S. (1993) *Managing The New Public Services* (London: Macmillan).

Farnham, D. and Horton, S. (1996) *Managing the New Public Services* (forthcoming).

Farnham, D., Horton, S. and Giles, L. (1994) 'Human resources management and industrial relations in the public sector; from model employer to hybrid model?.' Paper presented at the Eighth Employment Research Unit Annual Conference, Cardiff Business School, September.

Farnham, D. and Pimlott, J. (1995) *Understanding Industrial Relations* (London: Cassell).

Ferner, A. (1985) 'Political constraints and managerial strategies'. *British Journal of Industrial Relations*, Vol. 23 No. 1.

Ferner, A. (1988) *Governments, Managers and Industrial Relations* (Oxford: Blackwell).

Financial Times. 26 January, (1995).

Flude, M. and Hammer, M. (1990) *The Education Reform Act 1988* (Basingstoke: Falmer).

Flynn, N. (1993) *Public Sector Management* (Brighton: Harvester Wheatsheaf).

Fowler, A. (1975) *Personnel Management in Local Government* (London: IPM).

Fowler, A. (1980) *Personnel Management in Local Government* 2nd Edition (London: IPM).

Fowler, A. (1988a) *Human Resource Management in Local Government* (London: Longman).

Fowler, A. (1988b) *Personnel Agenda for Change* (Luton: LGTB).

Fowler, A. (1993) *Taking Charge* (London: IPM).

Fredman, S. and Morris, G. (1989) *The State as Employer* (London: Mansell).

Friedman, A. (1977) *Industry and Labour* (London: Macmillan).

Friedman, M. (1962) *Capitalism and Freedom* (Chicago: University of Chicago Press).

Fry, G. (1985) *The Changing Civil Service* (London: George Allen and Unwin).

Fry, G. (1988) 'The Thatcher government, the financial management initiative and the "new civil service"'. *Public Administration*, Vol. 66, No. 1. (London: RIPA/Blackwell).

Fryer, R. (1989) 'Public service trade unionism in the 20th century' in Mailly, R., Dimmock, S. and Sethi, A. (eds) *Industrial Relations in the Public Services* (London: Routledge).

Fulton Lord (1968) *The Civil Service Vol 1*, Cmnd 3638 (London: HMSO).

Further Education Funding Council (1992) *Funding Learning* (London: FEFC).

Gamble, A. (1988) *The Free Economy and the Strong State* (London: Macmillan).

Garrett, J. (1980) *Managing The Civil Service* (London: Heineman).

Giles, L. (1992) 'Breaking the glass ceiling: a case study' Unpublished MA Dissertation: University of Warwick.

Gilligan, A. (1994) 'Health boards becoming "job centre" for Tory backers'. *Observer*, 11 September, 2.

Gladden, E. (1966) *Approach to Public Administration* (London: Staples Press).

Gorman, T. (1995) 'Nottinghamshire County Council', in Perry, B. *Changing Role of the Human Resource Function* (Luton: LGMB).

Goss, S. and Brown, H. (1991) *Equal opportunities for women in the NHS* (London: NHS Management Executive).

Gray, A., Jenkins, B., Flynn, A. and Rutherford, B. (1991) 'The management of change in Whitehall: the experience of the FMI'. *Public Administration*, Vol. 69, No. 1 (London: Blackwell).

Greater London Council. Police Committee Support Unit (1986) *Guide to the MET: The Structure of London's Police Force* (London: GLC).

Griffiths Sir Roy (1983) *Report of the NHS Management Inquiry* (London: HMSO).

Griffiths, Sir R. (1988) *Community Care: Agenda for Action* (London: HMSO).

Griffiths, W. (1976) *Local Government Administration* (London: Shaw and Son).

Griffiths, W. (1990) 'Kent County Council: a case of local pay determination'. *Human Resource Management Journal*. Vol. 1, No. 1, Autumn.

Griffiths, W. (1993) 'Facing the future'. in Armstrong, G. (ed) *View from the Bridge* (London: IPM).

Guest, D. (1987) 'Human resource management and industrial relations'. *Journal of Management Studies*, 24.

Guest, D. (1990) 'Personnel management: the end of orthodoxy?'. *British Journal of Industrial Relations*, Vol. 29, No. 2.

Guest, D. and Peccei, R. (1992) *The Effectiveness of Personnel Management in the NHS: main report* (London: Department of Health).

Guest, D. and Peccei, R. (1994) 'The nature and causes of effective human resource management'. *British Journal of Industrial Relations*, Vol. 32, No. 2.

Gunn, L. (1987) 'Staff appraisal'. Paper to CVCP seminar, Manchester.

Hadow Lord (1935) *Report of the Committee on Recruitment, Qualifications, Training and Promotion of Local Government Officers* (London: HMSO).

Hain, P. (1983) *The Democratic Alternative* (Hardmansworth: Penguin).

Haldane Lord (1919) *Report of the Machinery of Government Committee*, Cd. 9230 (London: HMSO).

Hansard (1979) *House of Commons Budget Statement* 12 June 1979 (Parliamentary Debates Commons 1979–80, 968) (London: HMSO).

Harrison, S., Hunter, D. J., Marnoch, G. and Pollitt, C. (1992) *Just Managing: Power and Culture in the National Health Service* (London: Macmillan).

Health Service Circular (1975) *Management Education and Training in the NHS: Review of Guidelines* (London: Department of Health).

Healy, G. (1994) 'Professionalism, trade unionism and teaching'. Paper presented at the University of Wales College of Cardiff, Employment Research Unit Conference.

Health Service Report (1994) Ancillary and hotel services staff: a survey of 58 trusts. Summer.

Hendry, C. (1995) *Human Resource Management* (Oxford: Butterworth-Heinemann).

Heseltine, M. (1980) 'Ministers and management in Whitehall'. *Management Services in Government* 35.

Heywood, J. (1992) 'School teacher appraisal: for monetary reward or professional development, or both? in Tomlinson, H. (ed.) *Performance Related Pay in Education* (London: Routledge).

Hill, L. (1935) 'The Municipal Service', in Laski, H., Jennings, W. and Robson, W. *A Century of Municipal Progress 1835–1935* (London: George Allen and Unwin).

Hirsch, F. (1976) *Social Limits to Growth* (Cambridge, Mass: Harvard University Press).

Holdaway, S. (1991) 'Race relations and police recruitment'. *British Journal of Criminology*, 31.

Holland, S. (1975) *The Socialist Challenge* (London: Quartet Books).

Holmes, M. (1995) 'New Forest District Council', in Perry, B. *Changing Role of the Human Resource Function.* (Luton: LGMB).

Home Office (1961–94) *Annual Returns for the Police Source* (London: HMSO).

Home Office (1983) Circular 114/83. *Manpower, Effectiveness and Efficiency in the Police Service* (London: Home Office).

Home Office (1987) Circular 12/87. *Career Development in the Police Service* (London: Home Office).

Home Office (1987) Police Regulations 1987/851 Schedule 2.

Home Office (1988) Circular 105/88 *Civilian Staff in the Police Service* (London: Home Office).

Home Office (1989) Circular 87/1989 *Equal Opportunities Policies in the Police Service* (London: Home Office).

Home Office (1991) Circular 104/1991 *Career Development of Police Officers in England and Wales: Guidance to Forces on Training in Reporting and Appraisal Procedures* (London: Home Office).

Home Office (1991) Circular 105/91. *The Evaluation of Training in the Police Service* (Home Office).

Home Office (1992) *A Report of HMIC on Equal Opportunities* (London: HMSO).

Home Office (1993a) *Annual Report 1992.* Cm. 1909 (London: HMSO).

Home Office (1993b) Circular 39/1993. *Part 1: The Future Management of Police Training; Part 2: Police Training Council Strategy Document* (London: Home Office).

Home Office (1994) *Annual Report 1993.* Cm. 2208.

Hood, C. (1990) *Beyond the Public Bureaucracy State? Public Administration in the 1990s.* Inaugural Lecture, LSE, London.

Hood, C. (1991) 'A public administration for all seasons?', *Public Administration*, Vol. 69, No. 1 (London: Blackwell).

Hood, C. (1994) *Explaining economic policy reversals* (Buckingham: Open University Press)

Horton, S. (1976) 'Post-Fulton Developments'. Paper presented to the Civil Service College/ Public Administration Committee Seminar on the Civil Service since Fulton, London.

Horton, S. (1993) 'Employee relations management in context'. Farnham, D. *Employee Relations* (London: IPM).

House, D. and Watson, D. (1995) 'Managing Change' in Warner, D. and Crosthwaite, E. (eds) *Human Resource Management in Higher and Further Education* (Buckingham: Open University Press).

House of Commons (1977) *The Civil Service Vol. 1 Report*, (English Report). 11th Report of the Expenditure Committee 1976–77 (London: HMSO).

House of Commons (1992) *NHS Trusts: interim conclusions and proposals for future inquiries* (Health Committee, London: HMSO).

House of Commons (1994) *Report of Her Majesty's Chief Inspector of Constabulary for the year 1993* (London: HMSO).

Howard, M. (1994) *Conservatives and Community.* The Disraeli Lecture, Conservative Party, June.

Huddart, G. (1994a) 'NHS pushes on local pay'. *Personnel Today.* 11 October, 1.

Huddart, G. (1994b) 'Local pay debate stays on top billing'. *Personnel Today.* 25 October, 4.

Hughes, A. (1995) 'Employment in the public and private sectors'. *Economic Trends* No. 495, January (London: HMSO).

Humble, J. (1961) *Management by Objectives* (London: British Institute of Management).

Humphreys, B. V. (1958) *Clerical Unions in the Civil Service* (Oxford: Blackwell and Mott).

Hutt, R. (1985) *Chief Officer Profiles: regional and district nursing officers*. IMS report 111. (Brighton: Institute of Manpower Studies).

Hutton, W. (1995) *The State We're In* (London: Cape).

Incomes Data Services (1988) *Salaries and Benefits in Local Government: Policies and Practice*. Incomes Data Services Public Sector Unit/KPMG Peat Marwick McLintock, May.

Incomes Data Services (1989) *Paying for Performance in the Public Sector: A Progress Report*. Incomes Data Services Public Sector Unit/Coopers and Lybrand, April.

Incomes Data Services (1991) *Incomes Data Services Report 602*, October.

Incomes Data Services (1994a) *Public Sector Labour Market Survey*. IDS Report 676, November.

Incomes Data Services (1994b) *Local Government Unions Accept Revised Two-Stage Offer*. IDS Report 676, November.

Incomes Data Services/Institute of Personnel Management (1989) *Customer Care: The Personnel Implications*, October.

Industrial Relations Services (1989) *IRS Employment Trends*. IRS Employment Trends, No. 441, June.

Ingham, M. (1985) 'Industrial relations in British local government'. *Industrial Relations Journal*, Vol. 16, No. 1.

Institute of Personnel Management (1987) *Contract Compliance: the UK Experience* (London: IPM, October).

Institute of Personnel and Development (1995) *People Make the Difference* (London: IPD).

Ironside, M., Seifert, R. and Sinclair, J. (1993) 'Change in the teacher unions,' Paper presented for the University of Wales College of Cardiff, Employment Research Unit Conference.

Isaac-Henry, K. (1993) 'The management of information technology in the public sector', in Isaac-Henry, K., Painter, C. and Barnes, C. *Management in the Public Sector* (London: Chapman and Hall).

Jarrett, A. (1985) *Report of the Steering Committee for Efficiency Studies in Universities* (London: CVCP).

Jary, S. (1991) *Decentralisation in the Civil Service: the implications for industrial relations*. A paper presented to a Thames Polytechnic Business School Symposium.

Jessop, B. (1989) *Thatcherism: The British Road to Post-Fordism.* Essex Papers in Politics and Government No. 68 (Department of Government: University of Essex).

Johnson, N. (1990) *Reconstructing the Welfare State: A Decade of Change* (London: Harvester Wheatsheaf).

Johnson, G. and Scholes, K. (1993) *Exploring Corporate Strategy* 2nd edition (Hemel Hemstead: Prentice Hall).

Joint Review Group (1982) *Employment Opportunities for Women in the Civil Service* (London: HMSO).

Jones, S. and Silverman, E. (1984) 'What price efficiency? Circular agreements and financial constraints on the police in Britain'. *Policing* Vol. 1, No. 1 August.

Judge, T. (1994) *The Force of Persuasion* (Surbiton: The Police Federation).

Juran, J. (1989) *Juran on Leadership for Quality* (New York: The Free Press (Macmillan)).

Keep, E. (1992) *Schools in the Marketplace? – Some problems with private sector models. Multi-Lingual Matters* (Clevedon: Multi-Lingual Matters).

Keep, E. (1993) 'The need for a revised management system for the teaching profession, from National Commission on Education, 1993', *Briefings for the Paul Hamlyn Foundation National Commission on Education* (London: Heinemann).

Kemp-Jones Report (1971) *The Employment of Women in the Civil Service: The Report of a Departmental Committee* (London: HMSO).

Kessler, I. (1990) 'Personnel management in local government: the new agenda'. *Personnel Management.* November.

Kessler, I. (1991a) 'Pay determination in the British civil service'. Mimeo.

Kessler, I. (1991b) 'Workplace industrial relations in local government'. *Employee Relations.* Vol. 13, No. 2. Special issue.

Kessler, I. (1993) 'Workplace industrial relations in local government: themes and issues', in Ironside, M., Kessler, I. Seifert R. and White, G. *Public Sector Industrial Relations in the 1990s.* Thames Business Paper No. 19, University of Greenwich.

King's Fund Task Force (1991) *The Work of the Equal Opportunities Task Force 1986–1990: a Final Report* (London: King's Fund).

Knowles, R. (1971) *Modern Management in Local Government* (London: Butterworth).

Koch, H. (1992) *Total Quality Management in Health Care* (Harlow: Longman).

Kotter, J. (1990) *A Force for Change – How Leadership Differs from Management* (New York: Free Press).

Labour Party (1994) *Health 2000* (London: Labour Party).

Labour Party (1995) *Renewing the NHS* (London: Labour Party).

Labour Research Department (1990) 'Compulsory competitive tendering – the effect on jobs, wages and conditions'. *Bargaining Report*, May,

Laffin, M. (1989) *Managing under Pressure: Industrial Relations in Local Government* (London: Macmillan).

Laffin, M. and Young, K. (1990) *Professionalism in Local Government* (Harlow: Longmans).

Lanchbery, E. (1995) 'Developing a human resource strategy' in Warner, D. and Crosthwaite, E. (eds) *Human Resource Management in Further and Higher Education* (Buckingham: Open University Press).

Langlands, A. (1994) *Letter to chief executives of NHS trusts.* 6 June.

Lawton, A. and Rose, A. (1994) *Organization And Management In the Public Sector* (London: Pitman).

Leishman, F. and Savage, S. (1993a) 'The Police Service' in Farnham, D. and Horton, S. *Managing the New Public Services* (Basingstoke: Macmillan).

Leishman, F. and Savage, S. (1993b) 'Officers or Managers? Direct entry into British police management' in *The International Journal of Public Sector Management*. Vol. 6, No. 5.

Leishman, F. and Savage, S. (1993c) *Police Management and Organisation.* Course Unit 3 BSc (Hons) in Policing and Police Studies. Institute of Police and Criminological Studies University of Portsmouth.

Legge, K. (1978) *Power, Innovation and Problem Solving in Personnel Management* (London: McGraw-Hill).

Levacic, R. (1992) 'Local management of schools: aims, scope and impact'. *Educational Management Administration.* Vol. 20, No. 1.

Lilley, R., and Wilson, C. (1994) 'Change in the NHS: a view from a trust'. *Personnel Management*, May.

Lipietz, A. (1992) *Towards a New Economic Order* (Oxford: Polity Press).

Littler, C. (1982) *The Development of the Labour Process in Capitalist Society* (London: Heinemann).

LACSAB (1987a) *Recruitment and Retention.* Volumes 1–4, October, LACSAB.

LACSAB (1987b) *An Employers Strategy? A Consultative Document.* November, LACSAB.

LACSAB (1988) *Summary of Replies Received to the Consultative Exercise.* April, LACSAB.

LACSAB (1990) *Pay and Personnel Information Systems.* LACSAB.

LACSAB/LGTB (1990a) *Recruitment and Retention Survey 1989, Report 4, Employment Strategies (APT&C Staffs), III Use of Staff.* December, LACSAB.

LACSAB/LGTB (1990b) *Recruitment and Retention Survey 1989, Report 7, Employment Strategies (APT&C Staffs), VI Working Hours and Related Measures.* December, LACSAB.

LACSAB/LGTB (1990c) *Recruitment and Retention Survey 1989, Report 2, Employment Strategies (APT&C Staffs), I Pay Policies.* December, LACSAB.

LACSAB/LGTB (1990d) *Recruitment and Retention Survey 1989 Report 6, Employment Strategies (APT&C Staffs), V Labour Market Searches,* December, LACSAB.

LGMB (1992a) *Survey of Employment of Older and Mature Workers in Local Authorities* (Luton: LGMB).

LGMB (1992b) *Recruitment and Retention Survey* (Luton: LGMB).

LGMB (1993a) *Pay in Local Government* (Luton: LGMB).

LGMB (1993b) *Equal Opportunities in Local Government* (Luton: LGMB).

LGMB (1993c) *A Guide to Performance Management* (Luton: LGMB).

LGMB (1994) *Pay in Local Government 1994* (Luton: LGMB).

LGMB (1994a) *The Changing Role of the Human Resource Function* (Luton: LGMB).

LGMB (1994b) *CCT Information Service.* Survey report No 9. June (Luton: LGMB).

LGMB (1994c) *Performance Management and Performance Related Pay Survey* (Luton: LGMB).

LGMB (1994d) *Performance Management and Performance Related Pay – Local Government Practice* (Luton: LGMB).

LGTB (1987) *Getting Closer to the Public* (Luton: LGTB).

LGTB (1988) *Personnel: the Agenda for Change* (Luton: LGTB).

Lodge D. (1987) 'Working equality into manual job evaluation'. *Personnel Management,* September.

Loveday, B. (1993) 'Civilian staff in the police service'. *Policing,* Vol. 9, Summer.

Loveday, B. (1994) 'The Police and Magistrates' Court Act'. *Policing.* Vol. 10, No. 4, Winter.

Lubans, V. and Edgar, J. (1979) *Policing by Objectives* (Connecticut: Harford).

Lyotard, J-F. (1984) *The Postmodern Condition: A Report on Knowledge* (Manchester: Manchester University Press).

MacDonnell, Lord (1914) *Report of the Royal Commission on the Civil Service* (London: HMSO).

Maddock, S. and Parkin, D. (1994) *Barriers to women hospital doctors in the North Western Region* (Manchester: Corporate Management and Policy Services).

Mailly, R., Dimmock, S. J. and Sethi, A. S. (eds) (1989) *Industrial Relations in the Public Services* (London: Routledge).

Mallaby, Sir George (1967) *Staffing of Local Government* (London: HMSO).

Management Charter Initiative (1987). (London: IM).

Management Matters (1993a) 'Staff Appraisal'. January (London: HMSO).

Management Matters (1993b) 'New Principles of Personal Review and Promotion', February (London: HMSO).

Management Matters (1994) 'Equal opportunities AA AO course'.

Management and Personnel Office (1984) *Civil Service Management Development in the 1980s* (London: Cabinet Office).

Manning, R. (1995) 'Coventry City Council', in Perry, B. (1995) *Changing Role of the Human Resource Function* (Luton: LGMB).

Massey, A. (1993) *Managing The Public Sector* (Aldershot: Edward Elgar).

Massey, A. (1994) *After Next Steps*. A Report to the Office of Public Service and Science.

Masterman Report (1953) *Political Activities of Civil Servants*. Cmd. 8783 (London: HMSO).

Maud, Sir John (1967) *Management of Local Government Vol. 5 Local Government Administration in England and Wales* (London: HMSO).

McCarthy, W. and Ellis, N. (1973) *Management by Agreement* (London: Hutchinson).

McVicar, M. (1993) 'Education,' in Farnham, D. and Horton, S. (eds.) *Managing the New Public Services* (Basingstoke: Macmillan).

Mead, G. (1990). 'The challenge of police leadership – the contribution of the special course', *Management Education and Development*, Vol. 21, Part 5.

Megaw, Sir John (1982) *Report of an Inquiry into the Principles and the System by which the Remuneration of the Non-Industrial Civil Service should be Determined*, Cmnd. 8590 (London: HMSO).

Merrick, N. (1995) 'NHS trust finds little employee support for PRP'. *People Management*. 26 January.

Metcalfe, L. and Richards, S. (1990) *Improving Public Management* (London: Sage).

Millward, N., Stevens, M., Smart, D. and Hawes, A. (1992)

Workplace Industrial Relations in Transition (Aldershot: Dartmouth).

Ministry of Reconstruction (1918) *Final Report* (London: HMSO).

Morgan, S. (1994) 'Taking policing a degree further. Constables in the classroom'. Unpublished MSc. Dissertation (University of Portsmouth).

Morning, R. (1995) 'Coventry City Council', in Perry, B. *Changing Role of the Human Resource Function* (Luton: LGMB).

Mortiboys, R. and Oakland, J. (1991) *Total Quality Management and Effective Leadership* (London: Department of Trade and Industry).

Moss Kanter, R. (1985) *The Change Masters* (London: Allen and Unwin).

Moss Kanter, R. (1989) *When Giants Learn to Dance* (London: Routledge).

Moss Kanter, R., Stein, B. and Jick, T. (1992) *The Challenge of Organizational Change* (New York: Free Press).

Mueller Report (1987) *Flexible Working Patterns* (London: Cabinet Office).

Murray, R. (1989) 'Fordism and post-fordism', in Hall, S. and Jacques, M. (eds). *New Times* (London: Lawrence and Wishart).

Mustoe, N. (1932) *The Law and Organization of the British Civil Service* (London: Pitman and Sons).

Nash, M. and Savage, S. (1994) 'A criminal record? Law, order and conservative policy', in Savage, S., Atkinson, R. and Robins, L. *Public Policy in Britain* (Basingstoke: Macmillan).

NHSME (1990) *NHS trusts: a working guide* (London: HMSO).

NHSME (1992a) Personnel Development Division, *Report of one day workshop* 15 June (Leeds: NHSME).

NHSME (1992b) *Women in the NHS: an implementation guide to Opportunity 2000* (London: Department of Health).

NHSME (1993a) *Human Resource Survey: final results report* (Leeds: NHSME).

NHSME (1993b) *Ethnic minority staff in the NHS: a programme of action* (Leeds: NHSME).

NHS Training Authority (1985) *Annual Report 1984–85* (Bristol: NHST).

Neave, G. (1991) *Models of Quality Assurance in Europe* (London: CNAA).

Niskanen, W. (1973) *Bureaucracy: Servant or Master* (London: IEA).

Northcote-Trevelyan Report (1854) *Report on the Organization of the Permanent Civil Service*, C1713 (London: HMSO).

OECD (1987) *Universities under Scrutiny* (Paris: OECD).

OECD (1990) *Public Management Developments Survey 1990* (Paris: OECD).

OECD (1992) *Public Management Developments Update 1992* (Paris: OECD).

Oakland, J. (1989) *Total Quality Management* (Oxford: Butterworth Heinemann).

Oliver, I. (1987) *Police, Government and Accountability* (Basingstoke: Macmillan).

Owen, D. (1981) *Face the Future* (Oxford: Oxford University Press).

Parker-Jones, J. (1993) 'The success of the graduate entry scheme'. *Policing* Vol. 9, No. 3.

Parrett, L. (1992) *Past, Present and Future Roles of Civilians in the Police Service*. Police Research Group, Home Office.

Parris, H. (1969) *Constitutional Bureaucracy* (London: George Allen and Unwin Ltd).

Parris, H. (1973) *Staff Relations in The Civil Service* (London: George Allen and Unwin Ltd).

Parry, J. (1990) 'Organizational culture in a district general hospital' (Unpublished MA Dissertation: University of Portsmouth).

Partridge, P. (1994) 'Human resources management and development in higher education'. Paper presented to the Quinquennial Conference of the Conference of European Rectors, Budapest.

Parvin, H. (1995) 'Northampton Borough Council', in Perry, B. *Changing Role of the Human Resource Function* (Luton: LGMB).

Pascale, R. and Athos, A. (1980) *The Art of Japanese Management* (New York: Simon and Schuster).

Pearson, N. (1994) 'Employment in the private and public sectors' in *Economic Trends*, December.

Peat Marwick (1994) *CCT for Local Authority White Collar Services* (London: KPMG).

People Management (1995) '"PRP divisive" in health service'. 9 February, p. 6.

Perrin, J. (1988) *Resource Management in the NHS* (Wokingham: Van Nostrand Reinhold).

Personnel Management (1994) 'Push for more women in senior health posts'. June, 6.

PM Plus (1994) 'Trust changes nurses' hours to cut costs'. June, 3.

Personnel Standards Lead Body (1993) *A Perspective on Personnel* (London: PSLB).

Peters, T. (1987) *Thriving on Chaos* (New York: Harper & Row).

Peters, T. (1992). *Liberation Management* (London: Macmillan).

Peters , T. and Austin, N. (1985) *A Passion for Excellence* (New York: Harper & Row).

Peters, T. and Waterman, L. (1982) *In Search of Excellence* (New York: Harper & Row).

Pitt, D. and Smith, B. (1984) *The Computer Revolution in Public Administration* (Brighton: Harvester Press).

Plowden Lord (1961) *Control of Public Expenditure,* Cmd 1432 (London: HMSO).

Police Review (1994) 'Courses for forces' 24 June 1994 p. 26.

Policy Studies Institute (1983) *Police and People in London* (London: PSI).

Pollitt, C. (1993) *Managerialism and the Public Services* 2nd edition (Oxford: Blackwell).

Ponting, C. (1986) *The Right to Know* (London: Sphere).

Pratchett, L. and Wingfield, M. (1994) *The Public Service Ethos in Local Government* (London: Commission for Local Democracy).

Priestley Lord (1955). *Report of the Royal Commission on the Civil Service 1953–55,* Cmd. 9613 (London: HMSO).

Prime Minister's Office (1991) *Citizen's Charter*. Cm. 1599 (London: HMSO).

Pyper, R. (1991) *The Evolving Civil Service* (Harlow: Longman).

Radcliffe Report (1962) *Security Procedures in the Public Service.* Cmd. 1681 (London: HMSO).

Rainbird, H. (1994) 'The changing role of the training function: A test for the integration of human resource and business strategies?'. *Human Resource Management Journal*. Vol. 5, No. 1.

Ranson, S. and Stewart, J. (1994) *Management for the Public Domain* (Basingstoke: Macmillan).

Ranson, S. and Tomlinson, T. (1986) (eds) *The Changing Government of Education* (London: Allen and Unwin).

Rawlingson, D. and Tanner, B. (1989) *Financial Management in the 1990s* (Harlow: Longman).

Rear, J. (1994a) 'Defender of academic faith'. *The Times Higher*. 2 December.

Rear, J. (1994b) 'Freedom and responsibility'. *The Times Higher*. 21 October.

Redlich, J. and Hurst, J. (1903) *Local Government in England* (London: Macmillan).

Reiner, R. (1992) *Chief Constables* (Oxford: Oxford University Press).

Richards, H. (1995) 'V-C's pay packages hit 6 figures'. *Times Higher*, 24 March, p. 1.

Robinson, R. and Le Grand, J. (1994) *Evaluating the NHS reforms* (London: King's Fund).

Rogers, S. (1990) *Performance Management in Local Government* (Harlow: Longman).

Ryan, P. (1994) *The Future of Police Training* (London: National Police Training Directorate).

Sanderson, I. (1992) *Management of Quality in Local Government* (Harlow: Longman).

Saran, R. (1992) 'The history of teachers' pay negotiations,' in Tomlinson, H. (ed.) *Performance Related Pay in Education* (London: Routledge).

Savage, S. and Robins, L. (eds) (1990) *Public Policy under Thatcher* (London: Macmillan).

Savage, S., Atkinson, R. and Robins, L. (1994) *Public Policy in Britain* (London: Macmillan).

Scarman, Lord (1981) *The Scarman Report: The Brixton Disorders*, Cmnd. 8427 (London: HMSO).

Schofield, A. (1989) *Some Issues in Performance Appraisal in Higher Education* (London: Higher Education Consultancy Group).

School Management Task Force (1990) *Developing School Management: the Forward Way* (London: HMSO).

School Teachers Review Body (1993) *Second Report 1993*, Cm 2151 (London: HMSO).

School Teachers Review Body (1994) *Third Report 1994*, Cm 2466 (London: HMSO).

Scottish Office (1993) *The NHS Guide* (Edinburgh: Scottish Office).

Scottish Office Central Statistics (1994) 'Pupils and teachers in education authority primary and secondary schools'. *The Scottish Office Statistical Bulletin Education Series*. (Edinburgh: The Scottish Office Central Statistics).

Scottish Office Education Department (1992) *Devolved School Management: Guidelines for Progress* (Edinburgh: Scottish Office).

Scraton, P. (1985) *The State of the Police* (London: Pluto).

Seifert, R. (1989) 'Industrial relations in the school sector,' in Mailley, R., Dimmock, S. and Sethi, A. (eds). *Industrial Relations in the Public Services* (London: Routledge).

Seifert, R. (1992) *Industrial Relations in the NHS* (London: Chapman & Hall).

Seifert, R. and Ironside, M. (1993) 'Industrial relations in state schools,' Thames Business Paper No. 19, presented at Symposium on Public Sector Employee Relations in the 1990s, September 1991, University of Greenwich Business School.

Sheehy, Sir Patrick (1993) *Report into Inquiry into Police Responsibilities and Rewards* (London: HMSO).

Sinclair, J., Ironside, M. and Seifert, R. (1993a) 'Classroom struggle? Market orientated education reforms and their impact upon teachers' professional autonomy, labour intensification and resistance,' Paper given to the 11th Annual International Labour Process Conference.

Sinclair, J., Seifert, R. and Ironside, M. (1993b) 'The road to market: management and trade union initiatives in the transition to school level bargaining under LMS.' Paper presented at the British Universities Industrial Relations Annual Conference.

Sinclair, J., Seifert, R. and Ironside, M. (1994) 'The restructuring of non-teaching jobs in schools: the two-pronged attack of CCT and LMS.' Paper presented at the University of Wales College of Cardiff, Employment Research Unit Conference.

Sisson, K. (1994) 'Personnel management: paradigms, practice and prospects', in Sisson, K. (ed.) (1994) *Personnel Management* (Oxford: Blackwell).

Sisson, K. and Storey, J. (1993) *Managing Human Resources and Industrial Relations* (Buckingham: Open University Press).

Skelcher, C. (1992) *Managing for Service Quality* (Harlow: Longman).

Smellie, K. (1968) *History of Local Government* (London: Unwin).

Smith, M. (1986) *The Consumer Case for Socialism*. Fabian Pamphlet No. 513. (London: Fabian Society).

Smithers, A. Hill, S. and Silvester, G. (1990) *Graduates in the Police Service*, School of Management, University of Manchester.

Society of Chief Officers of Personnel (1994). *CCT – Personnel Services* SOCPO.

Spence, P. (1990) 'The effects of performance management and performance related pay in local government'. *Local Government Studies*, Vol. 16, no. 4.

Spoor, A. (1964) *White Collar Union: 60 Years of Nalgo* (London: Heineman).

Storey, J. (ed.) (1989) *New Perspectives in Human Resource Management* (London: Routledge).

Storey, J. (1992) *Developments in the Managing of Human Resources* (Oxford: Blackwell).

Storey, J. (1995) *Human Resource Management* (London: Routledge).

Taylor, F. (1911) *Principles of Scientific Management* (New York: Harper Press).

Taylor, C. and McKenzie, I. (1994) 'The glass ceiling at the top of the greasy pole'. *Policing*, Vol. 10, No. 4.

Thatcher, M. (1994) 'Learning a lesson from the private sector'. *Personnel Management*. April.

Thurley, K. and Wirdenius, H. (1989) *Towards European Management* (London: Pitman).

Times Educational Supplement (1995) 'Colleges split on contract: talks resume'. 20 January.

Times Newspapers (1994) *Times 1000* (London: Times Books).

Toffler, A. (1980) *The Third Wave* (New York: Bantam Books).

Tomkins, C. R. (1987) *Achieving Economy, Efficiency and Effectiveness in the Public Sector* (London: Kegan Paul).

Tomlin, Lord (1931) *Report of the Royal Commission on the Civil Service 1929–31*, Cmd 3909 (London: HMSO).

Tomlinson, T. (1993) *The Control of Education* (London: Cassell).

Torrington, D. and Hall, L. (1991) *Personnel Management A New Perspective* (London: Prentice Hall).

Touraine, A. (1974) *The Post-Industrial Society: Tomorrow's Social History* (London: Wildwood House).

Trades Union Congress (1994) *Register of Affiliated Unions* (London: TUC).

Transfer of Undertakings (Protection of Employment) Regulations (1981) SI 1981/1794.

Travis, A. (1994) 'Rich pickings for Whitehall chiefs'. *The Guardian* 13 December 1994.

Treasury and Civil Service Committee 1983–84. Eighth Report *Acceptance of Outside Appointments by Crown Servants*, HC 302 (London: HMSO).

Treasury and Cabinet Office (1991) *Pay and Management Flexibilities* (London: HMSO).

Treasury (1994a) *Civil Service Statistics. 1994 Edition* (London: HMSO).

Treasury (1995) *Chancellor of the Exchequer's Small Departments.* Cm 2817 (London: HMSO).

Tropp, A. (1957) *The School Teachers* (London: Heinemann).

Tyson, S. (1995) *Human Resource Strategy* (London: Pitman).

University Committee for Non-Teaching Staff (1988) *Investing in People* (London: UCNS).

University Manpower Review Committee (1988) *Investing in People* (London: UCNS).

Vize, R. (1995) 'Howard's police shortlists show bias to businessmen'. *Local Government Chronicle*, 6 January.

Wainwright, H. (1987) *Labour: A Tale of Two Parties* (London: Hogarth Press).

Wall, D. (1993) 'The outsiders'. *Police Review.* 30 July.

Walsh, K. (1981) 'Centralization and decentralization in local government bargaining'. *Industrial Relations Journal*, Vol. 12, No. 5.

Walsh, K. (1982) *The Role of the Personnel Officer in the Corporate Personnel Department.* SOCPO.

Ward, R. (1995) 'Industrial relations strategies and tactics' in Warner, D. and Crosthwaite, E. (eds) 1995 *Human Resource Management in Higher and Further Education* (Buckingham: Open University Press).

Ward, S. (1995) 'Appeal system safeguards against unfair dismissal'. *BMA News Review,* January, 21.

Ward, S., Warman, D. and White, G. (1988) *Competitive Tendering in the Public Sector* (London: IPM/ID).

Warlow, D. (1989) *Report of the conditions of employment of staff in the National Health Service* (London: Department of Health).

Warner, D. and Crosthwaite, E. (eds) (1995) *Human Resource Management in Higher and Further Education* (Buckingham: Open University Press).

Wedderburn, Lord (1986) *The Worker and the Law* (Harmondsworth: Penguin).

Wedderburn, Lord (1991) *Employment Rights in Britain and Europe* (London: Lawrence and Wisehart).

Welsh Office (1994) 'John Redwood announces five health authorities for Wales'. *Press release,* 2 November.

Whitchurch, C. (1994) *A Handbook for University Administrators and Managers* (Sheffield: CVCP).

White, L. (1933) *Whitley Councils in the British Civil Service* (Chicago: University of Chicago Press).

White, G. (1993) 'Public sector industrial relations – change and continuity', in Ironside, M. Jary, M. Kessler, I. Seifert, R. and White, G. *Public Sector Industrial Relations in the 1990s.* Thames Business Paper No. 19, University of Greenwich.

White, M. and Trevor, M. (1983) *Under Japanese Management* (London: Heinemann).

Wilding, R. (1979) 'The professional ethic of the administrator', *Management Services in Government,* Vol. No. 4.

Williams, B. (1985) 'Whistle blowing in the public service'. *Politics, Ethics and Public Service* (London: RIPA).

Williams, A. (1993) 'Transfer of undertakings – the recent changes'. *Public Sector Review,* Issue No. 6, November (London: IPM).

Williams, R. (1992/3) 'Management selection in local government: A survey of practice in England and Wales'. *Human Resource Management Journal.* Vol. 3, No. 2.

Williamson, O. (1975) *Markets and Hierarchies: Analysis and Antitrust Implications* (New York: Free Press).

Winchester, D. (1983) 'Industrial relations in the public sector,' in Bain, G. (ed.). *Industrial Relations in Britain* (Oxford: Blackwell).

Wood, L. (1994) 'Bottomley signals delay on NHS local pay deals'. *Financial Times*, 1/2 October, p. 6.

Woodruffe, C. (1993) *Assessment Centres, Identifying and Developing Competence* (London: IPM).

Wright, F. (1994) 'Growing by degrees'. *Police Review*, 22 April.

Young, M. (1991) *An Inside Job* (Oxford: Clarendon).

Index